Ribbons in Time

INTERDISCIPLINARY STUDIES IN HISTORY

Harvey J. Graff, General Editor

Ribbons in Time

Movies and Society since 1945

Paul Monaco

INDIANA UNIVERSITY PRESS

Bloomington and Indianapolis

Photographs 1–10 by courtesy and permission of the Museum of Modern Art, Film Stills Archive, New York, New York. Photographs 11–16 by courtesy and permission of the Deutsches Institut für Filmkunde, Bild Archiv, Frankfurt/Main, German Federal Republic. Photographs 11–16 were reproduced through the efforts of Donald Pilotte, Photographic Services Director at Montana State University, Bozeman, Montana. Photographs 17–20 by courtesy and permission of the Academy of Motion Picture Arts & Sciences, Beverly Hills, California.

MANUFACTURED IN THE UNITED STATES OF AMERICA

Library of Congress Cataloging-in-Publication Data
Monaco, Paul.
  Ribbons in time.
  (Interdisciplinary studies in history)
  Bibliography: p.
  Includes index.
  1. Moving-pictures—Social aspects. 2. Moving-pictures—History. I. Title. II. Series.
PN1195.9S6M65 1987   302.2'343   86-42996
ISBN 0-253-35074-3
ISBN 0-253-20447-X (pbk.)
1 2 3 4 5 91 90 89 88 87

Dedicated to
Birdena O. Monaco &
K.L.E.

CONTENTS

ILLUSTRATIONS

INTRODUCTION

From the very beginning, the links between movies and society need to be thought of as associative, not direct. We can take a movie and associate it with other movies with which it may have a connection, and then beyond with other spheres of culture, thought, economics, and society. In each chapter in this book that is what I have done. The value and meaning, as well as the social, cultural, and political significance, of any movie is contained in the movie itself, not in the process by which it came to be made, or in an analysis of how much money was invested in it by whom. In any society in which movies are produced this is a given.

My approach in writing this book is highly selective. Selectivity means choosing certain films to discuss, but, more importantly, it mandates deciding upon specific topics for chapters. In the first chapter we are concerned with how two of the most famous postwar directors in Italy, Federico Fellini and Michelangelo Antonioni, developed their film art out of the traditions of Neo-Realism, which both of them eventually superseded. Chapter 2 looks at the famed movement in moviemaking, the "New Wave" in France, through the prism of four films which might be called the New Wave's first crest. The third chapter focuses on a particular subject in films made in West Germany from 1945 to the mid-1980s: portrayals of Nazism, World War Two, and the Holocaust. Chapter 4 examines movies produced in the United States since the late 1960s which depict a mood that we call nostalgia.

Each of these topics has been selected because it is especially important to understanding movies and society in each of the nations respectively. Each chapter manages—at the same time—to raise salient issues of creativity, consciousness, and innovation in filmmaking. Nonetheless, a question arises as to why the overriding element for organizing this book is essentially "national"?

There are many theories, and much speculation, about the phenomenon of nationalism. The modern nation-state has been for centuries a repository of economic, political, and cultural power. Especially in the twentieth century, the nation has appeared to come to play an inordinately large role in the feelings and imagination of its citizens. The nation provides us with a fantasy partner who looms large in our perceptions of self-worth and achievement.[1] Our common parlance personifies the nation, imbuing it with a personality often: "France is in trouble; *her* economy is lagging behind government expectations," or "Great Britain's mood this year is somber, after. . . ." The nation remains unique in its collective psychological importance. And this is so, even as culture becomes increasingly international.

Historically, pioneer movements in film art consistently have been most highly regarded abroad before they were appreciated at home. This was the case with German "expressionism" and with Soviet "expressive realism" during the silent era of the 1920s, and it has also been true of Italian "Neo-Realism" and the "New German Cinema" since 1945.[2] While movies commonly have an international dimension, and exceptional ones first may be appreciated by foreign audiences, they are nonetheless rooted in national thought and culture. This dialectic of international/national is a complex one, and, it is an issue that has not been given adequate attention in cultural studies. Hopefully, this book advances our understanding of the complexity of this issue.

It was the sociologist Herbert Gans who coined the term "taste culture."[3] He applied this nomenclature to culture in the United States exclusively, but I find it even more valuable for illuminating the increasing internationalization of culture. There exist clusters of persons who share particular tastes which transcend national boundaries.[4] This is most apparent, perhaps, with teenage culture, but it is also evident with groups such as left-liberal urban intellectuals, or with elderly conservative women living in small towns or rural areas. Political opinions, religious values, and attitudes toward life and toward other people, all follow patterns which cut across national boundaries. So, too, do the categories of taste, whether it be for rock music, or classical music, or for music "Frank Sinatra style." This is true for films as well. There are those movies which appeal primarily to an audience composed of persons under twenty-five, while another audience of a particular composition exists for "foreign films." There are, across the length and breadth of the cinema, movies produced for specialized audiences and tastes. In fact, the emergence of these more specialized audience cohorts for particular kinds of movies is one of the subtopics which runs through every chapter of this book.

Another subtheme, which became evident during the course of my research, is that there appears to be an important high point or shift in the thought and culture of the western world that occurred at the end of the 1950s. This is intriguing and warrants—and receives—interpretive attention in the conclusion of this book.

A kind of golden age of the movies occurred in the 1920s and 1930s, when around the world audiences packed the great, palatial movies theaters. Since the Second World War, changing patterns of lifestyle, competition from television, the increase in the number of opportunities for leisure which are available, and social and demographic patterns have contributed to the erosion of the mass audience for feature films that had characterized the cinema of the 1920s and 1930s. This mass audience appeal waned unevenly from place to place, and was resisted by movie producers, especially those in Hollywood, for years.

But this erosion has not necessarily meant a decline in the social significance and importance of film. Much of what is shown on television in every country originates as film, and may, in fact, be a movie specifically produced for television with little or no expectation for its release to commercial theaters. Then, too, it is precisely the increasing specialization of the particular audiences for certain films which has enriched the variety of overt political, intellectual, and cultural associations found in movies produced since the Second World War. The erosion of the mass audience for movies meant at least two things.

> Television, in siphoning off the most passive element in the old film audience, actually did the movies a favor. Film-makers were forced to cultivate segments in the mass audience whose tastes were not satisfied by tepid and repetitious television fare. These included the sophisticated "lost audience" which historically had identified its cultural interests with novels and the theater; young people with unprecedented economic power. . . .[5]

To many this meant that in some instances the cinema became less strictly associated with entertainment. Entertainment has been an especially problematic and deceptive word, however. There is really no antipathy between entertainment and seriousness of purpose or message, although this is often believed to be the case. If we are disposed not to like the message in the first place we may come to especially resent its being "disguised" as entertainment. This is assumed to be a particular drawback of Hollywood.

> American film . . . tends to support the dominant ideology when it presents itself as unmediated reality, entertaining us while reinforcing accepted notions of love,

sexuality, history. More recently it has qualified our assumptions, as some directors have become more independent and more in control of their work, and equally as important, as television has taken over the dominant role of entertainer in our culture.[6]

All film tends to support the "dominant ideology" wherever it is produced. Yet it must be recognized that all ideology contains contradictions. All systems have shadows. Fiction functions often to mediate such contradictions and shadows.

The social significance of the mass, popular cinema was an instance in which the collective psychological dynamic between a movie and the mass audience was of paramount importance.[7] The social significance of the more differentiated and specific cinema since 1945 is a more complex, variable, and intriguing phenomenon. Moreover, the very erosion of the cinema of theatrical exhibition has meant that moviemakers have become more self-reflexive about the art and style of what they make. This turning inward, examining the medium itself and its possibilities more intently and richly, is one of the increasing characteristics of contemporary filmmaking, and yet another subtheme in this book.

As research and writing about film have developed during the last two decades, an increasing emphasis on theory has emerged. The application of French schools of theory in particular, however, such as Structuralism, Lacanian psychoanalysis, and semiotics, in considering the relationship of films to society has proven less than satisfactory in my estimation. While these theoretical structures may bear an intellectual respectability that was often lacking in earlier anecdotal approaches to film history, they provide a framework for analysis that is unnecessarily convoluted and pretentious. Between the simplicity and inadequacy of the anecdotal approach and the overblown pretenses of an overemphasized French theoretical model is the terrain I think most productive.

That middle ground consists of the challenge of comparative studies of movies anchored in their native social and cultural environment—that is, in the context of the nation in which they were produced. The comparative angle is of ultimate importance. It provides us with a way of modifying what we take to be "truths" about phenomena and about whose nature we are tempted to generalize.

The process of aping the social sciences in trying to build models of explanation is a pitfall in the study of the arts. Human creativity conforms to certain patterns of behavior which are influenced by myriad factors—national cultural history, the development and technical demands of the medium in which one is working, pressures from audiences and their tastes, the personal biographical experiences of the artist, and so on. Yet that conforming is not limited to a single determinant. To comprehend this necessitates suspending the anticipation and expectation of a model of explanation that reveals all. From Marxism through Freudianism through structuralism and semiology, a flaw in western thought is the desire for the all-explanatory, single model. The overemphasis on theory in film studies has led in this direction, but film studies hardly stand alone.

Ten years ago I published my first book on film and society. In the ensuing decade I have altered many of my perspectives on the cinema, and I have reconsidered my approaches to the social value and meaning of motion pictures. At the same time, every shred of evidence I have gathered has reinforced my belief that movies provide an extraordinary path of insight into the rich—and often disturbing—political, social, and cultural experiences of this century. All along, I have kept trying to see my way clear to what it is that is of essential importance in assessing the social significance of the movies. This quest has taken me down avenues which have deviated from those pursued by many of my professional colleagues. I have remained unconvinced that the cinema is a structure that reveals what a film is about only when we reconstruct its conditions of production and its financing to identify the deeper ideological motive or intent behind it. The *auteur* approach to film, too, has revealed itself as shallow, and only marginally rewarding. It is not what individual artistic stamp a director may leave upon a body of works, but rather how each individual film relates to the broadest social, political, and cultural issues of its era that is most provocative.

ACKNOWLEDGMENTS

A Fulbright Professorship in 1982/1983 to the German Federal Republic permitted me to research the chapters on Europe in this book. During a 1984 summer stipend from the German Academic Exchange Service (DAAD) I followed up on that research.

On both sides of the Atlantic I have received assistance from many institutions: Basis Film-Produktion (Berlin); Bibliothek der Deutschen Kinemathek (Berlin); Bibliothèque d'Idehc (Paris); Cinémathèque de Toulouse (Toulouse); Cinetecca Nazionale (Rome); Deutsches Institut für Filmkunde (Frankfurt and Wiesbaden); Doheny Library Cinema Research Collection at the University of Southern California (Los Angeles); The Margaret Herrick Library of the Academy of Motion Pictures Arts & Sciences (Los Angeles); Montana State University Library (Bozeman); Museum of Modern Art (New York); Staatliches Filmarchiv der DDR (East Berlin); University of California at Los Angeles Research Library.

Harvey J. Graff (UT-Dallas) read the first draft of my manuscript and made valuable comments upon it. Evan William Cameron, who directs the Graduate Programme in Film/Video at York University in Ontario, brought an extraordinarily wide-ranging expertise and a cautious eye to his critique of it. David Lovekin, a former graduate student of mine who now teaches at Sauk Valley Community College, assisted my research on chapters 1 and 2. Their comments have helped me immeasurably. Neither Graff nor Cameron nor Lovekin, of course, is responsible to any degree for what some may regard as my errors, misinterpretations, or poor judgments.

Elizabeth Stern-Scherr typed the manuscript of *Ribbons in Time*.

Bozeman, Montana   Paul Monaco

Ribbons in Time

ONE

Realism, Italian Style

Since the Second World War Italy has experienced rapid change. Literacy and prosperity have increased steadily. Like the other losers in the conflict, Germany and Japan, Italy experienced a rapid recovery from the war itself, and during the 1950s had one of the leading growth rates of any nation in the world. Italy also found its way back into the international community faster than either of the other Axis powers.

As in many other societies which have experienced rapid modernization and change, Italian life has been fraught by inconsistencies and inequities. Postwar Italy has witnessed an inordinate amount of internal migration, most of it back and forth between the north and south of the country. It has also experienced the sustained viability of the west's largest and most successful Communist party. This, in itself, seems an anomaly given the undeniable surge in the spread of literacy and prosperity across the country since 1945, as well as the traditional basis of the society in Catholicism.[1]

Since the Second World War both Federico Fellini and Michelangelo Antonioni have fostered successful directorial careers. Their films have put them at the forefront of attention in their native Italy, as well as propelling them into the spotlight internationally. Over a period of four decades both have continued to explore, and to work beyond, the tenets of Neo-Realism with amazing consistency.

> For Antonioni, as for Fellini, neo-realism remained the most important formative experience, whereas the innovative urge of their films stemmed from the reaction against its established formulas.[2]

Both Fellini and Antonioni have interpreted the values and experience of Italian society in radically different ways. Increasingly, they have created movies which relate to the Italian experience from opposite perspectives. The central topic of this chapter is to explore the complex relations between the work of these two directors, the principles of Neo-Realism proper, the Italian context, and the broader patterns of postwar development in Western Europe. Such an undertaking may be grounded in the ideas expressed by the famed French critic André Bazin whose aesthetic principles, developed in the late 1940s and early 1950s, were based on his assessment of the Neo-Realist movement:

It is up to the theorist to study the various processes (means) by which a filmmaker can make reality (the raw material) significant, and, more particularly, to make it significant in a certain humanly valuable way (form).[3]

Bazin's comment is telling, for it points to the filmmaker's engagement with creating meaning and value on celluloid for the world. To do so from the perspective of a realist posture of any sort requires working through the raw material of nature and experience. That is, the central problem becomes for the filmmaker how to transcend the camera's function as a mere recording instrument.

Neo-Realism in Italy is normally associated with the response of filmmakers (and other artists and thinkers) to the end of the Second World War and the immediate legacy of Fascism. It is denoted by its attention to contemporary social and economic problems as these appeared in the years immediately after the war. Nonetheless, it is important to bear in mind that, from the beginning, Neo-Realism had a broader dimension. That dimension might be labeled "philosophic" or, more correctly, "cinematic."

A more careful analysis is needed to reveal that the consistent focus of major neo-realist films was "not only upon social reality but also upon the dialectics of reality and appearance, usually the appearance or illusion of reality produced by artistic means."[4]

How both Antonioni and Fellini moved beyond Neo-Realism, and how they did so against the backdrop of a rapidly modernizing Italy, focuses on that dialectic.

Neo-Realism proper has been perceived as arising out of the experience of Italian Fascism which led to Italy's alliance with Nazi Germany and involvement in World War Two. Fascism arose in Italy at the end of the First World War, and triumphed there with the famed March on Rome and Benito Mussolini's takeover as chief of state in 1922. Fascism—which seemed such a distinctively twentieth century movement—served to protect a strong feudalistic class structure that had survived in Italy longer than in most other places in Europe.[5] Italian Fascism was not revolutionary in character, as Hitler's Nazism might be claimed to have been.[6] Italian Fascism preserved the monarchy, the class structure, elements of a feudal economy, and a dominant, conservative role for the clergy of the Catholic Church. Fascism's effects on the cinema, however, were generally erosive.

After a promising beginning before 1914, the fortunes of film in Italy had waned by the end of the First World War. The pretensions of the poet Gabriele d'Annunzio, who inspired several ill-conceived art films right after the First World War, were followed by the machinations of the Fascists who—after their political takeover in 1922—hoped to control moviemaking for their own ideological ends. That did finally occur, after Mussolini's alliance with Hitler in 1936. Nonetheless, the main innovation in the Italian cinema during the 1930s was the

"White Telephone movie," a singularly shallow genre depicting minor vicissitudes and temptations in the lives of Italy's urban upper-middle class.[7]

Neo-Realism was not confined to the cinema but nonetheless found its deepest, richest, and most thoroughgoing expression in nearly a hundred movies produced in Italy between 1945 and 1955.[8] Neo-Realism appeared simultaneously with the battle for Italy by Nazis and Fascists against the Anglo-American forces and Partisans that raged in 1943 and 1944, was intertwined with the resistance against Fascism and Nazism, and became identifiable with new voices and new hopes for a different direction in the Italian experience immediately after the war.

As the much acclaimed Italian novelist and social critic Alberto Moravia put it:

> Italy's theater and literature had never been especially important in the national culture, when compared to opera, painting, and sculpture. In 1943, however, as two foreign forces began the struggle between the occupying Germans and the Anglo-Americans bent on driving them out, the people awoke. And this awakening was expressed through film.[9]

In George Huaco's *Sociology of Film Art* (1965) the author enumerated these characteristics of Neo-Realist films:

(1) the use of nonprofessional actors in major dramatic roles
(2) rejection of studio sets and documentary use of "reallife" settings
(3) naturalistic photography using the "available-light" approach (e.g., the use of real sunlight instead of artificial light, the shooting of scenes at night instead of faking them with a red filter, and so)
(4) the use of individual heroes who are, however, nonidealized and frequently isolated
(5) detailed psychological characterization of major and minor characters
(6) the camera technique presents the environment by an accumulation of small concrete details[10]

General descriptive principles such as these, however, hardly begin to describe what the phenomenon was all about. Neo-Realist cinema was a creation of a moment, primarily identifiable by its spontaneity. It was a response to the political, social, and ideological environment in Italy as the war drew to its end there. As the master theoretician of Neo-Realist film, Cesare Zavattini, observed in a diary entry in 1944:

> The film's progress depends on the opportunities we encounter, or better, that we will make ourselves encounter in the liberated part of our country. . . . The project came to me months ago, born from the conviction that only in this moment people have a power to sincerity that they will lose again very soon. Today a destroyed house is a destroyed house; the odor of the dead lingers; from the North we hear the echo of the last shellings; in other words, our stupor and fear are whole, it's as if we could

study them in a test-tube. Our cinema must attempt this documentation, it has the means to move about like this in space and time, to collect within the spectator's pupil the multiple and the diverse, provided it abandons its language to the content (even the most modern content is still expressed in an antiquated language determined for the most part by the whims of capital).[11]

Neo-Realism emerged at the end of the war, when Italian society had to face up to severe material shortages and unemployment, as well as facing up to Italy's own political and moral dilemma in having followed Mussolini, and, in turn, Mussolini's ally, Hitler. These months must have been bleak and depressing; deprivation and want were widespread, as were destruction and resentment. Yet this situation affected the generations differently. As the famed author Italo Calvino noted:

> Italy's literary explosion in those years was less an artistic event than a physiological, existential, collective event. We had experienced the war, and we younger people—who had been barely old enough to join the partisans—did not feel crushed, defeated, "beat". On the contrary, we were victors, driven by the propulsive charge of the just-ended battle, the exclusive possessors of its heritage. Ours was not easy optimism, however, or gratuitous euphoria. Quite the opposite . . . Neorealism was not a school. (We must try to state things precisely.) It was a collection of voices, largely marginal, a multiple discovery of the various Italys, even—or particularly—the Italys previously unknown. . . .[12]

Neo-Realism in film turned out to be both a negation and a continuation of selected tendencies from Fascist cinema simultaneously.[13] Moreover, several traditions which spawned Neo-Realism could be found embedded in Italian culture, going back to a populist melodrama that had thrived in the previous century.[14]

Neo-Realism was eminently pragmatic as well. Directors took over the habit of shooting film scenes and then post-synchronizing sound to the footage in the studio which had been established in the late 1930s. The Fascist regime had introduced this way of making movies in order to more effectively censor the contents, and to make sure that lines in the scripts were actually said by actors and actresses with the "ideologically correct" emphasis, inflection, and intonation. The Neo-Realists found in post-synchronization a technical device that freed the camera from limits imposed on its work by the presence of sound equipment which made resetting for a shot clumsy. This added facility in filming intermeshed with the desire to shoot on location and with available light. At the same time it was also a device which held down production costs.

On the other hand, the Fascist regime had built enormous studios in Rome, and sponsored the building of others. The Neo-Realists emphatically rejected the confined, hothouse atmosphere of the studio in favor of shooting on location and with available light. In this regard, the Neo-Realists opted for production techniques which refuted the mentality of artificiality inherent in any studio

situation, and the devices of control of the environment which could be interpreted as reflecting a basic and underlying tenet of Fascist ideology in general.

The critic Guido Aristarco noted that the "neo" in Neo-Realism referred to
the renewal of Italian national life that was reborn in the armed Resistance
toward the end of the Second World War.[15] This artistic movement existed as a
vanguard of cultural change in a way paralleled in the history of film only by the
"Expressive Realism" of the silent cinema in the Soviet Union in the 1920s.[16]

This close connection to its social setting may be interpreted in the mode of
materialist determination. A contemporary, the French filmmaker René Clair,
opined that Neo-Realism ". . . produces masterpieces because it has no resources, but soon it will be rich."[17] While Clair's sentiment may be admired
morally—money has corrupted authenticity in art often enough—it is nonetheless both clichéd and incorrect. Clair is indulging in and endorsing the fundamental bourgeois myth of art and the artist: that creativity flows only from
conditions of impoverishment and deprivation.

Neo-Realism proper survived for a decade. In some instances its practition-
ers became rich, and in others they did not. The relationship between money
and breakthroughs in the art of the cinema is complex and intricate, and nowhere
is this clearer than in the instance of the European film movement that followed
Neo-Realism, the French New Wave (see chapter 2).

The most fruitful way of observing the phenomenon of Neo-Realism is to
recognize how the cinema captured the moment in Italy, both with regard to the
general pattern of intellectual and cultural developments at the end of the
Second World War and to the uniqueness of perception and perspective that was
particular to the Italian situation. That distinctive and unique element was
focused on the dramatic confrontation and the temporary symbiosis of Catholicism and Marxism. Indeed, that very confrontation and symbiosis is a central
thematic element in what I regard as the first Neo-Realist film produced,
Roberto Rossellini's *Rome, Open City* (1944). The story is of a priest, Don Pietro,
and a Communist, Manfredi, who are both working in the Resistance. Eventually they are captured; Manfredi is beaten to death by his Nazi interrogators, and
the priest is shot by a firing squad the next day. The two are from different
ideological worlds. Their relationship, however, is an effective one, for Manfredi
can count on the priest to deliver money to a group of Partisans after curfew, and
both can count on a shared loyalty to the higher cause of the Resistance itself.

Rome, Open City deftly achieves elements of humor, such as when Don
Pietro has to whack grandpa with a frying pan to keep him quiet as the priest
feigns giving him the last rites of the church in order to dupe the Nazi SS and the
Fascist police who are conducting a raid on the apartment house in search of
Manfredi and his chum. *Open City* also provides what has become a pervasive
stereotypical image of Nazis in popular culture, and especially in the movies,
ever since. The suggestion of sexual deviancy—in this instance, the effeminate
gestures of the SS general and the lesbian liaison between a Nazi agent and an
empty-headed young Italian actress—and of decadence is pervasive.

According to the analysis undertaken by George Huaco, between 1945 and 1955, of the Neo-Realist films produced, about half were directed by Catholic liberals such as Rossellini and Vittorio De Sica, with the other half being the work of Marxists, such as Giuseppe De Santis and Alberto Lattuada.[18] The social history of the directors of Neo-Realism itself reflects the "Marxist-Catholic symbiosis" that the movies themselves often portrayed.

Nonetheless, these films, as a whole, came to be seen as subversive, even if this condemnation was often vague. Such criticism was in step with the changing postwar political atmosphere. Increasing distaste toward Neo-Realism had much to do with Italy's position in the Cold War and the pressure placed on the Italian regime by Washington.[19] Directors' problems with the official censors in Rome increased,[20] and Neo-Realist films came repeatedly under attack by the Roman Catholic hierarchy.[21]

Soviet critics found Neo-Realist films ideologically acceptable, and praised them, observing, for example, that ". . . the hero of a neo-realist film is socialistic by instinct."[22] Neo-Realism, however, was never politically or ideologically rigorous. It began with a moral point of view that evolved into a distinct aesthetic idea, according to no better an authority than Roberto Rossellini himself.[23]

Neo-Realism marked the first unique mode of film art to emerge from the Second World War. While its own sociology is interesting, and while it produced memorable films which hold a treasured spot in film history—such as Rossellini's *Paisan* (1946) and *Germany, Year Zero* (1947); De Sica's *Shoeshine* (1946), *Bicycle Thief* (1948), and *Umberto D* (1951); De Santis's *Bitter Rice* (1949) and *Rome, 11 O'Clock*; Visconti's *The Earth Trembles* (1948); and Lattuada's *The Mill on the Po* (1949)—it is not with these, or even with the ideas and accomplishments in a particular historical milieu that we are concerned with Neo-Realism. Rather it is with the general concept of Neo-Realism, and the relationship of that concept to the subsequent careers of the two Italian directors whose films have gained great followings internationally, Federico Fellini and Michelangelo Antonioni.

Both Fellini and Antonioni had entered the film industry during the Fascist period, and both played roles in Neo-Realism proper as screenwriters. Also, they each directed one of the segments of the six-part, episodic Neo-Realist film, *Love in the City* (1954), which was one of the last in the genre proper. It was produced at the time that both Fellini's and Antonioni's own independent careers as feature film directors were being launched. Italy's two best-known directors in the postwar period, then, emerged from the give-and-take of Italian film history at roughly the same time and in nearly the same way. Their directing careers and the movies they have produced can be explored as departures from Neo-Realism; yet the departures are illuminated by continual references back to Neo-Realism as a source of their creative innovations. Neo-Realism remains for them a repository of specific ideas and notions through which both directors have been working.

The images and sounds created in their films have produced powerful and widespread impressions of the Italian experience, especially because of the large international audience for their movies. Nonetheless, both Fellini and Antonioni reflect deeply contrasting approaches to the interpretation on film of salient aspects of the Italian experience.

Antonioni's *Chronicle of a Romance* (1950) contains many of the characters, milieus, and fundamental narrative elements which the director eventually established in his mature and most widely acknowledged films, produced from the end of the 1950s to the early 1970s. In this first feature film Antonioni wove a complicated plot focused on a character named Enrico, a wealthy industrialist, who becomes suspicious of his wife Paola and hires a detective to investigate her background.

Quickly that investigation produces a number of provocative and mysterious photographs, and the detective learns that the wife had been involved in the past in a mysterious situation that had ended with the death of a friend named Giovanna. Apparently, Giovanna had walked into an open elevator shaft, with Paola and her lover Guido as witnesses. Moreover, that incident had caused Paola and Guido to break off their lengthy romance.

But the investigation reunites them, and Paola and Guido begin an illicit affair that Antonioni uses as the springboard to explore specific differences in social class, human expectations, and the possibilities of human emotion. Paola has come from an impoverished background, and her lover has remained poor. She is bound to him emotionally, and whenever she can she rushes to him. Yet she does not want to leave the luxury and comfort that her husband gives her.

When Enrico test-drives a Maserati he is considering buying for Paola, he speeds down a country road, where two giant bottles erected as advertising by a vermouth company stand on either side of the pavement. He nearly crashes and decides against buying the automobile for it would be too dangerous for his wife to drive.

Soon Paola and Guido have plotted Enrico's murder. Guido waits for him, revolver in hand, near a bridge over which Enrico passes each evening on his way home from work. Just that afternoon Enrico has learned the results of the investigations, which have uncovered his wife's infidelities with Guido. Before he reaches the spot where Guido lies in wait, the car crashes and Enrico perishes. The viewer does not know for certain whether it was an accident or suicide.

Antonioni's next feature, *The Woman without Camellia* (1953) shared many similarities in mood, theme, and point of view with *Chronicle of a Romance*. The female lead is once again, as in *Chronicle*, played by Lucia Bosé. And as Clara Manni, she plays a woman of impoverished background who is thrust into the world of wealth and comfort. She has been "discovered" and turned into a film actress by the producer Gianni. However, she finds her own situation even more problematic than did Paola in *Chronicle*. Clara's situation vis-à-vis the class to which she aspires is fraught with suspicion and insecurity. She has burned her bridges of class identity behind her, yet at the same time she has established only a marginal—and tenuous—relationship to the privileged class.

In both these movies Antonioni had already advanced beyond the main source of Neo-Realist film drama which focused on exploration of the working-class environment. Antonioni's purpose in these movies is an examination of the nature of Italian class structure, and the lines of distinction and discrimination associated with class identity. He took on the complex and sophisticated problem of critiquing the class system in Italy itself, rather than concentrating exclusively on protraying the results of that system—the impoverished underside of Italian society.

The milieu in which Antonioni's first two features are set points to the director's interpretive point of view. These settings suggest where it is that Antonioni was perceiving the major tension in modern and contemporary society. In the early 1950s Antonioni had begun to explore the nature of societal pressure and the conflict between the individual and his or her place in society. Antonioni's first two features were focused on female leading characters, indicating a pattern he would follow in many of his later films, and establishing his work as that of a "woman's director." It is more important, however, to recognize that Antonioni's fiction locates the essential crisis of modern life in the boredom, alienation, and *angst* of the upwardly mobile upper-middle classes. For the most part Antonioni eschews portraying the misery and impoverishment of the working classes and of the unemployed which had been a staple in the traditional Leftist critique of capitalist society.[24]

Federico Fellini was introduced to the cinema by Roberto Rossellini, who included him as a collaborator in the postwar Neo-Realist masterpiece *Paisan* (1946). *Paisan* bore strong elements of documentary film style, as well as an episodic structure, in portraying the stories of several fictionalized encounters between American GIs and Italians right after the war. The first feature film normally attributed to Fellini himself is *Variety Lights* (1950), which, however, he actually co-directed with another of the great directors of Neo-Realism proper, Alberto Lattuada.

In *Variety Lights*, Checco, "the wizard of fun," "the international wizard," is, in truth, an unsuccessful actor who promoted himself as the leader of a small group of comedians. One day a good-looking young country girl named Liliana joins the troupe, and acquires immediate popularity when her skirt falls off during a performance. Checco decides quickly that he prefers her to his longtime amour, Melina.

Checco promises Liliana that he will protect her, and bring her glory and fame on the stage. All this never happens, of course, as he leads his motley troupe through the poor villages of the Italian countryside. Finally, he runs off to Rome with Liliana, conceiving of a grand variety show that never materializes. There she takes up with an impresario, begins a romance with him, and deserts Checco, her dreams still intact.

Checco returns to Melina. She forgives him, and in the final sequence, when they are riding on a train, she falls asleep in Checco's arms. An attractive young woman enters their train compartment and takes a seat. Checco begins ogling her, and the viewer may well wonder if the tale with Liliana will be repeated.

Fellini's first two feature films outline the parameters of his subsequent directorial concerns less clearly than was the case with Antonioni's *Chronicle of a Romance* and *Woman without Camelia*. Antonioni's approach to scripting and directing emphasizes the subtleties of mood and their shifts, whereas Fellini's movies have more radical fantasy elements in them. In general, Fellini's features are less patterned.

Antonioni worked with Fellini on the screenplay of *The White Sheik* (1952), which was Fellini's second feature.[25] In it Wanda and Ivan, a young couple from the provinces, arrive in Rome for their honeymoon. He wants to see the tourist attractions, and is especially excited about the prospects of possibly attending an audience with the Pope. By contrast she can think only of meeting the man who portrays the "White Sheik" in a photographic cartoon.

While her husband is dutifully doing the rounds with relatives, she is off meeting Marilena, the editor of the "fumetti,"[26] who arranges for her to meet the "Sheik." In real life he is hardly the dashing romantic hero she had envisioned. Nonetheless, she is enamored of him and she accepts his invitation for a boat ride. Aboard an old, creaking craft he makes a pass at her, is beaned by a swinging sail beam, and is knocked unconscious. Meanwhile, her husband has started a frantic hunt for her, needing to produce her for propriety's sake when they are to be received by his relatives. Finally, the couple returns to shore. The "Sheik's" wife who is waiting for them at the dock gives Wanda a thrashing, and the "Sheik" sheepishly escapes on a motor scooter.

Wanda is remorseful and crushed. Her husband Ivan continues the hunt for her, running into several precarious—and possibly compromising—situations himself. Out of shame Wanda first hides in a forest, then decides to commit suicide by leaping into the Tiber. The water is low, however, and she winds up muddied, and is taken to the hospital. There her husband finds her. His primary concern is that they be on time for a meeting with her uncle so that a sense of social propriety may be salvaged. From there the proper couple goes to the Vatican for an audience with His Holiness.

Fellini's first two features point to his exploring peculiarities of Italian social practice and the assumptions which underlie it. Unlike Antonioni, however, Fellini's approach to such issues is through the devices of a broadly based humor. As Mira Liehm expressed it: "Fellini's *White Sheik* could be considered an attempt to resolve the basic dilemma of the time: how to move beyond realism to a new reality."[27] Fellini's fiction often borders on becoming truly tragic, but inevitably it steers away from this tendency in the direction of either a sentimental or a humorous resolution.

With *The Road* (1954), however, Fellini's vision and direction moved beyond the humorous and ironic perspectives on social conventions and shared illusions that he had established in his first two films. His direction of *The Road* followed the path of a 1953 feature, *The Big Loafers*, in which five men, each about the age of thirty, are caught in a continuing web of adolescent fantasies and desires. They live in a small resort town on the coast and the action of the film is set there during the off-season. The young men are types, and their typologies reflect the sociological range of shiftlessness, hostility toward society, dishonesty, and irresponsibility. This film marked an intensifying of the emotional stakes involved in his film dramas, and signified Fellini's shift toward his more successful work beginning in 1954.

In *The Road*, which was Fellini's first real international box-office success, the setting is once more the nomadic and problematic milieu of the circus and the fair. The itinerant performer Zampone, who entertains the crowds by breaking a chain wound round his chest, buys the young, childlike woman Gelosima from her mother. In time, she becomes attached to him emotionally. Zampone trains her, humiliates her, sleeps with her. He has affairs with other women openly before her. In one incident, while stopping at a wealthy man's farmhouse for the wedding festivities, Gelosima amuses a sick boy with comic gestures and tricks, and then goes in the middle of the night to comfort a trembling horse in the stable, while Zampone makes love to the elderly farmer's wife.

The next day Gelosima meets "The Fool" in the town square where he is giving a tightrope-walking display. It is Christmas eve, which serves to highlight the poignancy and pathos of Gelosima's situation. Soon Zampone has caught up with her again, and they take off on his oversized motorcycle, leaving "The Fool" behind. Fate, however, reunites the trio, after Zampone and Gelosima have joined a wandering circus. "The Fool" teaches Gelosima to play the trumpet in a poignant sequence. Then, he and Zampone fight and both land in jail. "The Fool" wants her to run away with him, but she is confused and uncertain about doing so. She stays with Zampone. One day soon after she has made this decision she asks him if he would miss her if she died; he calls her a jerk.

The next day they see "The Fool" by the roadside changing a tire. Zampone stops, leaps down from his motorcycle, and gives him a beating from which "The Fool" dies. Gelosima stretches out over his fallen body, mourning him. Zampone abandons her and disappears.

Several years later Zampone comes to a seaside village. In the streets of the town he discovers a younger woman playing the trumpet song that Gelosima had learned from "The Fool." She tells Zampone that she learned to play the tune from a wandering, melancholy woman who had come there a while ago and who had died. Zampone goes off, gets drunk, and in the last sequence of the movie staggers alone on the beach, weeping.

Many elements in *The Road* are typical of most of Fellini's movies—the circus or carnival environment, the macho figure who cannot acknowledge his own sensitivity, the pathos of wandering, the grotesque characters and situations found throughout the Italian provinces, and the music of the composer Nino Rota, who first began working with Fellini on *The White Sheik*. Are elements such as these to be reconciled with the principles of Neo-Realism, or do they mark a definitive departure from them?

The Road takes place in the milieu of the impoverished and the itinerant and the characters are simple folk, even though their personalities are eccentric and, in most instances, almost unique. Much of the movie was shot on location,

1. Gelosima and Mazeppa in *The Road*. Fellini's breakthrough movie established his search for a new realism. Museum of Modern Art

although sections of it were made in a studio. The actors and actresses were professionals, with Fellini's wife, Giulietta Masina, playing the lead role of Gelosima.

Yet the citing of certain characteristics, as if they were established clearly as topics on a checklist, and the attempt to estimate to what degree the elements of a specific movie fulfills them point clearly to the limits of such a rote and mechanistic response. There are varieties of Neo-Realism, not in the least because the notion of Neo-Realism itself suggests several possible interpretations of what it is that constitutes reality.

One of the most profound contemporary sources connecting Fellini to Neo-Realism is found in the commentary of André Bazin. Writing in the 1950s, Bazin argued that what Fellini shared with the mainstream Neo-Realist directors like Rossellini and De Sica was to give priority to portraying reality by means of specific dramatic construction and devices. Bazin maintained the singular talent of the Italian moviemakers in the years following the Second World War was their ability to establish through the Neo-Realist movement what Bazin called a "phenomenological" realism. "In it, the relationship between signification and appearance is, in a certain sense, reversed; the latter is always offered to us as if it were a singular discovery, an almost documentary revelation that retains all its detail and picturesque qualities. The art of the director resides, then, in the skill with which he can make the signification of an event surge forth, or at least the signification he wants to have, without destroying any of the ambiguities."[28]

In this argument Bazin claims that the quality and capacity of the image itself render meaning or value. The Neo-Realist aesthetic embraces a dualism. The image, on the one hand, is simply what it is as physically given; yet simultaneously the image invokes a power that exists over and beyond itself. Bazin finally best illustrates this in Fellini's case by referring to the fact that Fellini's characters, although powerful and evocative, are never drawn psychologically, and can be defined "only by their appearances."[29]

Bazin's arguments lead us away from focusing on the Neo-Realist movement as a historic appearance caused by the social situation of Italy immediately after the war. Hence, this means shifting the framework for appreciating Neo-Realist works, whether they are movies or novels, away from the ideological. The result de-emphasizes the ways in which such Neo-Realist works are rooted in a critique of poverty, particular social problems such as unemployment and political and social injustice.

According to Bazin, Fellini's realism is based philosophically on the notion of encountering the world as it has come to be. It means that the pursuit of what caused things to be as they are must be bracketed out, and necessitates suspending efforts to comprehend the basis for them. Fellini's movies represent an engagement with the material and emotional stuff of reality devoid of preconceived notions about its value or its meaning.

In an interview Fellini once commented that he thought that Rossellini was the only true Neo-Realist director, though he added that, yes, in a certain way he was a Neo-Realist, too. As to just what that certain way is, Fellini said that he was alluding to an "attitude of sincerity to the ideas we intend to develop or the characters whose story we want to tell."[30]

It is important to grasp Fellini's emphasis on both the sincerity and the intentionality of the director. Essentially Fellini was positing a view of "realism" that defined it as artistic integrity. Notice, for example, that in his statement Fellini refers to his fictional characters as if they existed outside the film and, hence, deserved a particular truthfulness and accuracy of representation. Reality becomes defined in terms of the authenticity of the film director's adherence to his or her own artistic principles. Fellini's movies, of course, are very much concerned, even in their overt subjects, with the entire idea of entertainment, performance, the image, and artistry.

Fellini's *Nights of Cabiria* (1956) again features his wife Giulietta Masina in the title role. Cabiria is a prostitute, although she is hardly savvy enough to negotiate all the peculiarities and underworld risks of her profession. In the first scene of the film Cabiria is deftly relieved of her handbag by a street thief and pushed into a river where she nearly drowns. Saved, but with wounded pride, her character has already been situated in the narrative. She has the viewer's empathy, and it is clear that is is not her whoring, but her vulnerability, that is the central issue of this movie.

Cabiria is adrift in the night world of Rome. She battles in the streets with her professional enemy, the hooker Matilde. She is driven to the Via Veneto to see her pimp Marizo, and is looked down upon by the fashionable ladies of the night who stalk Rome's most luxurious boulevard. Stopping outside the Kit-Kat Club, she sees the movie star Amedo Nazzari and his girlfriend having an argument. The angry Amedo impulsively invites Cabiria to join him, and off they drive in his sports car, she getting a fine revenge on the whores of the Via Veneto who stare at her resentfully. Before she can enjoy much of Amedo's hospitality, however, the girlfriend he abandoned outside the nightclub shows up and Cabiria must hide in the bathroom. From there she silently witnesses the rest of the evening's activities; she even feels happy about the couple's reconciliation.

Cabiria, who marked her exit from Nazzari's house by smashing a huge picture window, spends the next day drinking and picnicking at the "Madonna of Divine Love" sanctuary with other prostitutes and their pimps. Later, at a movie house, a magician doing a show at intermission hypnotizes Cabiria and introduces her to the imaginary Oscar, with whom she dances and falls in love. Awakened, she is angry at having been made a laughing stock.

Just at that moment, however, a gentleman introduces himself to her as Oscar D'Onofrio. Cabiria is attracted to him, and his courtship of her begins. Eventually she withdraws all her savings and is ready to move away with him. On the banks of the Tiber, Oscar snatches her money, throws her down, and runs off. Her story has come full circle. She lies on the ground for some time, then she wanders along a road in the moonlight. She joins a group of people who are singing and smiling, and continues on with them.

Cabiria focuses on crushed illusion—and the protagonist's recovery from it—in the midst of the modern city. The milieu is highly fantasized, rather than depicting naturalistically the metropolis and its dilemmas. While Cabiria lives and labors on the social margins of society, clearly the film is not geared to social criticism as we would normally understand that term. Yet *Cabiria* shows, perhaps better than any other earlier film by Fellini, just how he had worked through Neo-Realism, as Bazin suggested, managing to come out the other side. "Instead of using personal tragedies to understand a social problem, Fellini is interested in the effect that society and its institutions have on his rather singular characters."[31] In *Cabiria* Fellini "has focused down from a broad view of the hazards faced by prostitutes as a class—the Neo-Realist perspective proper—to a single, unique case."[32]

Yet, just how far can we push this distinction? Neo-Realist films proper hardly empty all their characters of individual presence or manage to eschew the kind of fictional power that elicits the audience response which we call "identification." From the priest, Don Pietro, in *Open City* to the little boy in *Bicycle Thief* to the characters of the various episodes—including the one directed by Fellini himself—in Cesare Zavattini's *Love in the City*, such characters are highly individual and are a source of empathy on personal, as well as on social or situational, grounds. Even though Neo-Realism shifted, for a time, the director's interest away from the professionalism of "actors" and "actresses," that does not mean that Neo-Realist theory could effectively empty all major characters of their dimensions of uniqueness. Moreover, cinematic representation could not simply be stripped of the fundamental appeals rooted in individual sentiment and the viewer's identification with a specific character. Neo-Realism succeeded even less than Soviet "Expressive Realism" had in the 1920s in putting forth its agenda on the issue of characterization.

The Soviet directors, such as Sergei Eisenstein, Vsevolod Pudovkin, and Alexander Dovzhenko, succeeded to an extent by making individual characters represent social types more fully by developing the "masses" as an element of force and motivation, as well as a determinant of action. Yet their success was anchored in the ideology of Marxist-Leninism, in the philosophy of historical determinism, and in the spirit of collectivization officially endorsed in the society in which these films were made. By staying within the conventions of bourgeois society, Neo-Realism in Italy could not really have it both ways, being forced in the end to promote Leftist social doctrine through the devices of nonsocialist aesthetics. There is no fundamental reason for reacting to Neo-Realist characters differently than one does to characters in films of a different sort. On this score Neo-Realism produced no breakthrough. The simple fact of depicting the proletariat does not translate necessarily into realistic codes. Fellini preferred to stylize people on the margins of society—entertainers and whores. But both those categories were a wellspring of unique individuals and eccentrics.

Moreover, with *La Dolce Vita* (1959) Fellini shifted from the social milieu of the lower-class setting of his earlier films. The "sweet life"—even though the title is intended ironically—prevailed amid the upwardly mobile middle classes. The central figure of this memorable movie is the journalist Marcello.

La Dolce Vita was an immense, immediate international success at the box office, and its legend has survived. And one of the significant reasons why this film has held such a grasp on collective memory is because of the way in which it captures a specific moment in time and in collective experience. In spite of its immediacy and its connectedness to the Italian scene, it was appropriate for a substantial audience across both Europe and North America right at the beginning of the 1960s.

La Dolce Vita opens with a sequence filled with stunning visual effects. Marcello, a reporter, and several press photographers are on board a helicopter which is carrying a statue of Christ across Rome from one spot to another. Below, on the rooftops, bikini-clad women wave to them. This opening, with the airborne Christ sweeping over the "sweet life," is the counterpoint to the ending of the film when Marcello sees the young Paola on the beach, and she fades away from him like an angelic vision.

La Dolce Vita is composed of a dozen distinct episodes, linked by the odyssey—and resultant deterioration—of Marcello, who is featured in each of them. Marcello's exploits begin in a nightclub where he meets Maddalena, the man-hungry daughter of a wealthy industrialist who seduces him. Returning to his apartment in the early hours of the morning he discovers his live-in girlfriend Emma has attempted suicide. After taking her to the hospital he rushes directly

2. *La Dolce Vita*'s visual metaphor of the dynamic of change, tradition, and decay in Italian life: Christ airborne over Roman arches. Museum of Modern Art

to the airport to interview Sylvia, the voluptuous Hollywood actress who is arriving in Rome from Hollywood with her fiancé. The day ends with the celebrated fountain scene in which Sylvia and Marcello frolic in the waters of the Trevi fountain, illuminated at night.

Then, during a photography session with a bevy of models, Marcello sees an old friend, the intellectual Steiner. They go to a church where Steiner plays the organ. In their conversation Steiner reminds Marcello of the novel Marcello had intended to write before he became caught up in journalism. Embarrassed by these comments on his loss of artistic impulse and by the allusions to his sellout to sensational journalism, Marcello leaves Steiner and goes to the seaside where he meets the young and vibrant Paola, who is waiting on tables. Later, with Emma, he goes to investigate the story of two children living in a lower-class suburb to whom the Madonna has appeared in a vision. Shortly after their arrival, however, the incident is revealed as an instance of parental exploitation. It ends in a rainstorm with the children reciting their prerehearsed piece while the others scatter, except for a dying man who had been brought to the place on a stretcher and who expires on the spot.

Marcello visits Steiner at his home. The family atmosphere, the comfort, and all the trappings of stability weigh heavily on Marcello, who admits to his friend that he is unhappy with his life. To Marcello's surprise Steiner responds that "the most awful life is a sheltered one, in a world where everything is in its place."

Marcello is visited by his father from the provinces, but early in the evening Marcello leaves the older man to his naïve and awkward appreciation of big city pleasures at an out-of-the-way bistro and returns to the Via Veneto, the heart of the "sweet life." At the outbuilding of an ancient castle a séance is held, and couples embrace and kiss in darkened corners. By dawn they leave, some of them wearing medieval costumes.

A few days later Marcello learns that Steiner has murdered his two children and then killed himself. Marcello winds up at an orgy at a wealthy estate where he degrades himself. He wanders with several others from the party down to the beach where a monstrous dead fish is hauled out of the water. He sees Paola, the young, energetic woman he had met at the café. He starts after her, but is drawn back into the group.

Perhaps, as the Italian critic Renzo Renzi wrote, *La Dolce Vita* is destined someday to find a special place as a work of fiction in the history of European decadence.[33] Certainly, at the time it appeared, it created such strong images and associations that they symbolized the era of the early 1960s throughout the industrialized western world. The movie's title itself—"the sweet life"—quickly became a colloquial phrase, in more than one language, that ostensibly described a major cultural impulse at the beginning of the 1960s. "However, viewed objectively, this cluster of motifs takes on a more affirmative historical significance. . . . *La Dolce Vita*, by implication, summed up a certain moment in the development of the Italian nation, just as *Rome, Open City* . . . had done long before."[34]

Nonetheless, Fellini hastened to reject commentary that saw the film as "an almost documentary piece of social criticism."[35] Indeed, he claimed that in the movie, "the Rome of which I speak is a city of the inner self; its topography is entirely spiritual."[36] Here Fellini comes close to pointing to the dialectic of reality through which he had been working consistently. His balancing of the imaginary, the filmmaker's subjectivity, and the external reality of appearance and society have blended fully.

In parallel fashion, Antonioni, too, kept striving toward representing the contemporary moment and doing it with a particular acuity, as situated in the milieu of the upper middle classes at the end of the 1950s. And he too, brought his own dialectical perspective to this undertaking. His path to that point had moved through a different, although a more logical, progression to this end than had Fellini's. Antonioni's two transitional films of the mid-1950s were *The Girlfriends* (1955), and *The Cry* (1956).

In the former, the protagonist is an outsider who has entered the world of wealth and luxury. The movie centers on Clelia and four of her female friends. Still, much attention is given throughout the film to Carlo, whom she likes but who still lives in the working-class district in which she was raised.

Clelia has come from Rome to Turin to oversee the opening of a fashion salon. The new friends she has made have a friend named Rosetta who has attempted suicide, and Clelia is introduced to her. They make an outing to the beach. Here is a scene of dislocation, where the characters are out of their own milieu. It is a movie situation for which Antonioni has become famous and one that he seems able to render tellingly on the screen time and again. Rosetta begins to realize that all the others really know a great deal about her suicide attempt, and that they have gossiped about her motives for it. The youngest woman, Mariella, impulsively shouts that they should run to the water's edge from the high dunes. They do so, but when they reach their goal, with the men lagging behind, they are disoriented. Put off by it all, Clelia, anxious to return to her lover Carlo, offers Rosetta a ride back to town. As they drive back to town, she also offers Rosetta a job at the salon.

In spite of her attraction to him, Clelia's relationship to Carlo begins to deteriorate as soon as she reflects on his class origins, for they threaten deeply her perceptions of her own upward mobility. Meanwhile, Rosetta has become ever more entangled with the artist Lorenzo, whose wife Nené is really more creative and successful than he. Eventually, at a restaurant, tempers flare. Lorenzo leaves in a rage, followed by Rosetta, whom he rejects. Rosetta goes to the river, jumps in, and drowns.

The next day, at the salon, Clelia expresses her feelings of guilt about Rosetta. She has decided to leave Turin and go back to Rome. At the station Carlo watches as her train pulls away.

In *The Cry*, Antonioni shifts his focus to a working-class character who has remained in a working-class milieu. Here it appears that the director has abandoned his exploration of the tension caused by social mobility and has become concerned with the sense of dislocation and psychological displacement inherent in a basic "modern" situation.

Aldo, a mechanic in a sugar refinery in a bleak village in the Po Valley, has been living with Irma, a woman whose husband left her years ago. Yet, one day, upon learning of her former husband's death, she despairs. This prompts Aldo to propose marriage in a relationship that has already produced a daughter. Now she reveals that she loves yet another man, which shocks Aldo and he becomes violent. They break up, and he takes the daughter, Rosina, off with him.

From a failed romance with a woman named Elvira, to the fact that he can't take a job offered to him because children are not allowed in the workers' barracks, to his sexual encounter on the beach with Virginia who runs a filling station, Aldo becomes more and more detached and alienated. He meets the impoverished, but animated, Andreina who lives in dire poverty in a shack on the river's bank. She is too full of life for him, sunk in remorse and despair as he is.

Finally, Aldo takes the bus back to his village, where Irma and Rosina wait. On the trip back the bus is stopped by a workers' protest against lands being expropriated by the government for the building of an airstrip. Aldo gets to town, rushes to the house, and peers through the window. He sees Irma bathing an infant. Crushed, he rushes off to the refinery. There he scales a tower and, becoming dizzy, falls to his death.

It is possible to argue that *The Cry* marks Antonioni's rejection of the basic social and political assumptions behind Neo-Realism. For in it both the characters and the milieu are working class, yet the point of view is one that is distanced from them as subjects. Moreover, the movie does not possess the adequate level of ideological advocacy favorable to the working classes to qualify as Neo-Realist in its theme. Yet in *The Cry*, Antonioni has penetrated central issues of proletarian life and has captured the marginality and alienated aspects of working-class experience. It might be argued that Antonioni attains to a kind of objectivity on his subject that not even the Neo-Realists proper had reached. From this perspective one concludes that *The Cry* fulfills Neo-Realist intentions of exposing the actual, contemporary social situation extremely well.

We can identify in Antonioni's movies, even as early as the mid-fifties, the close identification of his viewpoint with the emerging intellectual perspective of the "New" Left. Antonioni's vision recognizes an expanded definition of oppression, deprivation, and alienation. For him these definitions refer to feelings which are internalized and psychologized as opposed to the old, simplistic Marxist view rooted in a purely materialist definition of "want."

In *The Lovers* and *The Cry*, Antonioni traversed some of the emotional landscape he explored more elaborately in the great trilogy of films that he subsequently directed, consisting of *The Adventure* (1959/60), *The Night* (1960), and *Eclipse* (1961). All three are set in the upper-middle-class milieu of modernizing Italy. All three are underscored by a strong thematic sentiment that could be called existential.

In *The Adventure*, Anna goes for a cruise on a yacht with her fiancé Sandro and some friends. Anna and Sandro make love, while Claudia waits for them in a nearby art gallery. Eventually their trip takes them to an island. Patrizia, the aristocratic hostess stays on board, working a jigsaw puzzle. Claudia and her friend Corrado wander through ancient ruins. Sandro and Anna wander, bicker, and finally exhaust themselves in arguing. A storm comes up and the entire party decides to leave the island, but Anna is discovered to be missing. Sandro, Corrado, and Claudia decide to stay behind and search for her.

At first, Claudia suspects Sandro of having done harm to Anna, but that suspicion passes. The eye contact between them suggests that their affection for one another is growing. Anna's father comes to the island to help in the search, and the local constabulary mobilizes the police, but to no avail. Sandro goes off to contact smugglers at Milazzo, but returns without a clue. He catches up with Claudia at the station, just as she is about to leave by train. He wants her to stay with him, but she is unwilling to do so. He gets off the train at Messina and is immediately fascinated by the American, Gloria Perkins, who sports a dress slit up the middle.

In time, Sandro and Claudia are reunited and become lovers. They continue to travel about the island together until they wend their way back to Taormina. Sandro, however, encounters Gloria Perkins again and immediately becomes enamored of her. Claudia surprises them together. She runs off, but Sandro follows her. He overtakes her finally in a piazza. There he sits on a bench and weeps. Claudia comes up to him from behind and caresses the back of his head with her hand.

In the second part of the trilogy, *The Night*, we recognize that it is the mood, the situation, and the philosophical "insight" that holds these three movies together as a trilogy, rather than the specificity of characterization or the continuation of a common storyline. Again, the ambiance is contemporary and upper middle class, hence making the milieu in which Antonioni had by the end of the fifties come by choice to work. It was also the milieu in which he had come to establish the ideological positioning for his work.

That ideological alignment, indeed, may be measured against the original Neo-Realist project. For Antonioni's shift points to a reconsidering of the locus of psychological importance and significance as perceived from the perspective of social class. For Antonioni the crisis of the human condition in contemporary times has become located among the upwardly mobile, who are well off financially and who have relatively great amounts of leisure time. He has shifted from dealing with deprivation as a material problem, treating it, instead, as a socio-psychological phenomenon. The deprivation with which he deals is of the spirit. This choice positions him as being still a critic of the capitalist order. Yet he is a "New" Left critic, and on top of that, neither a Marxist, nor a neo-Marxist, ideologue. He explores the terrain of psychological alienation in the boundary-less condition of modern and contemporary awareness.

The Night begins with Giovanni, a writer, and his wife Lydia going to visit a dying friend. After that, they rush to a press reception honoring Giovanni's new book entitled *The Season*. Lydia, however, becomes bored and leaves. She phones Giovanni later from a romantic spot they used to visit, but he simply drives by and picks her up there, without evincing any expression of sentiment or feeling.

Then, a wealthy industrialist invites them to a party that Lydia does not want to attend, commenting cynically about the attempt to "buy intellectuals." Instead they go to a cheap nightclub where Giovanni becomes transfixed by a stripper's act. Lydia, still unenthusiastic, finally agrees to go to the party.

At the party Lydia goes off with the tall and handsome Roberto, and Giovanni takes up with an industrialist's daughter, Valentina. During the party Lydia learns that the friend they had visited, Tomasso, has died. However, she does not share this news with Giovanni.

Later, Lydia and Valentina end up in a room together, become acquainted, and vow to become friends. Giovanni, however, provokes a fight with Roberto. At dawn, Giovanni and Lydia leave the party. She tells him that Tomasso is dead and tries to explain how much he meant to her. She begins berating Giovanni for being self-centered. Finally they sit down on a golf green together. She pulls out a long letter describing a man's view of his lover, who is asleep. Giovanni, however, does not recognize his own words. Suddenly he embraces her, but Lydia declares that the love between them has passed. There, on the golf green, in the early light, he mounts her, locked in sexual embrace. The camera tracks back from them, and then leaves their image, replacing it with the empty stretches of the golf course.

Both *The Adventure* and *The Night* focus on female characters, Anna and Lydia, respectively. And in *Eclipse* the point of view is even more feminized, as the narrative follows a dimension of the experience of Vittoria, played by Monica Vitti.

In the opening sequence of *Eclipse*, Antonioni deftly emphasizes the human—and the dramatic—importance of silence. Vittoria is breaking up with her lover Ricardo. The viewer experiences the scene with directness and intensity, although almost no verbal information is exchanged between the characters, and although no conflict or violence is portrayed.

Later that day Vittoria goes to the stock exchange in the heart of Rome. There she finds her mother who is standing about with the other investors, absorbed in the big board. The atmosphere is loud and excited; irrationality appears to reign. The pandemonium in the hall is broken only to observe a moment of silence in honor of a stockbroker who had died at home of a heart attack the day before.

In the meantime she has met Piero, who is about her age and who is her mother's broker. They stand, separated in the film frame by a massive interior column, behind which they lean from time to time exchanging observations on the brief respite in the mayhem. Finally, Vittoria gains her mother's attention long enough to tell her that she has left Ricardo.

That evening Vittoria is visited by a neighbor, and then the two are invited over to the apartment of Marta. Marta spends most of the year in Kenya and returns to her apartment in Rome only occasionally. At Marta's they play African music on the phonograph, while Marta talks about her feelings toward the place and its people. Vittoria gets into black face and does an imitation of a native dance, which is interrupted when the trio must rush out into the Roman night to look for Marta's poodle who has run away while they were dancing.

The next day Vittoria goes with her friend Anita and her husband, who is a pilot, for a plane ride to Verona. They land at the flat, vacant airfield and Vittoria wanders into a bar where American servicemen are drinking. After standing about for a while, and observing the barrenness around her, she says how much she loves the place.

Back in hectic and crowded Rome the next day, she returns to the stock exchange. Panic has gripped the financial market; prices are dropping sharply. Many investors, including Vittoria's mother, are threatened with substantial losses or with being wiped out. Vittoria tries to convince her mother to leave, but she insists on staying, joining others in screaming at the brokers on the floor that the whole business is rigged. Finally, Vittoria wanders out into the busy street. She follows an older, nondescript man from the stock exchange who obviously has also been a loser. He buys a medication at a pharmacy, goes to a sidewalk cafe, takes the pill with a mineral water, doodles on a napkin. She sees that he has drawn flowers, and she is fascinated that a man losing millions has done so.

3. *Eclipse* (1961): Antonioni establishes visually the alienation between Vittoria and Piero, her stockbroker boyfriend. Museum of Modern Art

Later she tells Piero about this incident and shows him the drawing that she had picked up. They are at a bar and he seems distracted and not to care about such things. They drive to her mother's apartment where he makes a pass at her. That evening Piero visits Vittoria at her own apartment. While he's there, a drunk steals the sports car Piero has parked outside Vittoria's window. The next day the car is hoisted from the river, with the dead driver still at the wheel. Later that evening they go together to his house. They look through old things in the room he had as a boy, just as they had noticed and commented on things in her childhood room the day before. Finally, they find themselves separated by a pane of glass; they both press their lips to it, as if kissing through the glass. They promise to meet again soon, but in a tone of desperation.

The last seven minutes of *Eclipse* consist of a montage of shots at a construction site near Vittoria's apartment. The viewer may be thought to be anticipating that Piero and Vittoria will be meeting there. Time passes, other figures come and go, but Piero and Vittoria are never seen. They have disappeared from the film, no longer physically present in it.

Antonioni's trilogy marks a significant shift toward what might be called "modernist" concerns. Along with the works of the French "New Wave" directors which appeared at the same time (see chapter 2), the Swedish director Ingrid Bergman's features, and Fellini's *La Dolce Vita*, Antonioni's three movies mark a departure from cinema as "escapism" to a new role for it in exploring ideas and values.

In this context, the success of Antonioni's "realism," and, indeed, the overall nature and character of that "realism" is worth discussing. Antonioni is the cinematographic master of the long take, keeping the camera situated in one place and allowing a scene to unfold before it in a temporal framework akin to lived time, and in spatial relationships which alter normal perception but which do so in subtle ways. What is even more important is not that he shifts the social locus or setting of realist filmmaking to the upper middle class, but that he simultaneously explores the entire process of filmmaking itself in relationship to the source of modern and contemporary awareness.

Fundamental to Antonioni's realism is the revealing in his movies—through the techniques of the cinema—the disorientation and alienation caused by technology itself. This is sporadically present as a point of view in all his films, but becomes clearly articulated in the closing minutes of *Eclipse* and then increasingly in his subsequent movies. That articulation has less to do with content or characterization than with the self-conscious way in which Antonioni's movies work. The material world, the world of things, is granted a recognition not normally accorded to it in narrative film. In Antonioni's movies this is not restricted to the elaborating of a "sense of place," which is the simpler preoccupation of a good number of filmmakers. Antonioni presents the world as fractured. Experience has become broken into sounds and silences, represented as places we remember sentimentally and strange ones we have not been to before, but which we yearn to see. Or the surroundings are portrayed as contexts, full of objects which seem out of place. Or often the places themselves seem to be out of touch.

The technological world has permeated Antonioni's movies, and yet tracings of it are but rarely present as an actual, direct image on the screen. For what Antonioni has not only understood but has also assimilated is the fact that the reality of the medium of the film itself is technological, and is, therefore, especially suited to enacting in fiction the situation of the human confrontation with technology. In the *Red Desert* (1963/64), Antonioni's first film made in color, a scene can be cited that strongly illustrates this point. The industrial manager, Corrado, played by Richard Harris, is talking to workers about plant conditions:

> His eye rests first on an electric wire-end sticking out of a well, on the necks of empty bottles, on a pile of baskets, then on an apparently arbitrary blue line that climbs a wall and turns off to one side; the practical reality of objects drains away, and the world becomes a strange confusion of abstract shapes. We understand that Corrado's vitality and decisiveness are being paralyzed by a growing sense that the whole enterprise, perhaps all human endeavor, is futile.[37]

To comprehend the importance of a scene like the one just described, however, requires a slight digression into film theory. Film has the abrupt capacity to overcome and to alter our perspective of time and space. Indeed, this power can be understood as that element that is recognized and made central in what is called "formalist" film theory. The emphasis of the Soviet film director and theorist Sergei Eisenstein on "montage" effects which favor abrupt cuts to alter time/space relationships and build a dialectic of meaning is one approach to the relating of film to its social possibilities.[38] The realist tradition of film theory, especially as it has been expressed by the French critic André Bazin, emphasizes that when cinema renders the pure photographic image meaningful and powerful it is the supreme act of film art. The long take and the technique of deep focus (that is, keeping all elements in lens-focus to give an illusion of a realistic depth perspective) are regarded as aesthetically superior devices in moviemaking.[39]

Yet, what Antonioni does is to combine the two, apparently contradictory, goals of formalism and realism aesthetically. While a realist in his approach to the visual image itself, he is not unwilling to resort to formalistic devices which may make the viewer aware of the camera, the editing, and the director's techniques. Moreover, the duration of his shots are dictated less by the narrative demands of the movie story than by the philosophic and emotive desires of the director.

Antonioni's work consistently explores the tension between what have been called "story" and "non-story" traditions. "The dialectic movement away from the story and again back to it can be traced by two conflicting principles . . . suppression of the story and acceptance of the story."[40] If one holds to the view that photography is a product of alienation, this would mean that good cinema is inconsistent with intrigue and drama. Yet, the notion of pure contemplation of the visual world is complex. As the Spanish philosopher and cultural critic José Ortega y Gasset noted: "It appears that those elements which seem to distort pure contemplation—interests, sentiments, compulsions, affective preferences—are precisely its indispensable instruments."[41] And Antonioni is a great master of this tension between the given world of appearances and the potential of dramatic action between characters within it. His movies all function on a kind of principle of "surrender" and "catch"—letting go of the connectedness of a dramatic situation to its setting, then abruptly recapturing it. In other words, the dialectic of realism and formalism is continuous in these films.

Antonioni's movies have increasingly explored the tension inherent in our modern culture which lives by technology on the one hand, but which does not yet fully accept all the alterations that technology causes in our consciousness on the other. Indeed, Antonioni himself has acknowledged this. His own philosophic point of departure is one in which he lines up closely with the late nineteenth-century German philosopher Friedrich Nietzsche. Antonioni maintains that the world in which we live is scientific, technological, modern. Nonetheless, our value systems have remained pre-scientific, pre-technological, pre-modern. It is with this dissonance that Antonioni deals philosophically.[42]

Antonioni's films correspond to broad movements in post-Second World War European thought and culture: phenomenology, existentialism, and the emergence of the New Left. His movies contain subtle explorations—through ways in which the visual image is captured and the film material is constructed—of how our consciousness has come to be dominated by technology. This is likely best illustrated in Antonioni's most popular film, and the first he made in a foreign language, *Blow Up* (1968).

Set in contemporary London, *Blow Up* portrays the swinging life of the late sixties from the point of view of a photographer/artist named Thomas. While taking photographs in a park—random shots of landscape and scenery, we presume—a woman suddenly comes running at him. He flees, develops the film and keeps enlarging his photos. Finally it appears that in one of the photos there is the image of a gun barrel protruding from the bushes. He deduces quickly that his photograph, when blown up, gives evidence of the murder of a man who had been walking with the woman who came running after Thomas.

Thomas tries to interest a neighbor in his discovery. She, however, can muster only a brief and slightly uncertain expression of curiosity. His friend Ron, who is editing a volume of Neo-Realist photographs of factory workers by Thomas (shots of the urban poor and of the alienated castoffs of society) prefers the interiority of his own drug world to any pursuit of solving the crime in the park that has come to Thomas's attention. The woman he had encountered in the park eventually comes to Thomas's studio to retrieve the film. She begins undressing, is then given a roll of film by Thomas, but continues, evidently willing to have sex with him even though her goal of seducing him into surrendering the roll of film had already succeeded. He, of course, has tricked her, by substituting another film. This deception, however, is not the point of the scene between them.

Later two teen-age "birds" come by his studio looking for a chance to be photographed and, perhaps, a break into modeling. Instead, they wind up with Thomas in a sexual romp on lavender paper, leaving him too exhausted to do their shots and giving mainstream movie audiences, in the United States at least, a rare glimpse of pubic hair.

Episodes which point repeatedly to ambivalence and tentativeness shake the viewer's hold on "reality." Antonioni's grasp on the legacy of Neo-Realism results in an exploration of what it is that constitutes the nature of "reality," and what it is that defines our place in "reality" as we perceive it. Indeed, in Antonioni's subsequent films, *Zabriskie Point* (1969), *The Passenger* (1974), and *Identification of a Woman* (1982), the question of reality/unreality is always close to the surface.

In *Blow Up* the murder is never solved. There is nothing certain to establish that it actually did take place. Did the camera capture an image that was misinterpreted by the naked eye after the shot was blown up, or did the technical process of blowing up the photograph produce a distortion of reality? More likely, the murder occurred, the camera captured the visual tracings of that physical reality, but that reality was emptied of meaning and value when the simple knowledge of the event was put up against the fractured disjointedness and indifference of the real world. To that reality the murder itself—real as it likely was—remained peripheral.

For reality, alas, has to do with the viewer's perspective of it.[43] The photograph, or the film image, achieves its meaning and value not only in what occurs before the camera, but also in how that image is responded to. The screening of any movie or the viewing of any photograph may be treated as a performance—

4. A London photographer encounters this woman when taking random
pictures. Antonioni's most accessible exploration of reality and illusion
is in *Blow Up*. Museum of Modern Art

the images are set, like a text, but each viewing of a film or a photograph occurs
under different physical conditions (degree of darkness, sound quality, etc.) and
under different sets of emotional and affective conditions as well (when, where,
who is in the audience, etc.).

In another English-language feature, *The Passenger* (1974), Antonioni ex-
tended and elaborated many of these ideas. David Locke, a television journalist
for the BBC exchanges identities with a fellow Englishman named Robertson
who dies unexpectedly of a sudden heart attack. Locke then takes Robertson's
diary/calendar, and proceeds to live out the other man's life by keeping his
appointments.

Robertson, it is soon revealed, had been working as a gunrunner to rebel
forces waging a civil war against the government of an unidentified African
nation. Locke had, in fact, been trying to investigate and report on those very
rebels. One of the most revealing sequences of *The Passenger* occurs in footage
Locke had filmed which is now being reviewed by his producer back at BBC. In
it a Black rebel asks Locke for his camera and, once he has it, turns it on him. The
rebel leader points out that Locke's questions really reveal much more about the
asker than the African's answers could possibly reveal about himself and his

situation. By taking on Robertson's identity and role, Locke has moved from an "academic" encounter with the rebels and their project to becoming a live participant in that project.

Following Robertson's schedule of appointments, Locke reaches Barcelona. There he meets a young woman. It seems to him that he had seen her once before, when he returned to London briefly toward the beginning of the movie to check on his being declared dead. And it seems to the viewer that this is the case. Of this, however, the viewer is not entirely certain, nor does the movie subsequently "fill in" the missing information. By now, Locke's wife and his producer are suspicious that he is not really dead. They arrive in Spain, and Locke and his newfound companion just manage to escape them and leave the city. Riding in a convertible down a long, straight, treelined road, she asks him what he's running from. He tells her to turn around and look behind them. She does, seeing nothing except the road.

Locke follows Robertson's daybook and arrives at a small whitewashed hotel in a remote Spanish village. He has been followed there, however, by government agents who believe that he is Robertson, the gunrunner. They assassinate him in a sequence that Antonioni draws out with superlative control of the temporal framework. Locke's wife and his producer arrive a few minutes later

5. David Locke, played by Jack Nicholson, is a BBC-journalist reporting on revolutionaries in Africa. Suspense merges with the question of identity in *The Passenger*. Museum of Modern Art

with Spanish police. When they enter the room where Locke lies dead, however, his wife says she does recognize him. The younger woman whom he befriended in Barcelona comes into the room and acknowledges that yes, indeed, she knew him.

Zabriskie Point, set in the United States, was produced at the acme of the youth and protest counterculture, in 1969. Antonioni's exploration of the American scene has features such as shots of massive billboards, which appear and reappear throughout the course of the movie. This particular visual emphasis, however, evoked the negative response from some critics in the United States that Antonioni had misunderstood and was misrepresenting American culture through the exaggerated device of spotlighting such billboards. One must ask, however, what is the essence of the reality of the United States? Might it not, indeed, be found visually in the image of a purple, oversized "Elsie the Cow" peering down at a freeway? Moreover, are not the unnaturalistic results of the explosion at the end of the movie—when so many recognizable material goods and artifacts of the consumer culture are projected skyward in slow motion from the source of the blast—expressive of a central element in the American experience?

There is a tentativeness—even an incompleteness—in *Zabriskie Point*, matched only in Antonioni's 1982 film produced in Italy, *Identification of a Woman*. This latter film manifests an eroticism which goes beyond the casual sexuality in *Blow Up*, well beyond the surrealistic "coupling" scene in the desert in *Zabriskie Point*, and far beyond the restrained, and invariably thwarted, physicality that is present in nearly all his other films. Yet, the central issue of this movie, too, is appearance, image, and reality itself.

The critic Mira Liehm sees in *Identification of a Woman* the residue of an enigma—the "post neo-realist enigma of facts." Antonioni admits in this film that the "reality of life" has evaded him.[44] *Identification of a Woman*, she claims, "may represent his thematic return to Italy but not to the roots of his art.[45] Yet, this is arguable. For the central quest of Antonioni's moviemaking has remained extraordinarily stable. Going back to the earliest protagonists of his films in the 1950s, Antonioni has demonstrated a curiosity about women that goes well beyond superficiality or the normative cinematic objectification of them. In *Identification of a Woman*, with the autobiographical suggestions of the film director seeking to solve both a personal and an artistic crisis by discovering the true identity of the movie's heroines, Antonioni has fully accomplished his dialectical inquiry once more.

Blow Up comes closest to evoking the main elements of Antonioni's ongoing concerns; *8½*, made in 1963, elicits these elements for Fellini. If this movie is not Fellini's quintessential accomplishment, it is nonetheless the one that is most pivotal in understanding his work. *8½* is about a film director, and it gives us a clue to Fellini's particular extension of the Neo-Realist idea into his later works.

The fictional film director, Guido, is to begin a film. He cannot, however, recollect the plot that he has figured out for it; his imagination and his "sense of reality" have become confused. This confusion is manfested in a visual metaphor that Fellini presents near the beginning of the movie. Guido is trapped in his car in a traffic jam in Rome. His constraint and his limitations are emphasized through the camera angles and editing of various shots. Suddenly, however, his body simply rises out of the car and into the air—liberation!

This visual metaphor refers not only to Guido's situation as an artist faced by problems, but also more generally to Fellini's confrontation with the entire question of reality in cinema. This sequence counterpoints the two tendencies which are invoked simultaneously whenever and wherever film is made. The motion picture captures, or re-presents, the corporeal, physical world, and all the objects and personages before the camera, with apparent verisimilitude. Yet this photographic quality of the image-in-motion is set off against the capacity of the material in the movie itself to be manipulated, or edited, and of various cinematic techniques to introduce elements which may be called magical. It is this tension that Fellini explores, but from a perspective diametrically opposed to Antonioni's.

The doctors recommend that Guido retire to a spa for rest and recuperation, yet he cannot manage to free his mind's eye of the film project he must prepare. His imagination, however, can conjure up neither plot nor storyline; in it the image of Claudia, a divine, yet sensual, creature persists. She is juxtaposed to the living women in his life: his mistress, Carla, and his wife, Luisa.

One evening, during a magic act, an illusionist reads out "Asa Nisi Masa," which is an anagram for "anima," or soul. Hearing this evokes Guido's thoughts on problems of creation and of the soul's transmigration. He fears that he is a liar and fraud, without either imagination or talent. He then conjures up the vision of the monstrous Saraghina—the devil as a whore.

His tensions with his wife persist. A friend, Rosella, in answering his question as to why Luisa cannot accept him as he is, tells Guido that it is because Luisa really loves him. Guido seeks escape in his imagination, conjuring up the image of himself in a large house with all the women in his life. He announces to them, "happiness is being able to tell the truth without hurting anyone." Yet he can only subdue the women in this dream by posing as their master and whipping them into line.

Guido holds a press conference at his producer's urging, but he discovers that he has no ideas and nothing to say. He contemplates suicide, but decides that such an act would solve nothing. All the movie's characters appear at the base of a spaceship as the sun sets. There is a reconciliation between Guido and Luisa, who now promises to try to accept him as he is. At a gesture from the Magician, all link hands and dance gaily over a narrow bridge. Guido and Luisa join the circle. As the last figure in the film cast, a clown, disappears, the image of Guido as a child remains.

8½ is, in many ways, similar to Fellini's 1965 feature *Juliette of the Spirits*. That film focuses on a central character, a woman named Juliette, played by Fellini's wife. The objective world again is fully integrated—both visually and emotionally—with the subjective perceptions of the main character.

There are a number of powerful images in this complex movie. Perhaps the strongest of them is Juliette's recollection as a schoolgirl of performing in a play in which she portrayed a saint being burned on a grid as the martyr ascended toward heaven. Her irascible grandfather, obviously none-too-sympathetic to the antics and teachings of the nuns to begin with, disrupted the play at this moment. After all of Juliette's adventures of the mind and the imagination, it is a vision of her grandfather who appears to her. He urges her to let go of him in her imagination and to let go of the image of herself sacrificed on the burning grid.

In Fellini's next two features, *Roma* (1972) and *Amarcord* (1974), he finally connected through each movie's fantasy structure his character's subjectivity to the objective, or so-called real, world. Moreover, in both cases, this real world could be described as enriched by exploration of the collective Italian experience. The first of these films deals, both longingly and sentimentally, with the nation's capital. Yet, rather than presenting a vibrant, modern city, Fellini's movie envisions a city defined by vignettes, burdened by history, and sunk in the morass of advancing technology, as manifested in the pandemonic traffic jam scene, which is reminiscent of the opening of 8½.

"Amarcord" is a dialect phrase meaning "I remember," and the film is presented, at one level, as being autobiographical. It concerns Fellini's growing up during the late 1920s and early 1930s in the seaside town of Rimini. At the same time its temporal setting portrays the experience of Mussolini's Fascism, as perceived through the point of view of an adolescent in a provincial setting. Many images which appear and reappear in Fellini's films are drawn richly and developed fully in *Amarcord*: the corpulent prostitute, Vopina, or the attraction of the great ship, *The Rex*, which draws the townspeople to row out to sea to catch a glimpse of the luxurious liner. Fellini, moreover, is the master of the visual vignette, and he exploits this talent especially well in *Amarcord*. Take, for example, the sequence in which old uncle Teo is briefly released from a mental institution in *Amarcord*. Teo climbs a tree, finds a perch in it, and begins tossing rocks at all who pass by, screaming "I want a woman."

In *Roma* the boardinghouse where the youthful Fellini lives when he first arrives in the great city is a veritable sideshow, peopled by all sorts of fascinating and grotesque characters. The most revealing sequence in the movie itself, however, is self-reflective. After a chaotic scene on the road coming into the city, when a truck overturns and the carcasses of slaughtered animals are strewn over the highway, a cut is made to Fellini. He appears on camera, talking to a group of students who are arguing with him about what they perceive as the film's lack of social consciousness or a perspective ideologically rooted in social criticism. "I haven't solved the problems in my own life," Fellini tells them, "how, then, can I solve the problems of society?"

Fellini's posture might best be described as that of "romantic realism." His primary directorial concerns are with the complex interrelationships between the real and the imagined, between the external world and the interiority of an individual's perception of it or, in other words, between the inside and the outside of experience. Fellini's art leans in the direction of psychology, yet remains bound essentially to the notion of artistic imagination. Fellini stands

6. *Roma* (1971): Fellini shifted his exploration of objectivity, subjectivity, and Italian awareness onto a new plane with this movie. Museum of Modern Art

with those contemporary thinkers who have tended to maintain the primacy of an internalized psychological perspective. For when we survey the total corpus of his creativity, including movies such as *The Clowns* (1971), *The City of Women* (1980), *The Orchestra Rehearsal* (1979), and *The Ship Sails On* (1982), it becomes evident that Fellini's realism has been rooted over the years in the notion of the integrity and the authenticity of the director's artistic vision.

Fellini's proposal to do a documentary on the last of Europe's great clowns turned instead into a feature-length exploration of his own obsession with the circus. Ths threat of his individualism and subjectivity "subverting" his films toward reactionary social and political postures has been noted by many critics. His *City of Women* (1980) may be contrasted, for example, unfavorably by feminists to Antonioni's *Identification of a Woman*. The former seems either unwilling or unable to transcend, even for an instance, the director's male bias. The odyssey of Fellini's male protagonist passes through stations—like a penitent believer passing through the Stations of the Cross?—where the women in his life await him. Finally, he can fulfill his image of the ideal woman in his life only by falling in love with a doll who mechanically performs his wishes and demands. Already, his *Orchestra Rehearsal*, produced a year earlier, had explored the pandemonium in an orchestra whose members refuse to follow the conductor. Many critics found this film to be ideologically nihilistic and reactionary, as had those who criticized *City of Women* for being sexist and dominated by the traditional, conservative male myth.[46]

Fellini's broad popularity and international appeal must result, in part, from the ways in which he satisfies audience expectations which are rooted in widely shared images of the "artist" and of the "Italian." The first of these is that Fellini is a model for the now classic stereotype of the artist: eccentric, flighty, and spirited. To have produced movies so rich in an imaginative imagery born of his own perceptions, Fellini strikes a blow for individualism in the artistic vision and for its ability to dominate even so collective, and commercial, a form of expression as the movies. Even his films which are apparently anchored historically and based on established texts, *Satyricon* (1969) and *Casanova* (1976), bear the imprint of Fellini's personal obsessions.

Moreover, throughout his films Fellini juxtaposes the images of individual fantasy over and against images drawn from the rites and practices of Catholicism. In processions, in statuary, in the presence of priests and nuns, and in scenes such as the statue of Christ airborne—carried by helicopter across Rome over the rooftops of the city—Fellini's movies consistently expose the viewer to Catholic and Italian sources of collective creativity and imaginative power. Then, too, especially in films such as *Roma* and *Amarcord*, Fellini's imaginative images often give way to what may be interpreted as standard and clichéd stereotypes of Italian social behavior—theatrical, emotional, strong on gesture, and loud of voice. Nonetheless, Fellini's film art never quite reaches the level of surrealism, which seeks to attain a superior kind of reality that is created as the result of establishing a dialectic between external, observable reality and interior, dreamlike awareness as conjured up by the imaginative forces of one's interiority.

Antonioni, by contrast, eschews the imaginative flights of imagery and underplays the Church. This latter omission is evidently consistent with Antonioni's Nietzschean conviction that God is dead.[47] Throughout his movies Antonioni points to the modern source of myth and belief which has supplanted religion: namely, science and technology. His films are devoid of stereotypical Italianate types. Early in his career Antonioni abandoned the homely charm of peasants and workers to explore the psychology of an increasingly affluent middle class, smug in its external appearances but floundering spiritually upon a shaky and uncertain psychological terrain. Antonioni's art manifests a phenomenological approach to reality and whose works invariably explore each human situation from a perspective in filmmaking which can itself be called "existential."[48]

Antonioni's films explore the social realism of a modernizing society through its situationism and through its apparent impact upon the moral prerogatives and the psychological values of its characters. It is in this regard Antonioni can best be understood as going furthest in extending the parameters of Neo-Realism, while appearing on the surface to reject the ideological premises of that movement.

Their visions of filmmaking reflect diametrically opposed perceptions of the reality of an experience that both have shared culturally. In the 1960s when

Antonioni acknowledged that Italy was becoming part of a greater fabric of modern experience he moved outside the narrow confines of the Italian setting per se. By contrast, Fellini burrowed more deeply into Italian experience, exploring historical perspectives of its development, exploiting its imagery, and, in fact, intensifying its stereotype.

How we see culture, history, development, postwar society, modernism, reality, and truth may, in this context, determine whether we prefer the works of Antonioni or Fellini. Both make powerful points about our perception of the world, and the possible meanings that those perceptions may yield. Their life's work, in both instances, attest to the central issue of realism in cinema.

Reality and illusion clash in every society. All ideologies, and the political systems that they spawn, are rife with contradictions. Italian political life has stabilized far less than that of any other country in Western Europe. The parade of some forty different governments in the last forty years indicates this strongly. Communism has remained a viable political force in the country. Terrorism has been especially bold, and in particular the actions of the "Red Brigades" in the 1970s. The North-South tension still prevails throughout the peninsula.[49]

Fellini is, on the surface, the more "Italian" of the two directors. In spite of his international acclaim, he has resisted all offers and temptations to direct elsewhere. Antonioni has responded differently. He has directed films in other countries and in other languages. He has even produced a nonfiction work in China: *Chung Kao* (1972). Yet, that fact does not make Antonioni less of an Italian director. Indeed, he has continued exploring a central theme of Neo-Realism, and he has done so more persuasively and effectively than Fellini.

Fellini portrays an Italy of clichés and stereotypes. Undeniably, he often breaks through these. Nonetheless, his vision of the society and its history remains linked to the obvious. Antonioni, even when his films are set elsewhere, still engages the central problems that he had established in the movies he directed in Italy. The final question should not be misunderstood. It is not who presents the more "realistic" portrayal of the evolving Italian situation. Rather, it is the capacity to penetrate a situation and to explore it through the means of the medium. The phenomenological approach to reality emphasizes presentation, which might be best understood as the act of presenting. For it is the dialectic between that act and its subject that is of paramount importance. When by presentation we understand not what is presented but the presenting of it, the essence of Neo-Realism is comprehended.[50]

TWO

The First Crest of the New Wave

At the end of the 1950s a movement in the cinema in France registered as a forerunner for a number of new directions and styles in filmmaking. At the same time this movement manifested an impulse to independence among filmmakers. In a number of ways this phenomenon, called the "New Wave," most closely resembled the vanguard movements which have come to characterize distinct "breakthroughs" in the other arts—music, writing, painting, theater, and dance—in the nineteenth and twentieth centuries: Futurism, Surrealism, Expressionism, and so on.

Neither the subsequent influence of the New Wave nor its historical sources are our focus here. The emphasis is on the moment of the New Wave's emergence. This concern gives rise to specific questions about the nature of the movement itself, as well as its relationship to a specific era. We can pinpoint the time of the New Wave's emergence, namely, in the years from 1958 to 1960, and simultaneously we can recognize that those dates define a period of public turmoil and transformation in France.

In 1958, Charles DeGaulle, after over a decade of self-imposed political exile, again dominated center stage in France. DeGaulle's re-emergence was intriguing because of the varied and complex forces which produced his re-entry into politics, and because the political movement to which he lent his name, Gaullism, was multifaceted.[1] "Gaullism was not simply a strategy of conservative defense," although obviously the movement gained its central impulse from the special brand of conservatism in France. "Conservatives had to share Gaullism with other goals and claims on its strengths: economic modernization, institutional rejuvenation, and nationalistic assertion."[2]

The Gaullist initiative to take power and to redirect France's fortunes, and the fact that this initiative was not always what it seemed to be, reflected the complexity of the situation. Within what appeared as the establishment of a "conservative" force at the center of French politics were to be found the germs of a movement that was essentially transitional. In this instance conservatism, usually associated with preservation of the status quo, heralded the advent of wide-ranging changes in French life.

More importantly the years 1958–1960 marked the pinnacle of the cultural initiatives pioneered by a generation of intellectuals who had risen to prominence in the aftermath of the Second World War. Existentialism was at its peak, the "new" writing—and with it a self-proclaimed "new thinking"—was emergent, and the basis of French structuralism was being established.[3] In this regard it must be pointed out that intellectual life in France appeared to have a different quality and character than elsewhere. The intellectual establishment possessed a special place in the nation's life and culture that dated back at least to the Enlightenment era of the mid-eighteenth century. And although this intelligentsia's shared ideas might be characterized as progressive, its structure and status as an elite was traditional and conservative.

The intellectual establishment had a special role to play in all aspects of French experience. And by the time the New Wave appeared, this role had had its impact on the cinema. Film already had been accepted as an art by the intellectual establishment in France. So while the concept reflected in the term "New Wave" suggests a counterculture phenomenon, its appearance meshed well with established shared concerns of the Parisian intelligentsia. The New Wave marked the beginning of a trend, that subsequently spread far beyond France, whereby the cinema began to gain respectability in academic and intellectual circles.[4]

The New Wave appeared, then, at a particular interstice of a complex, conservative thrust in politics, counterpointed to an increasingly leftist, or progressive, intellectual atmosphere, which was itself underscored by the particular generational moment that existed at the end of the 1950s. Those "coming of age" at the end of the 1950s were young men and women born in the 1930s, who had experienced the Second World War as children or as young adolescents. Collectively, they shared certain critical perspectives. Their antagonism toward their parents' generation was linked to their attempt to comprehend that older generation's culpability for France's collapse before the invading German army and the nation's acquiescence to the Nazi occupation.

The audience for New Wave movies consisted of younger men and women who were drawn to the independent, low-budget productions. This taste for a different kind of movie was a generational inheritance. It should be emphasized that talking about generational characteristics refers to the audience for New Wave features, not to the affinities and shared intentions of the filmmakers who brought these low-budget, independent creations to the screen.

This emphasis differs from the point of view found in most of the literature on the New Wave, which focuses on the personalities of certain directors and on their subsequent filmmaking careers in light of whether, and to what degree, they continued to adhere to New Wave principles of moviemaking. Such an approach meshes well with principles enunciated by the New Wave itself— namely, an emphasis on the artistic power of the director. One of the New Wave aims was to establish the director of the film as having a similar strong artistic imprint upon the work he or she directed as would be ascribed to an author of a novel. This *auteur* notion deflected interest away from the social and cultural milieu in which a movie is produced to the personal thematic choices of the director and his or her stylistic idiosyncrasies.[5]

As film theoretician J. Dudley Andrew has pointed out, however, the *auteur* theory is, strictly speaking, no theory at all.[6] Rather, it is a claim—and one that has persistently been promoted in certain quarters—whose intent is to establish the connectedness of creative activity in the cinema to a traditional view of creativity in the arts. The assumption behind this view is rooted in an aesthetic of individual genius and virtuosity. And this aesthetic has prevailed in our valuation of painting and music, as well as our passion for literary creativity, since the Renaissance. Yet, this aesthetic must first of all be acknowledged as culture-bound. Hence, it must be pointed out that it is a point of view applicable to the traditional arts of the western world, but not necessarily to the new forms of electronic and visual communication which have emerged in the twentieth century, among them the motion pictures.

That the *auteur* notion is not really a theory is, in itself, not so important. Rather, it is that *auteurist* concepts steer us away from recognizing that film possesses a distinct, collective relationship to the social and cultural base in which it is created. The movie's director, even if he or she is the dominant creative agent behind the entire film production, is still himself or herself a part of the culture and society in which he or she creates. It is the symbiosis between the creators, who in the case of a movie must work collectively, and those who respond to the film, that characterizes the totality of the cinematic experience.

The timing of any phenomenon is one of the elements defining its rooted-ness in the social and cultural milieu from which it came. The New Wave originated in the particular interest in and attitude toward the cinema that existed in certain quarters in France during roughly a decade prior to its appearance. The forerunners of this movement were the critics and theoreticians André Bazin and Alexandre Astruc. The prime movers in it were young men who wrote for the *Cahiers du cinéma* from the late 1940s onward, or who formed the devoted audience for older films shown by the Cinémathèque française under the auspices of its founder Henri Langlois. The basic challenge to which the New Wave responded was an intellectual one, and its roots were essentially philo-sophical.

As Alexandre Astruc expressed it in his influential article of 1948, what was needed was a cinema that could be as flexible and subtle, and as rich in its nuance and variety as written language.[7] Astruc's challenge to filmmakers was rooted in a perspective that was embedded in the cultural and intellectual traditions of the West. The basis for this challenge can be traced back to the assumption of the supremacy of written language, and to the cultural ascendancy of what Marshall McLuhan, writing nearly two decades after Astruc, called the "Gutenburg Galaxy."[8]

Astruc, as a promoter of the cinema and a theoretician, was bent on developing principles which supported what he believed to be the correct vehicle for asserting the artistry of the motion pictures. Nonetheless, his models of creative expressiveness were essentially literary, and his turn of mind was to promote a cinema that was as "valuable" and as "good" as literature.[9] In Astruc's oft-quoted phrase, what was necessary was for the visual image to become, clearly and compellingly, created by an intelligent instrument, *le caméra stylo*, in other words, "the camera that writes."[10]

Interestingly, this notion was linked both with established traditions, as well as with emerging patterns in thought and culture. Beyond its connectedness with the overwhelming bias for the word in western tradition, in the French cinema itself there was a past pattern linking movies to literary and theatrical sources. This link dated back to the attempt, at the end of the first decade of this century, to produce films based on classic literary sources, the so-called "Films d'Art." Even during the silent film era the passion for literary adaptations to the screen was strong. The French silent cinema labored under these burdens after the First World War, and broke through to a revival of its artistic and productive energies only after the advent of sound production at the end of the 1920s.[11] The relationship of French cinema to the word—perhaps one could better say its "dependency" on the word—was well established.

What the New Wave itself aimed at, however, was breaking down these older and traditional forms of dependency upon the word by substituting a more lively and vibrant film language. Nonetheless, verbal text and dialogue are tremendously important in the movies of New Wave directors.

Astruc's article appeared—and with it the entire issue of the cinema becoming as subtle, as expressive, and as thoughtful as writing—just at the time when the traditional novel was waning. The philosopher/humanist José Ortega y Gasset was arguing that a "literary genre may wear out," and that after the Second World War just this was happening to that bulwark of modern literary productivity—the novel.[12] On the one hand, we might see the call for moviemaking that would somehow be more like writing as appearing just when cultural critics were becoming aware of the exhaustion of the particular literary forms.[13] On the other hand, within the literary circles in France in the early 1950s new forms of written expression were being pioneered. In the experiments of Alain Robbe-Grillet,[14] Michel Butor, and Nathalie Saurraute, the narrative and its psychological bent was emptied in favor of a more direct and simplified form of writing. Thus, the New Wave had connections to broader cultural and intellectual problems which were current. The New Wave, it must be repeated, pointed to various connections with the concerns of the intelligentsia in France, even if the "New Wave" directors themselves did not come from the upper echelons of France's educated elite.

The sociology of New Wave films established an immediate appeal to a young, educated, urban audience internationally. The New Wave was important within the entire field of cinema worldwide, and an aspect of that significance was commercial. Although it is presumably the aesthetic qualities of the New Wave which distinguish it, the spate of films which announced the arrival of the New Wave proved also to be commercially farsighted. In effect, New Wave directors demonstrated compellingly that low-budget, personal movies could be made which would appeal to selective audiences whose particular allegiance to such works could be anticipated. Moreover, the commitment of these targeted audiences to supporting such films would subsequently develop and grow. In many ways, this was ingenious, anticipating as it did the shift during the 1960s toward production of movies targeted for increasingly more specific age cohorts and specific taste groups.[15]

We recognize that the term "New Wave" has, since the beginning of the 1960s, become well established in our cultural vocabulary. Yet, unlike many of the movements which have characterized modern cultural experience, the New Wave neither registered nor spread into other areas of human creativity and expression. That happened, to a great extent, because the New Wave cannot be understood as having represented a broad impulse of creativity emerging from a particular perspective that touched upon many areas and aspects of human expression and communication. Movies had not yet, when the New Wave occurred, established themselves internationally as possessing cultural respectability adequate to have an occurrence in the cinema proliferate in other artistic forms. The impulses and inspirations which led to the New Wave ideas were specific, precise, and narrow. The aim of the New Wave, put simply, was to respond to the specific conditions of movie production, and to transform them in the direction of becoming "more like the other arts," and also "more modernist."

The New Wave was a film movement in every sense of the word. It was generated by self-conscious filmmakers who addressed a large cultural dilemma—but strictly through the medium of the movies. The New Wave's goal was to make the director dominate a movie in much the same way as the author dominated a novel or a painter dominated a canvas. Given the nature of the film medium, this goal could be achieved only in part, although some New Wave adherents, as well as those who took a particular kind of inspiration from them, appreciated this fact only partially. The fundamental notion they shared was to overcome many of the commercial demands placed on moviemakers. Hence, they would carve out a new position for the film artist vis-à-vis the studio system in which most movies had been produced traditionally, at least in "free-market" economies.

It may seem ironic that the New Wave critic/directors—both before they began making films and afterwards as well—held directors such as John Ford, John Huston, Michael Curtiz, Orson Welles, and Alfred Hitchcock who had worked in the studio system of Hollywood in such high regard. But it was precisely because those individuals had succeeded within the studio system by placing their own stylistic marks on their films, that the New Wave lionized them.

When we inquire into the question of what the New Wave was, it becomes apparent that conflicting views of this cultural phenomenon exist. Perhaps the most pervasive view is that reflected in the subtitle of a recent popular article "The New Wave at Twenty-Five."[16] This view suggests that the New Wave emerged at the end of the 1950s, remained geographically in France, and persistently cut a course across time which may be viewed historically. To measure the New Wave in this manner is to take the movement itself as having been once established, and then to interpret its initial impulses as being a set of criteria by which subsequent adherence to New Wave ideas and principles might be judged.

The New Wave was *not* like other movements in the arts which proclaimed their intentions in elaborate manifestoes and which, in turn, demanded a kind of partisan commitment to them. The New Wave, in spite of the image of unity often ascribed to it, was extraordinarily diffuse. And in spite of all the well-earned recognition of its significance, the New Wave was, in actual number of active participants, stunningly small. Indeed, the New Wave normally only numbers six or seven directors: François Truffaut (died 1984); Alain Resnais (often considered not to belong to the New Wave at all); Claude Chabrol (considered a sellout to popular commercialism); Jean-Luc Godard (considered the most consistently experimental of the directors); Jacques Rivette; Eric Rohmer; Jean Rouch (a documentarist). Moreover, its membership still defines less a unified movement than simply several French directors who, at one point in time, bucked the traditional system of production in ways which marked the beginning of a realignment of the social and artistic significance of the cinema.

This chapter minimizes the notion of the New Wave as an established artistic movement with specific, central ideas which have been sustained through time. Instead, the focus should be on the sudden appearance of several movies—in each case the first feature-length production of the specific director—in France during the years 1958 and 1959. This approach places emphasis on the image to which the term "New Wave" itself gives rise—something powerful, abrupt, sweeping in, and then, just as quickly, receding and going away. The French New Wave betokens a precise eruption of an impulse in the cinema that was clearly focused on presenting works in which the director's relationship to the medium was altered in the direction of the aesthetics of virtuosity.[17]

The New Wave is situated at a moment in time. And it is on the appearance of just four movies produced in 1958 and 1959 that we shall concentrate our attention: *Handsome Serge*, directed by Claude Chabrol; *The 400 Blows*, directed by François Truffaut; *Hiroshima, mon amour*, directed by Alain Resnais; *Breathless*, directed by Jean-Luc Godard. But first, some comments must be made on the nature of the political situation in France in those two years.

By the late 1950s, France had not yet fully recovered from the abysmal military and societal collapse of the year 1940 which had permitted the swift German triumph over the nation. Or, to qualify that claim, France had not yet fully recovered *psychologically* from that defeat and humiliation. After the liberation of France by Allied forces in 1944, a wave of public euphoria had covered over the scars left in French society by the defeat of 1940 and obscured the moral and political questions which were a residue of the subsequent German occupation of the country. During that occupation the regime of Marshal Pétain at Vichy had been responsible for governing the south of France in coordination with Nazi wishes and policies. This cover-up was complicated and persisted until nearly the end of the 1960s. The return of Charles DeGaulle to politics in 1958 provided much of the impetus for superimposing a new myth of resistance and French glory over this distinctively dismal episode in the nation's history. And it occurred just when the original myth appeared about to erode.

The decline of France's claims to being a world power, which essentially had begun with the defeat in 1940, had continued in a downward spiral after 1945. In part, this was one aspect of the overall eclipse of Europe after 1945 signified by the rise of the United States and the Soviet Union as the superpowers which now dominated a divided Europe. Yet this eclipse registered differently in France than it did elsewhere.

France's overseas empire, much like Britain's, deteriorated quickly after the end of the Second World War. This deterioration, in France's case, was apparently more involved and more traumatic—and the resistance to it was more costly, in human, psychological, and even economic terms—than in Britain's. France found itself at war in Indo-China, facing the same formidable opponent that would later challenge and conquer the South Vietnamese Republic in the 1970s despite the latter's extensive support by the United States and eventual direct U.S. military intervention in Southeast Asia. France had to withdraw from the conflict in 1954, having undergone the painful bloodshed and expense of a nine-year war.[18] That war had cost France more than twice what it received in Marshall Plan aid from the United States during the same period.[19] And, immediately on the heels of this defeat in Indo-China, the French faced another native liberation movement in one of its colonies much closer to home.

The Algerian crisis was, in many ways, a classic instance of an independence movement taking up armed struggle against European colonialism. Its impact on French society was further complicated, however, by the fact that Algeria had been a site of French settlement from the beginning of its colonization. Unlike many European holdings in Africa, the Middle East, or Asia, a substantial European population had been resident in the country for a number of generations.

The Algerian conflict, coming on the heels of defeat in Southeast Asia and humiliation over the Suez crisis of 1956, produced widespread problems and unrest in France. To a great extent the governmental crisis that brought the reappearance of the aging "Free French" leader, General Charles DeGaulle, was caused by the struggle in Algeria.[20] Nonetheless, it is important to bear in mind that the severity of the impact of that struggle was underscored by the overall prolonged erosion of France's image and self-confidence as a world power. Eventually, it was to this general problem that DeGaulle addressed himself most effectively.

Another issue at the end of the 1950s was more subtle, but even more basic, than France's problems with her colonies and the erosion of her power and status worldwide. Put simply, France was challenged with the problem of modernizing, and doing so quickly, or else ceasing to have any claims at all on being a major and important nation. And with the single word "modernization," one could describe a series of economic and technological changes which would be linked to serious alterations in communications, productivity, and transportation, and which would dislocate certain segments of the population, while enhancing the status of others. In all, modernization meant vast economic, social, and cultural changes which were certain to have an impact on each of France's institutions—from universities to churches and to families. And it was for modernization that a call could be heard increasingly throughout France in the late 1950s. To "make France a modern nation," was a demand that attained currency in the years just prior to the end of the Fourth Republic and the founding of the Fifth.[21]

Far less than was the case with the concern about France's grandeur in the world, the desire for France's modernization could be justified statistically. By the late 1950s France's industrial productivity already lagged far behind that of either Italy or West Germany, both of which had suffered more extensive physical and material damage during World War Two.[22] Even in France's vaunted agricultural sector, the indices of production and development were weak. A U.S. farmer in 1955 was producing over three times as much, on average, as a French farmer; France had one agricultural university for every 57,000 farmers, while West Germany had one for every 3,300. The government in the Netherlands provided an agricultural adviser for every 240 farmers, whereas the ratio was 1:6,000 in France.[23] Both industry and agriculture in France suffered from traditions dating back well into the nineteenth century— small, family enterprises and small, peasant farming operations[24]—to which had been added various forms of governmental subsidy and protectionism in the post-World War Two years.

It was with the intent of responding to these two major areas of concern that Charles DeGaulle reentered the political arena. On both issues he seemed ill-suited to the task. DeGaulle was rooted in traditional conservatism, military values, French chauvinism, patriarchal attitudes, and Catholic religiosity. Given these circumstances, it was hardly to be expected that the government he led would prove to be flexible and open to compromise, or progressive and reliant on the advice of professionals. Nonetheless, it soon became apparent that DeGaulle meant to be creative, rather than recalcitrant, in his policies toward Algeria; he eventually withdrew France from Algeria paving the way there for independence. Moreover, DeGaulle's government immediately placed great emphasis on centralized planning in order to promote science and technology and to stimulate economic development in the direction of larger-scale and more-modern modes of production.

The New Wave appeared at the beginning of this changeover to the era of DeGaulle. Between spring, when DeGaulle was called from retirement as the political system disintegrated, and October, when the new constitution establishing the "Fifth Republic" was adopted, the year 1958 was one of turmoil for France. Constitutional crisis, civil unrest, disenchantment over the nation's malaise, and a continuing colonial war in Algeria framed a bleak picture for the nation and its prospects.

The first New Wave film production completed was *Handsome Serge* in 1958. It was both scripted and directed by Claude Chabrol, whose wife's recent inheritance had provided funding for the film, which was made by a firm established by Chabrol called AJYM.[25] Henri Deare was the cinematographer, and the movie was shot on location in the tiny remote village of Sardent where Chabrol had grown up.

Although set in the locale of his own boyhood, Chabrol's *Handsome Serge* is not ostensibly autobiographical. Nonetheless, one of the two central characters,

François Bayon, the sophisticated city dweller who had left the village years before the film's action begins, may be considered to be a character who incorporates traits found in Chabrol himself.

Handsome Serge opens with a long tracking shot across the French countryside. The camera searches through the leafless trees of winter, brings into focus a bus traveling along the curving road to the village and follows it until the bus stops. The scene itself is built around a relatively standard and conventional situation in fiction in which an individual returns to the place of his youth after a long absence. François is met at the bus, a sequence in which the viewer is informed that he is coming to Sardent for the winter to recover from an unspecified illness (probably tuberculosis).

Immediately François sees his boyhood friend Serge who has become the town drunk, and who is much changed from the young man he had known years before. Other changes have occurred. The butcher is dead, and "his wife went off to Aubisson with another guy." François's old homestead is in shambles. Serge explains to him, when they meet for the first time briefly in the tavern, that "all of us have changed." Nostalgia counterpointed to transformation is established immediately in the movie, but from a neutral point of view. And that is the point of departure for François to reconstruct, in a conversation, Serge's life. Serge had wanted to leave the town and study architecture. Instead, his girlfriend became pregnant, they married, Serge stayed in the village, began driving a lumber truck, and took to drink.

The viewer's awareness of Serge's situation in the narrative, however, is soon complicated by the relationship that quickly develops between François and Serge's seventeen-year-old sister-in-law, Marie. She is portrayed as a sexually precocious and aggressive young woman whose first sexual encounter was with her brother-in-law; now she becomes a lover to François. Throughout the movie she appears repeatedly, playing at enticement and often precipitating a crisis. She is seductive, natural, and elemental, but not entirely uncomplicated. Devotedly she takes care of the elderly Glaumard, who may or may not be her father. For the most part it appears that he is, but Marie goes out of her way to tell François that he is not.

There is also complexity in Serge's relationship to his wife Yvonne, and, this complexity is likely exaggerated in François's perception of the relationship. Initially Serge and Yvonne seem locked simply in a troubled marriage of convenience, in which the death of their baby at birth has led to an overwhelming burden of guilt that has resulted in Serge's drunkenness and abject alienation. Serge suspects that, at first, François does not like Yvonne, finding her plain and uninteresting, and moreover, blaming her as the cause of his old friend's alcoholic behavior and deterioration. Serge, in fact, confronts François about this, but the man from the city denies having negative feelings toward her. Nonetheless, shortly thereafter François says that Serge should leave Yvonne. At this, although he seems normally to treat Yvonne with both indifference and contempt, Serge says in an emphatic and telling way: "She's better than both of us."

Handsome Serge, at one level, is a devastating portrayal of family life, which

7. The urban sophisticate François looks to his old boyhood chum Serge (leaning out of the truck cab). Between them is Marie, in Chabrol's *Handome Serge*. Museum of Modern Art

amounts to a searing assault on the bourgeois myth of the family. Coupled with this, moreover, is the sense of grinding recognition in the film of the authenticity and depth of feeling among the villagers and in their private lives. As Serge responds after hearing that the old man Glaumard has forced Marie to have sex with him after he has discovered that she is not really his daughter, "It's really pretty normal." François is horrified and repulsed by such primitive behavior, but Serge points out that after all the old man had been lusting after her for years. Serge is not astounded by the rape, but rather by the fact that the old man had held back his urges for so long.

François is the city slicker who, even though the viewer never sees him in his urban habitat, reflects all of the prejudices, the emotional distancing, and the astonishment of his breed. He simply cannot comprehend what he views to be the brutal circumstances of village life. Yet, the film—because, in this case, the title does *not* mislead—is about Serge. And it is one of the notable elements of the movie that a shift in point of view is achieved during the course of the narrative that dispels any illusion that the movie is about François.

Serge sends his pregnant wife home from a village dance and then goes off into the night for a rendezvous with his sister-in-law Marie. François, both jealous and outraged by Serge's conduct, follows them out of the dance hall. He confronts Serge in the street and gets a thorough beating from him. From this moment on, increasingly the movie is seen from Serge's perspective.

François, after his beating, returns to his room. His landlady tells him, "You see how they are," and urges him to go back to the city. He ignores her, leaning against the window casing, and looking out. Snow begins to fall. The image of snow falling is superimposed over the scene of François, dejected, still in his room. Flute music accompanies the sequence. The passage of time is registered by shots evoking the stillness of a winter's day, and the overall shift in perspective and point of view within the film itself is, thus, attained visually. This shift is set against, but also in a subtle way predicated by, François's decision to "make himself an example" for the villagers. For in reacting to the priest, who also has suggested that François leave town, François has made just this commitment verbally. It indicates a shift born of his failure to attain his original, simpler goal—to "try to help them."

François sees himself driven to action; his vital impulse demands that he "do something" to alter the situation. He ignores the priest's warning—which he regards as weary and cynical—that the villagers "don't need you or anybody else." Yet as the narrative progresses, François has not taken things into his own hands or made himself a model or an example for the townsfolk. Far from it! Instead, he evolves into a kind of go-between in trying to rescue the relationship between Yvonne and Serge, even though he had originally urged his old friend to leave her.

Yvonne is pregnant. As the pregnancy has progressed Serge has left home and habitually goes on long benders that he sleeps off in barns and stables around the village. When, one night, Yvonne goes into labor she sends for François. He tries to get one of her neighbors to go to fetch the doctor, but the young woman complains that it's too cold outside. She stays home, and in so doing gives a final blow in this fictional film to the myth of pastoral tranquility and cooperative neighborliness of village life.

The doctor who is treating old Glaumard doesn't want to leave the elderly man to go and attend to Yvonne. François goes looking for Serge and finds him, passed out, in a barn. In a strongly expressionistic sequence, characterized by extremes of light and dark, he drags Serge through the snow back to his home. There he revives him. Serge comes out of his drunken stupor slowly. Yvonne has already delivered the baby and the doctor has arrived belatedly. Suddenly recognizing his healthy son, Serge screams in agitated delight, as if this awareness has suddenly purged the effects of the alcohol from him. The film ends with an image of him smiling, and laughing uproariously, that becomes increasingly blurred and distorted before it finally fades away.

Claude Chabrol's theoretical contribution to the New Wave was to proclaim unabashedly that movies should explore only what he called "little issues." Beyond this claim was a more general philosophic bent, and one which merged with the demands for authenticity or genuineness found in existentialism,[26] as well as with the "situation ethics" ascribable to certain European theologians in the late 1950s. Chabrol was one of the contributors to the awareness that movies provided a marvelous vehicle for certain ideas which were current. Thinkers during the 1950s had turned increasingly to fiction and drama to present the immediacy of selected moral and philosophic issues, and with the new seriousness of the New Wave a philosophic bent could blend with that entrée that movies had always provided into the world of action. The philosophic mode then in vogue in France especially, but throughout western Europe as well, existentialism, rejected speculation in favor of self-reflective spontaneity, immediacy, and choice. As an intellectual and cultural force, taking off from its roots in Friedrich Nietzsche's late-nineteenth-century critique of past systematic philosophy, it had developed increasingly toward a position rooted in a simplifying of themes and toward an immediacy and situationality to which film could be linked.

Handsome Serge is a film filled by the details and subtleties of transition and transformation. Change is an important—although displaced—theme in its narrative. This displacement, in fact, pushes the narrative frequently away from many of the filmic and theatrical conventions for dramatizing change. In *Handsome Serge*, such change is present, but also is understated. The story line reverses the traditional fictional mode of contrasting the city and the country that had been inherited from the nineteenth century, by thematically setting certain fictional conventions on their head. The view of the provinces as pastoral, traditionalist, and conservative is rudely shaken in *Handsome Serge*.

Moreover, the debunking of the myth of the family is pervasive. Religiosity no longer has any role to play in the life of the villagers; the curé, in fact, is the first to acknowledge this. Sophisticated values, temperance, and the constructive reexamination of one's life and responsibilities are the focus of François's awkward campaign to reform Serge. Yet Serge, who apparently has been sent into his terrible tailspin by a combination of having to marry Yvonne and then having their baby die at birth, resists his friend and eventually gives him a physical beating. More importantly, Serge triumphs in the last scene in an elemental and life-giving manner. The film's ending, stylistically rendered in the expressionist mode and tending to go out of focus visually, leaves our final interpretation of Serge's response to the birth of a healthy son open, but the mood is clear, nonetheless.

At the end Serge is triumphant and almost delirious in happiness. But whether this is "happiness" in the normative bourgeois sense we cannot know. What he has triumphed over we do not know for certain. We can hardly imagine that he is like someone in analysis who has finally overcome the psychological fallout of a past trauma. Instead, the film itself tends to suggest that it is Serge's basic vitality and life-force that at the end is triumphant.

Throughout *Handsome Serge*, as that shift of focus we have described from François's point of view to Serge's occurs stylistically, the point of view of the film itself shifts toward greater neutrality and lassitude with regard to the coarse and unconventional drinking and sexuality of the villagers. *Handsome Serge* is, perhaps, best seen as a film of transition in which the stylistic means of shifting from an objective to a more subjective point of view underscores the central theme of the film itself.

This theme of transition, indeed, is central to Chabrol's film and distinguishes it as belonging to the special order of film that feels to us more like a genre movie than a so-called "personal one" of the sort normally attributed to the New Wave directors. Nonetheless, *Handsome Serge* still points toward the New Wave concern for the possibilities of genre as a part of the larger, almost consuming, concern with the nature of the film medium and the process of filmic awareness itself.

Handsome Serge confronts the viewer with numerous pairings: the sophisticated, responsible François and the coarse, irresponsible Serge; Yvonne, the loyal, devoted wife and Marie, her seductive sister. There are two fights in which François is involved, two elderly men, two scenes of Serge and his lumber truck, two scenes with the village priest. The dialectic of city and country is moreover central to the film, even though the village is given on celluloid and the urban environment is only suggested. These dualities, too, define yet more formalistic elements in the film, which clash with the apparently naturalistic surface of much of the representation in *Handsome Serge*.

Fundamentally, the notion of the transitional is a mode that meshes well with notions of the dialectical.[27] And we must bear in mind that the New Wave emerged at what appears to have been a moment of significant transition in French society, while at the same time, a self-proclaimed transition in the medium of film itself was being heralded.

The New Wave was French only insofar as so much of what happens in Paris defines what is French. The New Wave was a phenomenon that was quite specific—both temporally and in terms of its locale. It existed in a culture in which a special role had been carved out by the intelligentsia and in which a single city, Paris, is the predominant center of intellectual and cultural life. The New Wave directors knew each other and had contact with each other. They shared several goals: establishing the director as the film's "author," exploring "small themes" on "small production budgets," and experimenting and innovating in "the language of film." Nonetheless, they only worked together in a few instances. Virtuosity of the director, not collaborative work, was their cherished idea. The surface unity in the New Wave covered a wide degree of thematic diversity. Indeed, their emphasis on virtuosity, *auteurist* ideas, and independence mandated that it be so.

Chabrol had set up the production company "AJYM Films" with money his wife inherited. François Truffaut, who had been taken in as a restless teenager by the theorist and critic André Bazin, was staked to production funds for *The 400 Blows* by his father-in-law, a wealthy movie distributor.[28] The commercial fortunes of the first two New Wave films were rooted in family gifts.

The 400 Blows is a work connected with the literary conventions to which *auteurist* notions of filmmaking might easily be linked in theory. The movie is much like a first novel, based as it is on autobiographical material in part, and concerned as it is with the particular experience of adolescence. Like many first novels, its themes have much to do with the search for one's identity, gaining emotional distance on a hostile adult world from which one has already become alienated, and coming to confront the injustices and hypocrisies of society at large from the weakling position of adolescence.

The opening sequence of *The 400 Blows* consists of a traveling shot through Parisian streets. The locale having been established, the next cut is to a classroom in a typical all-boys school in France before educational reforms (fostered by DeGaulle's administration) ushered in coeducation. The camera is set up at the back of the classroom so as to establish the viewer's identification visually with the point of view of the pupils. We see several of them passing a girlie photo, and soon it comes to a boy who will soon be identified as Antoine Doinel the young protagonist of *The 400 Blows*. Antoine is caught with the photo by his teacher, and he is brought to the front of the class for punishment. The remainder of the schoolroom sequence is taken up with the harried teacher's dictation of the poem "The Hare," which elicits teenage tittering over its romantic allusions to the lovelife of Mr. and Mrs. Rabbit.

At home, in their crowded family apartment, Antoine confronts his mother's vanity and self-centeredness along with his father's petit-bourgeois weakness of character. Both are obvious to him, and his resignation and sense of impotence in dealing with his parents is evident to the viewer immediately. With a friend he skips school, and the boys head for a movie theater, which is the first of several references to the cinema proper in *The 400 Blows*. Antoine and his sidekick hit the pinball machines, too, and Antoine's ride in a centrifugal force machine gives Truffaut occasion for a daring and unusual use of the camera. The viewer sees the whirling figures standing above as the drum of the machine rotates. As the floor drops from under the feet of those in the machine we abruptly see Antoine in several contorted positions as his small body clings to the wall of the machine. Here he is caught up in the freedom and joy of a new experience, but the undertone of the sequence is distinctly one of threat and terror evoked visually. Antoine's body has become strained and contorted, as if he is being tortured physically, and his face bears a grimace of discomfort and fear.

Then, on the way home from school Antoine sees his mother kissing a strange man on the street near a subway station. Later, at home, he laughs at the notion that his mother loves him.

The next day, having told his teacher he was absent from school because his mother died, Antoine's lie is discovered. His father gives him a cuffing, and after that Antoine complains to his pal that he can't bear living at home any more. He spends a night away from home, surreptitiously sleeping on the floor of a printing plant owned by his sidekick's uncle.

Yet, immediately after this sequence, the mood of the film turns humorous, at least briefly. As a kind of ellipsis, Truffaut's direction offers the viewer a neatly developed visual vignette, shot almost entirely from a high-angle camera position. The camera follows a group of the school boys being taken out for exercise. As their coach leads them through the streets of Paris toward the playing fields, in groups of two or three they peel off from the others and scurry away in various directions. They duck into hallways or sneak off down alleys; a few even pop into a convenient bistro. This is a significant piece of cinematic action in *The 400 Blows*, not because it moves the narrative forward, nor because it offers the viewer any new grasp on situations or characters, but because it deftly embraces the sharp contrasts of emotion characteristic to adolescence itself.

Indeed, the sequence described above provides an opening to the "Balzac episode" in the film, in which the viewer is treated to a lighthearted, but poignant, portrayal of real interest and enthusiasm on Antoine's part. He has discovered the novels of the early nineteenth-century French writer Honoré de Balzac, and reads them voraciously, a cigarette hanging from his lip Humphrey Bogart-style. One evening he erects a kind of shrine to his newfound literary hero, complete with a lighted candle as a token of Antoine's critical acclaim and burning admiration for the novelist. During the evening family meal, however, the candle ignites a drape and the tribute to Balzac becomes besmirched with smoke. His father, his mother, and Antoine retreat to a movie theater on one of the grand boulevards of Paris and enjoy their forced night out on the town.

The next morning the lingering joy of the night before is quickly erased. At school his teacher judges him harshly for having plagiarized a composition from the well-known writings of Balzac. Despite his pleas that he didn't copy the great writer directly, Antoine is expelled from school—and his pal with him. By afternoon they have landed at the other boy's apartment in Montmartre.

At the other boy's home, in an upper-middle-class environment, we hear the father telling his son that his mother manages to set her schedule to avoid seeing him as much as possible. *The 400 Blows* portrays a demolished myth of the family as is found in *Handsome Serge*. Antoine's family is a ruin based on hypocrisy. At the other end of the social scale his friend's family is held together only by the convenience of avoidance. Should this theme, which is found both in *Handsome Serge* and in *The 400 Blows*, be considered a function of the personal inclinations of both directors, as an auteurist interpretation might maintain, or be seen as a common symbolic element in which disintegration and disarray relate to broader social themes? The interpretation here leans toward the latter. For if the New Wave appears at what is essentially a moment of cultural transition—the "turning point" marked by the end of the 1950s—then its fiction must find some way to encapsulate the notion of change, in this instance in the form of disintegration of the familial myth.

Later in the narrative of *The 400 Blows* as Antoine and his pal walk through a park—after the requisite stint in the movie theater—they come upon a "Punch & Judy Show." The frame is filled with the faces of children, each four or five years old. There is an irony, pointed out by their innocence and their wide-eyed stares, as juxtaposed against our protagonist Antoine, just entering adolescence, but already in the process of becoming estranged and alienated from society. Indeed, right after this he and his friend steal a typewriter in hopes of fencing it, but when they can't, Antoine sneaks back to the office to return it. He is caught by the night watchman who phones his father.

This event, and the embarassment of it, convince his parents that Antoine has become incorrigible. At their insistence he is sent to a reformatory in the country. There, soon after arriving, he is interviewed by a woman psychologist in a scene that is memorable for its unique visual qualities. The camera focuses exclusively on Antoine. There are no cuts during the sequence, but rather a series of dissolves which represent the passage of time. This visual technique evokes a sense of repetitiousness and futility in the scene. The viewer's awareness of the camera's presence is heightened, while at the same time the visual attention of the lens remains strictly on Antoine.

As the critic Georges Franju observed to Truffaut regarding this sequence:

> If you'd cut to the girl, the psychologist, it would have been stupid, it would have been ruined, it would have been traditional . . . that's what I call a *new* technique, because you kept focusing on the face without cutting. Haven't we been hounded about cutting back and forth though? No, not cutting like that is much better— it's rare.[29]

The latter parts of *The 400 Blows* increasingly contain striking visual effects. Shortly after his arrest, Antoine is taken away in a paddy wagon. Sitting among a group of prostitutes, he looks out through the wire mesh opening at the streets of Paris. This singular point-of-view shot, in which the camera captures the moment as if from Antoine's eyes, marks an abrupt introduction of subjective cinematography into *The 400 Blows*. Used so sparingly, its effectiveness is heightened.[30]

Yet the most memorable visual effect in the film remains the final freeze-frame of Antoine at the shore in winter. He has escaped from the school for delinquent boys, and he has run across fields and directly down to the water's edge. There he stands, looking out at the sea, then turns to face the camera—and is frozen in that position.

This final shot is frequently cited in the pantheon of memorable movie moments. It captures the open-endedness and tentativeness of Antoine's situation. The visual device also suggests the fictional continuation of his saga— Truffaut carried it on in two subsequent films which, together with *The 400 Blows*, form the so-called "Antoine Doinel trilogy."[31]

Both *Handsome Serge* and *The 400 Blows* are highly personal films in which autobiographical material, drawn from the experience of the respective directors, is present. Godard's *Breathless* is personal, but in a sense distinct from the autobiographical. It is a movie that is extraordinarily self-conscious about its own position in, and relationship to, film history. Much of the value of the movie resides in its placing of personal concerns about movies and their making into an imaginative cinematic framework. *Breathless* is full of allusions to those darkly lit Hollywood movies of the 1940s belonging to the genre called "film noir."[32] Yet it would be incorrect to say that Godard's movie owes its own being to that genre. Instead, the relationship of *Breathless* to "film noir" is one of vigorous and imaginative extension, consisting of both a playing on, and a playing off of, the established cinema conventions to which it frequently and deftly refers. *Breath-*

8. Truffaut's famous freeze-frame at the end of *The 400 Blows* captures the isolation, alienation, and tentative situation of Antoine. Museum of Modern Art

less, most distinctively among the first New Wave films, is a work that can be labeled "modernist."

Breathless opens somewhere in Paris where a character played by Jean-Paul Belmondo steals a car. He drives to the countryside, humming and singing about how he loves France. He glances to the side, as if addressing the audience directly on the subject of not liking the seaside and the mountains. He then discovers a revolver in the glove compartment; he points it out the window, at the shining sun, and pretends to fire it. Soon enough he actually does get to shoot; moments later, he guns down a highway policeman who has stopped him for speeding. He then flees across an open field.

Already in this opening sequence *Breathless* establishes itself as nontraditional. We encounter a character and a crime, for which neither background nor motivation are provided. The cutting is abrupt, both within the sequence and from that sequence to the next. The convention of filmic naturalism, which normally prohibits a character in the action addressing the audience directly, is violated. A loud blast of music ends the first sequence as Michel Poiccard (the Belmondo character) runs away. We are aware of the camera, the editing, the music, and the soundtrack from the very beginning. Godard makes us so, hence revealing his intent to examine the film medium and its conventions while telling us a story. Yet, at the same time, *Breathless* immediately draws us into its characters and the thin, but intriguing, narrative in which they find themselves.

Belmondo, or Michel Poiccard, alias Lazlo Kovacs,[33] and Jean Seberg—at once an American actress in Paris as well as the American character Patricia Franchini, who is drawing money from home for university studies and peddling the *Herald Tribune*—are the unlikely couple at the center of the narrative. As the critic John Kreidl has written: "Each character [in *Breathless*] plays two roles; one in a social document of 1959, one in the complete fiction. . . . Never in the history of film has a fiction had so much to do with real life as in *Breathless*."[34] Our awareness of the "real" lives of both Belmondo and Seberg only strengthens the values which are characterized by them in the roles of Michel and Patricia.

Back in Paris, Michel/Lazlo proclaims himself ready to "live life dangerously to the end."[35] He's on the run from the cops, trying to arrange a pickup of money owed to him by a mobster, and, through all of this, doggedly, pursuing Patricia Franchini. He is obsessed with her, and she, being twenty and in Paris, is interested in a whole world beyond and removed from his obsession—journalism, literature, and so on. She's afraid, she admits at one point, for she wants him to love her and at the same time she hopes that he won't. She quotes from the novelist William Faulkner that between grief and nothing, Faulkner would choose grief. But in response to this Michel/Lazlo says he sees grief only as a compromise: "You've got to have it all or nothing." Later he tells her that his ambition is "to become immortal and then to die."

During the filming of Belmondo's cab ride through Paris to the destination where he is to pick up the money owed to him, Godard experiments with abrupt jump cuts. This experimenting evokes self-reflection on the nature of film as a medium. The ways in which stylistic and technical devices are made apparent—

indeed, almost disruptive—in sequences such as this one are underscored. Moreover, there are many direct allusions to movies in *Breathless*. Patricia escapes the two Parisian detectives tailing her by rushing into a cinema where an English-language Western is playing. Later Michel/Lazlo poses beside a poster with Humphrey Bogart on it outside a movie theater. Other communicative media are present, too, for as the couple leaves the movie theater across the street a neon news report on a building flashes that Michel Poiccard's arrest is imminent. *Breathless* is punctuated with poignant asides, not only on the situation that exists between Michel and Patricia, but also on dimensions of the human condition. One of these asides is when Patricia notes, "Even when two people are 'sleeping together' they're alone."

Slowly, the dragnet closes in on Michel/Lazlo. The clownish Parisian detectives have warned Patricia that they are aware of his contacts with her. The next morning, after she has phoned police inspector Vital to tip him off as to Michel/Lazlo's whereabouts, she tells him that she doesn't want to be in love with him and that's why she called the police. As for Michel/Lazlo, now that the end is near, he is left alone in the street and tossed a revolver by a fleeing gangster chum. He can only say: "I'm beat and I want to sleep. I can't stop thinking about her."

In terms of placing itself in the broadest streams of modern and contempo-

9. Jean-Paul Belmondo as a Parisian hood and Jean Seberg as his
   American girlfriend in *Breathless* (1959). Museum of Modern Art

rary culture and consciousness, *Breathless* is an extraordinarily important fictional work. In the combination of its self-reflection, which explores the nature of the film medium itself, its portrayal of the anti-hero, and its existential thematic, *Breathless* becomes a truly modernist work. Its visual depth-structure is filled with various posters and signs, telephones, newspapers, and American automobiles; the soundtrack is punctuated throughout by contemporary jazz. The conversations in *Breathless* may be described as non-revealing, discontinuous, and non-dialogical. This underscores the episodic nature of the film's narrative structure. *Breathless* is held together by its power of absorption into the nature of the medium itself. Conversation in this movie does not advance the story but, rather, serves as a commentary on the nature of film action and narrative itself. Moreover, the camera work in *Breathless* may be thought of as especially voyeuristic. There is a distancing present in the cinematography, which is reinforced by much of the editing, that seems calculated to make the viewer aware of the presence of the camera and the qualities of film as artifice. Indeed, in *Breathless* the entire tension that forms a dialectic between the naturalistic/photographic qualities of the medium, on the one hand, and the nature of the movie as artifice, on the other, is present throughout the movie itself. This dialectic flourished generally in the works of the New Wave, but in *Breathless* it is especially prominent.

Breathless is also one of the cinema's most self-conscious and provocative explorations of existential themes and motifs. Even the cinematography of *Breathless* is existential in its temper. The camera is a presence that endures through its own situationally; it is constantly and obviously in the process of searching out. By making the viewer aware of the camera's presence, its activity, and its point of view, the machine itself is established in its own authenticity. The settings, too, reflect existential priorities. The action in *Breathless* takes place almost entirely out-of-doors. Interior scenes are few; Michel/Lazlo has no place of residence, and Patricia has a hotel room. The tentativeness of life uprooted is manifest.

It is primarily Michel/Lazlo's commitment to live life dangerously to the end, and to make choices that define a philosophic point of view, which may be called existential. To some viewers, of course, the Belmondo character appears to be the embodiment of a European's misunderstanding of the caricature of an American criminal type. Yet, viewed from another perspective, we find in Michel/Lazlo an authenticity. He is a self-positing individual in the extreme; one who makes choices consistent with his own being.

What some viewers may consider to be an existentialist point of view in *Breathless* is intermixed richly with the director's taking advantage of—and also liberties with—the genre of the gangster thriller. Existentialism itself, however, already was rooted in an intentional rejection of the past assumptions of systematic western philosophy. In taking each situation to be unique, particularly as in the version of existentialism expounded in France by Jean-Paul Sartre, the individual's freedom to choose for himself or herself, and, in choosing, to make one's life into a destiny, was paramount. These elements of the existentialist point of view fall neatly into line with certain fiction genres, such as the thriller or the gangster film. A genre, after all, may be regarded as being a particular way of looking at life, whereby the implication of genre itself becomes a philosophic one. Specific genres betray clearly held values.[36] What could be closer to the spirit of Nietzsche's prime existentialist maxim to live life dangerously than the narrative and dramatic conventions of the thriller as developed in the twentieth century? Who can be regarded as more alienated and hence living on the razor's edge of choosing than the outlaw or the gangster? This is the logical fusion of modernist alienation with modern, popular genres—first established in literature and subsequently fully exploited in movies.

The box-office successes of *Handsome Serge* and *The 400 Blows* established the New Wave. By 1960 every distributor in France, at least, was anxious to be able to connect the term New Wave to nearly any new release as a marketing ploy, whether it fitted or not.[37] *Breathless* too was a box-office hit. That did not, however, translate into a political situation favorable enough for Godard to permit circulation of his film about the war in Algeria, *The Little Soldier*, which was produced in 1960.[38] The French censors were not as responsive to the marketplace as were the film distributors.

Here is an instance in which social awareness, a point of view that was harnessed to an overriding philosophic emphasis, and the imaginative exploitation of certain narrative conventions merged. Often, in a kind of romanticizing and mythologizing of the New Wave emphasis is placed on the non-commercial or even anti-commercial intentions of these young directors. Yet that is really an overemphasis. Whether it intended to be so or not, the New Wave was commercially farsighted. The New Wave brought forth a kind of cinema whose time had come.

The New Wave was established by an elite for an elite, and at the time of its founding both this creative elite and its audience were essentially "disengaged" politically and socially.[39] Nonetheless, the New Wave films were related to broad patterns of cultural change in France. The New Wave, however, found its audience internationally, primarily among younger, well-educated persons. As a group, that audience was composed primarily by students who were the children of an increasingly affluent middle-class in the western world. It also pioneered a strategy of production and distribution that was targeted at specifically defined audiences.

The New Wave came into being just as the demographic changes, the rise in affluence, and the impact of television were combining to end the nearly fifty-year ascendancy of the theatrical motion picture as the primary popular entertainment throughout the industrialized world. The New Wave broke on the scene at the end of the 1950s when even some of the diehard moguls in Hollywood were realizing that the era of an industry based primarily on big-budget productions which appealed to all ages and types of people as a potential audience was finished. In Western Europe, broadcast television had arrived later than in the U.S. and had just begun its ascendancy at the beginning of the 1960s. Hollywood, by the late 1960s, came to gear its standard production toward younger audiences. At the beginning of the decade the New Wave had pioneered targeting an audience of student-aged men and women who considered themselves "modern" and who had a certain grasp of the cinema that could be called "informed."

François Truffaut once claimed that the only thing the New Wave directors really shared in common was their love for the pinball machines found in nearly every Parisian bistro and sidewalk café.[40] There is a substantial ring of truth to this claim. In a more serious vein, the New Wave, as Truffaut pointed out at another juncture, emphasized the individualism and unique vision of each director.[41] While these directors may have shared certain attitudes and intentions, they did not share thematic concerns—at least on the surface—nor did they share an ideological terrain. Chabrol was generally conservative, and though he later broke with the Church, essentially Catholic. *Handsome Serge*, in fact, won a prize from the OCIC (International Catholic Office of Film).[42] Truffaut had lined up—at least for a time—to the right during the 1950s, publishing provocative articles in *Arts*, which some observers regarded as a neofascist magazine.[43] By contrast Godard aligned himself to the political Left. By the late 1960s he came close to proclaiming himself a full-blown Maoist. The other director in the first crest of the New Wave, Alain Resnais, was clearly leftist. Of all the new films which appeared between 1958 and 1960 in France, only Resnais's *Hiroshima, mon amour* could be considered fully new in technique and execution, as well as being revolutionary in its content.[44]

In strict interpretations of the New Wave, Resnais often is not included in the list of directors belonging to that movement. His exclusion is normally justified on three grounds: (1) Resnais was ten to fifteen years older than the other directors of the New Wave; (2) He did not share with the other New Wave directors a background in writing film criticism; specifically, he was not attached to *Cahiers du cinéma* or one of the other organs in which the New Wave directors published before turning to filmmaking proper; (3) Resnais is not as clearly an advocate of *auteur* cinema, and hence cannot be placed with complete accuracy as standing at the vanguard of the New Wave movement.

Yet, these objections are based on narrow and rigid assumptions as to what the New Wave was. The traditional view of the New Wave has seen it as a highly self-conscious and self-positing movement, relatively well organized, fostered by artists who shared the experience of writing for *Cahiers du cinéma*, being devotees of Henri Langlois's cinémathèque, and being of the same age. Clearly, there is much to this argument. But it is more valuable to see the New Wave as a moment in cultural experience, when a new agenda and set of priorities were being established throughout much of the western world. The New Wave was a part of a larger phenomenon that began in the mid-1950s with the "Beats" in the United States, with the "Angry Young Men" in Britain, and with the emergence of rock music on the margins of cultural respectability. The perception of the dawn of a new era, in turn, was punctuated by the astonishing popularity of the Kennedy presidency across the western world, and finally completed only by the end of the 1960s with the manifestations of a counterculture and the spasms of "New Left" politics, which then deteriorated, at varying rates, in the societies of Western Europe and North America during the 1970s. To assess its rightful place in cultural history, the New Wave needs to be seen as part of a breakthrough in awareness and perception in the cinema that began unobtrusively at the end of the 1950s, but which was a part of the continuum that erupted cataclysmically in the youth movements of the late sixties.

Resnais often is considered as part of that coterie called the "Left Bank Directors," who are distinct from the New Wave: Agnes Varda, Chris Marker, Alain Robbe-Grillet, and Marguerite Duras. Resnais, in my estimation, nonetheless stands out as having made the ultimate and quintessential New Wave movie with *Hiroshima, mon amour*.

As one European critic put it, "Resnais [with *Hiroshima, mon amour*] freed film from having to be limited to being just film; he established it as a medium into which *all* the arts flowed simultaneously."[45] Indeed, *Hiroshima* has a complex narrative that breaks through much of the classical form of editing and established storytelling.

Hiroshima, mon amour is engaging—even haunting—from the opening frame forward. Two naked bodies are intertwined in embrace, but the viewer does not necessarily immediately identify these forms for what they are. They might even better be called only surfaces moving and undulating. They seem, at first, covered with ashes; on closer look, perhaps it is moisture. The shot of the embrace dissolves, and the dialogue begins. The voices are disembodied as in a narration, yet they, too, are haunting. The language is, at once, both concrete and simple, but also full of passion and insight. Its development is poetic; its ambiguity is not so much confusing as it is enthralling. "You saw nothing in Hiroshima. Nothing." She responds, "I saw everything. Everything."

The woman is known throughout the film only as *Elle* (she), who is a French actress making an international film on behalf of the peace movement in Hiroshima. He is a Japanese architect, known only as *Lui* (him). Both are married to other people—happily, they say.

The opening section of *Hiroshima, mon amour* consists of footage that appears to be "documentary" in its character. It is accompanied by the voice-over narration which flows poetically. She claims to have seen the hospital in Hiroshima, and at these words the camera takes the viewer down empty corridors, probing ever so briefly into rooms where patients stare out from their beds. With his denial that she has seen anything, the camera tracks again through the corridors. There follows a shot outside the hospital; the sequence then fades, dreamlike, back to their embrace.

Next, we hear her voice: "Four times at the museum." The outside of the museum appears. It is a nondescript, low, modern building. Then, in four separate shots (does this suggest the subjectivity of the camera's point of view being precisely equivalent to the four times she says she has visited the museum?) we see the interior space of the building. The camera moves through a number of exhibits; a class of schoolboys gather around one of the images of destruction. We see a model of the city before its bombing, then the frame of a bicycle twisted and distorted by the intense heat. A film being shown in the museum portrays victims, their clothes on fire, running toward the camera. We see bottles containing human flesh writhing in a solution.

Again he denies that she has seen anything at the museum. We see a woman, her clothes aflame, emerging from the rubble, coming toward the camera. Of these newsreels, she says: "I've invented nothing," to which he replies "You invented everything." She continues in her conscious act of remembering. "Like you, I am overwhelmed by memory. I know what it is to forget." We see a sequence of shots of a skylight, of a building, of a window in a tourist shop, of a store selling balloons, of a commemorative plaque on a building; then, again, of a skylight. "Like you, I have forgotten. I've wished to have inconsolable memory—a memory of darkness and stone." As she says this, we see people before a monument, then a memorial shaped like a bomb, and then the figure of a person etched in stone by the explosive radioactivity. "Like you, I have forgotten." As she says this, we see a tour bus packed with tourists accompanied by a young, smiling, and attractive tour guide, microphone in hand who is describing the city as they make their motorized rounds through it.

The camera commences a long, rapid tracking shot through the streets of Hiroshima. Her voice intones: "I meet you, I remember you, you destroy me, you are good for me; how could I doubt this city was made to the size of my love? How could I doubt that you were made to the size of my body?" The long tracking

10. A flashback to World War II in Nevers, France. The actress *Elle* punished by her family over the disgrace of her having had a German lover, in *Hiroshima, mon amour*. Museum of Modern Art

shot through the city ends with the lovers, now photographed clearly in bed, appearing as if awakening from a dream. They look at each other's skin—hence, at each other's nationality and race. He asks, "Why do you want to see everything in Hiroshima?" She replies: "It interested me. I have my own idea of that. You see, one has to learn to see well."

This first segment of the film is extraordinary for its combining of disparate elements—the documentary, the poetic, the world historical, and the intimate. This sequence manages to draw the viewer into the film's visual and aural world with tremendous force, yet to do so on a basis that remains emotionally tenuous and problematic. This opening segment of *Hiroshima* simultaneously gives the viewer a great deal of information about the city and its bombing, but it also evokes a mystery surrounding what it is the characters really know or don't know about that experience. The present tense of the narration, the melange of images, and the constantly tracking camera provoke us as viewers to ponder what we know or don't know about the characters, as well as considering what we know or don't know about the historical event that is alluded to. The second segment of the film is predicated on feelings evoked by the effectiveness of the opening portion; the viewer enters the world of a more conventional narrative approach and structure as if awakening.

Yet the movie remains visually innovative, intellectually challenging, and poetic. There is, first of all, the self-reflexive quality of *Elle* being an actress who is seen making a film-within-a-film. Then there is the instant when, looking at her Japanese lover as he still lies in bed face down, the sight of him cues for her a visual recollection of her slain German lover in her small hometown of Nevers during the Nazi occupation of France. Interjected into this instantaneous recollection is her cynical insight: "People always notice things to suit themselves," followed by objective and distanced observations on herself, to the effect that she had been full of bitterness and could have made a career of it.

She tells *Lui* that she is leaving Hiroshima to return to Paris the next day, and that she will not see him again. He finds her later, however, at the site where the movie she is making is being filmed. In a bar she finally opens herself to him, and tells the story of her romance with a German soldier, who was then gunned down by French Partisans. Fourteen years have passed. "Tonight I remember, but one day I won't; none of it," she says. He replies that he will "think of her as the symbol of love without memory."

Her dead lover was an enemy of France. As punishment for her relationship with him her head is shaved, and she is paraded through the town. Her disgraced family has locked her in the basement. After this session of revelation and confession at the bar, she returns briefly to her hotel room. Then she goes back out into neon-lit late-night Hiroshima.

In her monologue as she walks she says, "This city is made to the measure of my love, his body is made to the measure of my love. . . . Deform me to your likeness, so that no one ever after will understand my desire." As she walks, the street scenes of Hiroshima transform visually into the streets of her hometown, Nevers. At this point the visual material of the film has become completely identified with her mind's eye; the camera work and the editing create a medley of passages which evoke the subjective first-person point of view.

"A time will come when we can no longer name the thing that unites us. . . . While the memory of you sets my body on fire, I'd love to see Nevers again." Through the night she walks alone; they are briefly together on a bench at the train station. She slips off and goes to a café (named the *Casablanca*); he follows her there. Back at her hotel they embrace. First she says "I forget you," and then she says to him, "I name you Hiroshima; You are Hiroshima." He responds, "And you are Nevers, Nevers in France."

Hiroshima, mon amour is a significant movie, not in the least because it brought the cinema into full embrace of modernist impulses akin to those established already in literature and in other modes of culture. *Hiroshima* demonstrated how well a movie could "think," because it established the capacity of film to express interiority and subjectivity fully. Moreover, it succeeded in achieving a narrative flow extraordinarily close to what in literature is called "stream of consciousness."

Writing in the journal *Arts*, the critic Henri Deutschmeister observed that the New Wave in France had liberated moviemaking from the unions, from studios, from self-imposed censorship, and even from actors and actresses.[46] The New Wave did all this, and set a model for others who followed—Third World cineasts, young German filmmakers, and even some of Hollywood's rebels. The greatest international influence was registered, of course, by the films themselves, and of all of them, the single one which most radically challenged established notions of film narrative and classical editing was *Hiroshima*. Moreover, this movie was obviously a more politically engaged work of art than the others in the first crest of the New Wave. *Hiroshima*, in fact, had to be entered in a special category at the Cannes film festival in 1959—rather than being presented as an official French entry—for fear of offending the U.S. government.[47]

Many observers have found the original source of inspiration for the New Wave in the call sounded by the critic Alexandre Astruc in 1948 for recognizing film as a new language when he talked of the "writing" camera.[48] And, indeed, this thinking obviously inspired notions of *auteurism* which flowed into the ethos of the New Wave. Other observers believe that the particular conditions of production in France determined the moment of arrival and the specific filmic nature of the New Wave. Jean-Pierre Melville, often considered a seminal figure in the Left-Bank circle of moviemakers, thought that the increased pressure on production funding in France from 1947 on led directly to the conditions in French film production from which the New Wave emerged.[49] The French government had become involved in supporting film production in 1946, but this activity increased abruptly and markedly in 1958.[50] It meant that a startling number of new and younger talents had opportunities to begin directing films. Nonetheless, the initial crest of the New Wave consisted of movies produced not from governmental support subsidies, but on the basis of independent private financial sources. They all were low-budget productions, averaging about 50 million old francs (i.e., roughly $75,000) per feature.[51]

Nowhere is there evidence to support the view that the New Wave was economically determined in any normal, causative sense of that phrase. It was true that between 1959 and 1962 in France a record ninety-seven directors each made their first full-length feature film.[52] So we can be safe in pointing out the quantitative creativity in the French film industry. This, however, offers no insight into the particular qualitative character of the New Wave movies, which were actually few in number.

When we seek to investigate the genuine nature of the relationship of these four films to French society, we may, initially, be tempted to agree with the critic Marcel Martin who, at the time, argued that films like *The 400 Blows* and *Breathless* were documents, not of French society, but rather of the French cinema.[53] On reflection, however, this seemingly accurate appraisal of these inventive and self-reflective works of film art must be challenged. For such an argument, at base, is circuitous and only semantic; it is a tautology. For the "French" cinema is, after all, a component of French society.

One of the elements being explored in the first crest of the New Wave was the question of the nature of the cinema itself. In turn this exploration can be seen as reflecting a concern for the media and their role in society, the concern for the image and how the image shapes reality. The initial crest of the New Wave appeared on the heels of massive constitutional change in France, and the arrival on the scene (or, really, the *re*arrival) of the French politician who was master of the image and its manipulation, Charles DeGaulle.[54]

The exploration of the nature of the image itself, and the playful, creative investigation of this subject in fiction is most clear in *Breathless*, where the characters are the result of an image created by Hollywood, living it out and conforming to it. Similar elements are present in *Hiroshima, mon amour* where the entire idea of a film-within-a-film functions as an exploration of the notion of "making a film to promote peace." The first segment of the movie raises numerous questions about the documentary qualities of much of the footage by blurring the distinctions between fiction and nonfiction. Indeed, the drawing of that very distinction is central to the entire notion of developing "an image."

In *The 400 Blows* and *Handsome Serge* such references are more shallow. Still, these movies are concerned with major crises in the "images of" venerable mythic institutions—the family; the pastoral rural town; adolescence; the entire process of change and transformation.

The initial movies of the French New Wave are strikingly related to the moment in time at which each appeared—right at the end of the 1950s. A movie may not be concerned with themes of world historical prominence, or may not be a work that we would consider to be ideologically or politically "engaged," and still may be of the broadest social significance. The notion itself of the "social problem film" being a distinct category of the medium is naïve, at best.[55] All movies are social documents.

The movies which form the first crest of the New Wave are not of uniform artistic pretense, nor has each gained a shared position of prominence in the pantheon of classic films. *Handsome Serge* is rarely shown, whereas *The 400 Blows* and *Breathless* maintain a strong presence in the repertory of the revival movie houses and on university campuses. Yet, we recognize that *The 400 Blows* may be most appreciated because it stands as a work that launched Truffaut's career; some might even say it marked a high point in his artistry, which he did not manage to equal again. As for *Breathless*, perhaps the interest in it is somewhat the reverse: It represents the initial feature work of Godard, a work of innocence and simplicity, as compared to his later explorations of New Left politics, radical distancing of the viewer from the film material, and experiments in montage and narration. *Hiroshima, mon amour* is not neglected, but also does not seem to be given the attention that its significance merits, perhaps because its thematic material directly confronts devastation by atomic weapons and underscores the burdens of the human condition in the nuclear age. Such recognition as is accorded to individual movies, however, remains predicated by a linear reading of where they stand in relationship to particular directorial careers, or how they stand critically, not on the basis of the social and cultural issues around which they might be clustered.

The New Wave was very much a product of its time. It is an intellectual and cultural myth to represent it as a marvelous breakthrough in cinema art carried out by a few determined young directors who had fashioned themselves into the standard bourgeois image of the independent-minded artist in a medium that had not known such independence of vision and creativity often. In the broader cultural context, the New Wave brought Modernism—the twentieth century's most pervasive artistic mode to the cinema—the century's most prescient and predominant art form. The New Wave was, at the same time, a commercial success that was the essential forerunner of an international movie industry that increasingly targeted its artistic works for more specific audiences. The New Wave was an international success, marking the first—with the "Beatles" being the second—triumph of Western Europe in reversing the flow of post-1945 cultural impetus from the United States to Europe. The New Wave commanded respect, and was at the heart of the rise of the so-called "art movie houses" in North America in the early 1960s. Yet, although its success, its inspiration, and its influence were all international, the New Wave remained, in a special way, doggedly and peculiarly French.

The New Wave too, for all its visual innovativeness, and for all its radical departures in the length of shots and scenes as well as the aural components of the sound-track, nonetheless established the film in a new relationship to the word, and the serious study and criticism of the cinema, by extension, to linguistics. These were particular French specialties, which had been present in its film culture even before World War Two, but which now were forced into the forefront of collective consciousness.

The New Wave appeared just as France was undergoing an enormous transition, not just from the Fourth to the Fifth Republic, or from his colorless predecessors to the grand old man DeGaulle, nor even simply from rural to urban, and from agrarian to technocratic. France also was undergoing a campaign to redirect its national image worldwide. This extraordinary act was carried out under DeGaulle's leadership. It reestablished French prominence in the world through the propagation of its "image," far outstripping any importance that could be based solidly in the actual economic, military, or diplomatic strength of the nation.

THREE

The Bitburg Syndrome

Just as the German cinema of the 1920s Weimar era was a point of departure for pioneer study in the sociology of the movies, so has this "New" German Cinema of the 1970s fascinated commentators. The fascination with Weimar movies, however, was triggered by interest in Hitler and the Third Reich and was forward looking—how did the movies of the 1920s and early 1930s relate to the political and social order that followed? By contrast, the interest in West German film in the 1970s and early 1980s, has focused on its distinctiveness and newness.

There is no arguing that the films of Alexander Kluge, Rainer Werner Fassbinder, Wim Wenders, Volker Schlöndorff, Margarethe von Trotta, Werner Herzog, Edgar Reitz, and others constitute a body of work, relatively unified. By emphasizing the "newness" of their film work, however, the label itself points away from our exploring their links to the past.[1] As an astute commentator has noted: "It surprises one just how little attention has been paid to the lines of continuity between recent and other German films."[2]

The German Federal Republic, which most North Americans still by habit call West Germany, is the self-proclaimed successor state to Hitler's Third Reich and the preceding governments of Germany. The German Democratic Republic (East Germany), by contrast, has declared itself a new form of state apparatus, maintaining that it is the first in German history to reflect the aspirations of the entire population rather than those of a narrow, dominant class. Whereas West Germany proclaims a continuity in history, East Germany emphasizes its break from it.

In North America we have had a vigorous exposure to the West German cinema of the 1970s and the early 1980s. We have established some critical and analytical literature about this phenomenon. The implications of this literature are clear. A common assumption is that the so-called "veil of amnesia" that the German feature film had shown toward Nazism and the Second World War was ripped away abruptly in 1977. One hypothesis has it that this occurred in direct response to the rise of left-wing domestic terrorism in the German Federal Republic in the late 1970s, and the subsequent repression of it by the Bonn government.

This interpretation often cites a film made collectively by a number of the Federal Republic's most renowned directors, including Edgar Reitz, Rainer Werner Fassbinder, Alexander Kluge, and Volker von Schlöndorff and entitled *Germany in Autumn* as marking this turning point.[3] And certainly a number of movies have been produced since 1977 in the Federal Republic about aspects of the Nazi experience, and a number of them have gained a following internationally: among them are *Lili Marleen, The Boat, The Tin Drum, The White Rose, Germany, Pale Mother, Hitler—A Film from Germany,* and *A Love in Germany.* Some significant movies produced since 1977 have hardly reached the United States: *The Children from No. 67, The Last Five Days, The Hour Zero, The Trip to Vienna, David, The Oppermann Family, From a German Life, Between Two Wars.* Nonetheless, West German film treatments of the Third Reich require close examination. Is it true that a spate of movies dealing with Nazism which have been produced since 1977 are a new phenomenon without precedent in West German filmmaking? Does their appearance mark an abrupt breakthrough into filmic consciousness on the issue of Nazism? I think not. During the period from 1949 to 1961, over forty feature films produced in the Federal Republic of Germany were set directly in the Third Reich. Claims that exploration of the Nazi past in the German cinema is a recent phenomenon seems inaccurate.

Between the war's end in 1945 and the founding of the two new German states in 1949, four films were produced which explored dimensions of the experience under Nazism: in the Soviet zone, *The Murderers Are Among Us* and *Marriage in the Shadows*; in the American and British zones, *In Those Days* and *The Film without a Title.*

In Those Days (1947) consists of five vignettes set between 1933 and 1945. Each one of the short stories is set off by an object found in an old car that two mechanics are trying to repair as refugees stream by. This movie provides a rich example of use of footage of destruction in Germany and of displaced persons pouring across the country from the east. Chronologically *In Those Days* penetrates the postwar era. The automobile itself talks and provides the narration. Before it finally goes to the junk heap, it comes once more into voice, providing an interpretation of the entire epoch: "I saw no great events; no acts of fate. I saw a few people. The times overwhelmed them, but there will always be such people."

In Those Days contains elements and themes common to nearly all subsequent movies about Nazism and World War Two produced in West Germany. The notion of the essential goodness of average people caught up in events beyond their control dominates. The five vignettes of *In Those Days* are, in microcosm, a summary of standard depictions in German film fiction of the Third Reich:

(1) The dizzying nature of the Nazi seizure of power as witnessed by essentially apolitical people.
(2) The repression of opponents of the regime, as represented by intellectual and professional elites.
(3) The Jewish sympathy theme, handled antiseptically outside the Holocaust.
(4) The portrayal of respect and pity for the German fighting man, distinguishing his sacrifice and valor from the war effort itself.
(5) The heroizing of the will to start anew in defeated Germany.

The following year, a second feature was produced in the Allied zone of occupation, *The Film without a Title*. Three characters begin the movie by discussing the problem of producing a film about the Hitler years. They are certain that they do not want to make a war movie, but they are uncertain what plots or themes to choose to address the recent past so dominated by war. In principle, elements of a comedy would be fine, for example, but then it is so difficult to portray anything from the Nazi era without seeming crass and heartless!

Supported throughout by the central device of periodically interrupting the storyline to return to the three characters who talk about the action, comment on it, and hold it in place, the plot itself remains simple. An art dealer named Martin and his maid, a country girl named Christine, become lovers briefly during the war in Berlin. Both are forced from the city; he to the front, she to the country to escape the bombing raids. After the war they are reunited by chance at her father's farm. They decide to marry. In spite of her father's feelings that Martin's profession is impractical the wedding takes place, complete with folk dancing in traditional costume.

One theme of *The Film without a Title* is straightforward: The postwar era offers an opportune setting for the breakdown of the traditional divisions between the social classes. The depiction of the war emphasizes the sadness of human suffering, as experienced by Germans themselves. There is no reference to Nazism as having been the driving force in German society, nor is there any critique of Germany's aggression having caused World War Two.

Both these movies are strikingly, indeed almost painfully, self-conscious. They utilize unusual dramatic contrivances such as the talking automobile or the characters who discuss the concept of the movie and interrupt its action. Both represent a distancing in trying to come to terms with the Nazi past and Germany's defeat.

Subsequent to these early, tentative productions the West German films set in the Third Reich which were produced between 1949 and 1961 can be grouped into three categories: (1) "Resistance" films which portray the valor of the struggle within Germany against Hitler; (2) "Neutral" movies, generally critical of the Nazi regime, but portraying the decency of the average German swept along by circumstances; (3) "Heroic, Patriotic" movies, primarily "war movies" devoid of any criticism of Nazism, Germany's aggression, or the conduct of Hitler's war.

Among the resistance films, the most easily classified are three from the mid-1950s about military officers who rebelled against Hitler's leadership: *Canaris* (1954), *The Devil's General* (1955), and *The Twentieth of July* (1955).

The production costs for *Canaris* were high for the period at 1,400,000 DM (roughly $350,000). The movie, however, was a good investment, as it proved to be an excellent box-office draw. *Canaris* earned the appellation "Especially Worthwhile" from the movie industry's self-censoring body,[4] and also was selected as the best German film at the annual Berlin Film Festival in 1955. The

West German newsweekly *Der Spiegel* praised the movie as a "real opposition film" (i.e., anti-Nazi), and generally the West German daily press agreed.[5]

Canaris is interesting filmically because it works so extensively with integrating documentary footage of the war itself into the fictional material of the plot. Ideologically *Canaris* offers calming opinions, which are placed in the dialogue convincingly, such as: "The common people down below really don't know what's going on." Admiral Canaris inveighs against Hitler, warns against his military madness, and at least peripherally, is involved in the famous plot against Hitler's life in July 1944.

Movies like *Canaris* enter directly into the business of reconstructing the past. They serve as interpretations of history, and the acknowledging of this point is extremely important. Although they are, of course, entertainment vehicles, there is no reason why entertainment and historiography are mutually exclusive.

In East Germany a bitter claim was advanced in the form of an accusation against the film. Spokespeople for the Communist regime maintained that the point of view portrayed in *Canaris* meshed neatly with the Bonn government's own favored interpretation of the Nazi past. That is, that all the mistakes and crimes of the Nazi war machine were attributable to the excesses of Hitler's personal, ideological corps, the SS (Schutzstafel). The regular German military, according to this view, actually had opposed Hitler.[6]

Interestingly, the theme of this opposition is repeated in G.W. Pabst's *The Twentieth of July*.[7] The aging Pabst had been a mainstay of the pre-Hitler German cinema, having directed features such as *The Joyless Street* (1926); *The Love of Jeanne Ney* (1927); *Pandora's Box* (1929); *Diary of a Lost Girl* (1929); *Threepenny Opera* (1931); *Comradeship* (1931). Just before the Nazi takeover in 1933 Pabst, in fact, had established left-wing political credentials, which was rare among the mainline creators of movies, even in the Weimar period.[8]

The movie portrays a small group of officers, ostensibly naïve politically, who want Hitler out of power. They argue that "the war was lost before it began," and they talk of the "social welfare monarchy" which will presumably follow the Third Reich. The authenticity factor in *The Twentieth of July* is exploited through dubbings of Hitler's voice on the phone, cuts to speeches by Goebbels, and documentary footage of battlefield action.

Lieutenant Stauffenberg, the leader of the plotters, is portrayed initially as leaving the front in shock as he has witnessed the killing of a thousand women and children—just because they are Jews. This is in direct contradiction to a scene earlier in the movie where Fräulein Klee has seen Jews being rounded up in Berlin; a Jewish man drops his glasses, and one of the soldiers says coldly, "He won't need them where he's going." Yet, her officer boyfriend has assured her "that the front is clean." *The Twentieth of July* does make perfectly clear that the roundup and destruction of Jews is being conducted on Hitler's orders. The movie ends with the final written information filling the screen that after July 20, 1944, more people died than in the entire first five years of the war.

An even more direct portrayal of a high-ranking German officer who hates both the Nazi party and the SS is found in *The Devil's General*. General Harras, the protagonist, is an open, vigorous man who loves life, and, hence, is counter-pointed to the dedicated, obsessive Nazis around him. The film was based on a stage play by the elderly Karl Zuckmayer which had gained international acclaim. In Hollywood, Warner Brothers wanted to get the rights to *The Devil's General*, and plans were to star Clark Gable in the leading role.[9]

Hollywood missed its chance on this property, but the West German state-owned airline, Lufthansa, did not. The film's production coincided with the resumption of civil aviation in West Germany, and Lufthansa believed that its investment in the production was a wise and timely one.[10] The film itself, directed by Helmut Käutner, portrays the dilemma of Air Force General Harras who is caught between a code of duty and a recognition of the evil in which the Third Reich is engaged. This dilemma is never resolved. It is merely alleviated by instances such as the one in which General Harras realizes that an adjutant, Oderbruch, is sabotaging German *Stuka* fighter planes. Harras decides not to reveal what he knows. Instead, he finds ways of holding the *Stukas* back from the front.

Käutner's adaptation follows the original stageplay closely. The medium of film, however, permits not only the sharing of the work with a much greater audience, but also the realization of weaving the complexity of Harras's dilemma into sequences portraying the actual workings of the German air force at war. Yet, like the play, the movie is ambivalent. Hence, particularly abroad, the reaction to *The Devil's General* was mixed. After its release in New York, the *Herald-Tribune* found the character of Harras confusing, morally obtuse, and unsatisfactory. The *New York Daily News* and the *Daily Mirror* both liked the movie, but noted perceptively that it omitted portrayal of any of the leading Nazis.[11] *The Devil's General* was well liked by critics in France.[12] Dutch student audiences, by contrast, protested the movie as evil in its basic intentions.[13] They saw it as a whitewash of German guilt and an improbable, ambiguous inquiry into a single character's reservations about the Führer.

These particular films, in fact, are easily linked to an evolving situation in West Germany. By 1954 Chancellor Konrad Adenauer's government in Bonn had agreed with the United States to West Germany's remilitarization and the integration of its new army into NATO. There is no evidence of government funding or sanction for these movies, except Lufthansa's subsidy of *The Devil's General*. By portraying the theme of resistance in the regular German military, and placing all blame on Hitler's elite SS, however, these movies could be interpreted as leaning in the direction of sanitizing the image of the military at a time when the Bonn government was reinstituting an army—a move that was widely opposed in many quarters in Germany.

Another group of movies portrayed resistance by common Germans, not strictly within the elite of the officer corps whose ranks were filled with men of aristocratic lineage. Of these, two were West German co-productions, one with the United States and the other with both Austria and Yugoslavia.

Decision Before Dawn was produced by 20th Century-Fox as a U.S.-

German co-production in 1952.[14] It was an adaptation from an American novel, with a German, Peter Viertel, writing the screenplay. The cast featured both U.S. and German players—Richard Basehart, Gary Merrill, Oskar Werner, and Hildegard Knef. In Bavaria, where Hitler's political career had begun, *Decision Before Dawn* was treated with official suspicion. An attempt was made at banning it—a characteristic reaction in West Germany's most right-wing state—based on fears that the movie was "anti-German."[15]

The moral dilemma posed in the movie is whether one's loyalty is to the Fatherland or to some deeper moral cause. A German soldier played by Oskar Werner has been captured by U.S. troops. He volunteers, after extensive soul-searching, to be dropped by parachute behind German lines and to spy for the Americans. He does this against the backdrop of a crumbling Germany; only the Gestapo seems still to be intact. They pursue him to Mannheim. There he seems trapped. He discovers, however, that he can pass the information he has to a U.S. agent, but if he does so he must sacrifice himself. This he finally decides to do.

Younger viewers in the Federal Republic generally responded well to *Decision Before Dawn*, whereas their parents did not.[16] Still, there was ample criticism even among younger people that treason "against millions of dead and wounded," even "out of high idealism," should not be portrayed as heroic.[17] Generally in leftist newspapers and magazines the film was praised.[18] Middle-of-the-road commentary often cited the movie as being conceived too much from the American perspective.[19]

The Last Bridge was another co-production undertaken by a West German producer, with Austrians and Yugoslavians. In fact, this film provided a good number of interesting connections for the future of representing resistance on film, and won great acclaim, especially in France.[20] *The Last Bridge*, in fact, was awarded a prize at Cannes in 1958. It had actually premiered in Berlin, however, in 1954! In the featured roles were Maria Schell and Bernhard Wicki. *The Last Bridge*, in spite of sentimental phrasing in the dialogue and maudlin Yugoslav peasant songs sprinkled throughout, comes close to the bare naturalism of the Italian Neo-Realist tradition. Likely this is why it won such high praise from the French critic André Bazin.[21]

Yugoslavia, of all the areas that German armies occupied between 1939 and 1943 was the site of the most vigorous resistance to the Nazis. In Norbert Kunze's script, a German nurse named Helga is the protagonist. She is captured by Yugoslavian partisans, and eventually decides that she will help them in getting a serum to fight an outbreak of typhus in their camp. The medicine is being dropped by the British. Helga's commitment to aid as a courier in delivering it marks behavior which some would call treasonable.

In a surprise attack, the Germans suddenly recapture the small town from the Partisans, and Helga is freed. Then she is reunited with Martin, whom she thought had fallen in battle. Her Yugoslavian captors have been routed to a spot just across the Poltava bridge. Still, she decides that she needs to get the medicine to them. This she does, only to be shot down on the bridge itself, in no man's land, when trying to return to the German side.[22] In the film her act is portrayed as an "humanitarian" one that has had no adverse effect on her own side. Nonetheless, the movie was banned in Franco's Fascist Spain.[23] The International Catholic Office of Cinema (in Brussels), however, honored *The Last Bridge* with a special prize for "fostering understanding among the European peoples."[24]

Other "resistance" movies produced in West Germany during the 1950s include *Children, Mothers, and a General*; *Delinquent Battalion 999*; and *Betrayal of Germany*. Of these, the most controversial was director Veit Harlan's "atonement piece," the confused *Betrayal of Germany*.

Betrayal of Germany was a spy movie, generously intercut with newsreel footage from the war. Most of the action is set in Japan and much of the production was filmed on location there. The plot is a fictionalized version of a story about Richard Sorge, a German, who worked in the embassy in Tokyo and spied for the Soviet Union.

Veit Harlan had established what many considered to be an especially scurrilous record in the film industry of Nazi Germany, capped by his 1940 direction of *The Jew Süss*. *Betrayal of Germany* had to be shown anonymously when it premiered in France.[25] The opposition to the film when it was released in West Germany, however, did not focus on Harlan's pro-Nazi past. Instead, the issue on which protest centered was that the movie portrayed "pro-Soviet biases." The movie industry's own self-control board picked up on this cold war theme and denied the film a license and clearance.[26] A major conservative daily, the *Frankfurter Allgemeine* criticized as shocking the last scene in which a Communist who considers religion to be the opium of the masses expires in front of a crucifix.[27] The film was recalled, after being premiered illicitly, but then finally passed muster after several cuts. This controversy did not help Harlan's movie at the box office. After the furor had subsided, *Betrayal of Germany* had a brief run for small audiences.[28]

Children, Mothers, and a General, also released in 1955, was connected with another old name in the German cinema, although one far less controversial than Harlan. It was produced by Erich Pommer, who up until the Nazi seizure of power had been the influential, independent-minded head for feature-film production at Germany's largest studio, UFA. Directed by Lazslo Benedek, who had spent years in Hollywood, this movie features, once again, Bernhard Wicki and Maria Schell, along with Klaus Kinski. It is distinguished by the many shots in deep-focus, the abiding darkness of much of the lighting throughout, and, in particular, by the ominous scenes of night warfare. The movie is set on the eastern front in the waning months of the war.

Six women, of different ages and social status, meet at a school and discover that their sons, all in their early teens, have been sent to the front.[29] They follow the boys there. The women travel in cattle cars. They arrive at German headquarters only to encounter a General who assures them of their boys' heroism and commitment to the Fatherland, seeking to dismiss them. The women are not taken in by his claims, nor are they convinced ideologically of the justification for Goebbel's call to total war.

The Captain, Dornberg, finally agrees that he can't keep the women from seeing their sons. Their reunions take the shape of individual vignettes which form the narrative structure of the film: the grandmother who finds one grandson but learns that another has been killed; the mother who meets her son in the ruins of a church, but as she glances at the fallen crucifix he coldly tells her that he's there to fight, not to pray; and so on.

Finally, Captain Dornberg surrenders the town and calls for retreat. The General inquires of him if the presence of the women had made him reach such an insubordinate decision. The General agrees that they all know the war is lost. As soon as he finishes saying this, he orders Dornberg's arrest, and this irony is given careful and evocative attention by the director.

In the final sequences of the movie, the surviving boys, more confused than ever, go off on trucks with their unit. The women are in the right foreground of the final frames, watching the trucks depart. "They'll always forget us," one of them says.

The Fox of Paris, directed by an old pro of the German film industry, Paul May, who worked rarely in the 1950s, likewise shows many of the tendencies of the twentieth of July movies.[30] It is about a General and his nephew in Paris. The General sets up his nephew to reveal Hitler's plans for the defense of Paris to a group of French Resistance fighters who transmit them to London. The General hopes that when it's learned in Berlin that the Allies know of the plans that they will be scrapped by the Germany military leadership. In this way thousands of German lives, which Hitler is ready to sacrifice, will be saved.

The nephew, Captain Furstenwerth, played by Hardy Kruger, is arrested by the Gestapo at a café where he's handing over more plans to his contact, Yvonne. He is sentenced to die by firing squad, and does. Even the plans he had transmitted through to the Allies make no difference; Hitler remains bound to his own, mad design.

Set also in 1944, the favorite year for the "resistance" movies, *Delinquent Battalion 999* (1959) contains elements of *The Last Bridge* combined with those of the July 20 movies, all held together by melodramatic scripting. The featured character is a scientist, Dr. Deutschmann, who has been pressed into military service for holding vaguely incorrect political opinions. When they encounter the Yugoslavian Partisans, Deutschmann takes care of an ailing elderly man. Meanwhile Frau Deutschmann suffers in Berlin without him, endures the air raids, and finally gives herself a lethal injection. With clanging music and whirring telephones the melodrama is built, linking Deutschmann back to his wife in Berlin. When he learns she is dead, he requests a leave and is laughed at.

The battle scenes in *Delinquent Battalion 999* are gripping; especially the sequence near the end of the film. The ditch where Deutschmann and his friends are hiding is hit first by a hand grenade, and then graphically assaulted by a tank. There are terrible fires and destruction. In an ending that lacks resolution, however, Deutschmann is ordered back to Berlin. He leaves Yugoslavia to the sound of drum music. Along the road silhouettes of men carrying shovels pass by.

The final resistance film, produced in 1960, was Wolfgang Staudte's *The Fair*. Staudte, whose *The Murderers Are Among Us* had been the initial hard-hitting postwar German film about the Nazi experience produced in the Soviet zone in 1946, had left East Berlin for the West. In 1960, at a gaudy carnival, a workman setting up a tent strikes a buried skeleton, a tin helmet, and a machine gun. His doing so occasions a flashback which is then protracted into the main action of the movie.

Toward the end of the Second World War a young recruit goes AWOL from his unit and returns to his home village. Yet, even with the Reich collapsing, neither his own parents, nor the priest, nor the innkeeper, nor his neighbors will offer him help. In his despair he shoots himself. In the final inferno of fighting, as the allies invade the town, his family buries him. *The Fair* connects its story to the present. In it resistance is portrayed that is extremely limited. There is a poignancy and a truth about this portrayal.

In retrospect, a critic informed by an understanding of the history of Nazism must acknowledge that the modern world's most evil regime was also one of its most popular. This is a lesson that has been difficult to establish, and one that many laymen and historians still deny. The July 20 assassination attempt occurred, but what real role did the actions of a disgruntled group of Prussian officers play in alleviating the overall moral culpability of German society at large for the programs and policies of the Third Reich? Questions like these must be asked of the resistance movies produced by West Germans.

A number of other movies of the 1950s should be categorized as neutral. Unlike the movies already discussed which portrayed resistance of one sort or another, these movies depicted weak figures swept into the tides of Nazism, its course through history, and the war.

08/15 was a three-part movie produced between 1954 and 1957. It might be thought of as the German equivalent to Joseph Heller's *Catch 22*—an absorbing, freewheeling, black comedy. Based on a novel by Hans-Helmut Kirst, who had served during the war itself in the Nazi Propaganda Ministry, the first two parts of *08/15* each drew over twenty-million moviegoers in the German Federal Republic. The third part, however, which Krist himself criticized as "watered down" did not do well at the box office. All three parts of *08/15* were banned in South Africa, where the regime considered them to be defeatist and anti-military. They were also never shown in the United States, not on political grounds, but rather because *08/15* portrayed a sympathetic attitude toward extramarital sex that was considered unacceptable by distributors in the United States in the fifties.[31]

Part I of *08/15* takes place in 1939 just before World War Two began. Rather than developing suspense or tension, however, the action of this movie exploits the monotony of life at a military post. Some names of the characters are allegorical—Vierbein (Four Legs), Asch (Ass)—and others are "types," such as Sergeant Schultz, his wife, the bar maid Elizabeth, and Major Lutsche.

Much of the action in the first episode of *08/15* has to do with Frau Schultz's amorous adventures, which the viewer understands as a response to the insensitivity—and the philandering—of her Sergeant husband. The peculiarities of life on the base are also explored. Vierbein runs into the military mentality at one point when he is ill. He can only be sick when an official form says he is sick, and since there is not one that does, although he looks extremely ill, he cannot be.

The continuity of the movie is drawn out and elaborated by the sweeping transitions which take the place of abrupt cuts. The camera work here is of medium-shots photographed straight on; this is in contrast to episode two of *08/15* in which the camera angles are more extreme, and in which angle shots are used far more frequently for effect.

A large portion of the humor of *08/15* is verbal, and toward the end of the first episode, in particular, the dialogue becomes engaging. This first episode ends dramatically. The final sequence shows the troops in formation, called from the barracks in early morning. Major Lutsche stands rigidly before them as Hitler's voice booms over a loudspeaker, announcing the German invasion of Poland.

The second episode is set on the eastern front in 1942, when the course of battle still was running in Germany's favor. The action is more pointed and more tense than in episode one, but the broad, and often racy, humor is maintained. A character named Kowalski, a sort of Teutonic version of the "Good Soldier Schweik,"[32] now takes on a position in the screenplay roughly equivalent to that of Vierbein and Asch. Kowalski is the ne'er-do-well—the seeming fool who cleverly follows each order given to the letter. Hence, in one sequence he drives Sergeant Schultz's jeep straight ahead just as he commands—into a snowbank.

Frau Schultz matches the pace of her sexual adventures in episode one, but her amours are overshadowed by the romance that develops between a German Lieutenant and the Russian peasant woman, Natascha, as well as the spontaneous mating between a Captain and a visiting female entertainer.

The final section of the movie, however, switches abruptly away from the barracks humor and the broader strains of comedy. A Soviet advance sets the Germans in retreat. Natascha and her son are revealed as having been spying for the Soviets all along. The shortage of supplies for the Germans becomes evident. Vierbein is killed. Asch and Kowalski remove their helmets and come to him. They find a letter he has written to his fiancée Ingrid. The episode ends as it began—whirling snow, across seemingly endless tracts of land.

Whereas the first episode could be seen as broadly humorous, given the many scenes of the recruits outwitting their sluggish officers,[33] the second episode of *08/15* was more controversial. One critic saw in it a combination of "front existentialism" and "bad taste,"[34] although in France it was compared favorably to Erich Maria Remarque's famed World War One saga, *All Quiet on the Western Front.*[35] Perhaps the broadest possible praise for it as an adaptation was found in the *Suddeutsche Zeitung*, which claimed that episode two of *08/15* succeeded in "sharpening all the contours of the book."[36]

The third episode of *08/15*, set at the end of the war, however, tended toward greater sentimentality than the first two episodes. It was much less successful at the box office than the other two, and less successful critically as well. The first two episodes stand as the highpoint of the "neutral film" set in the Third Reich or in the Second World War. These films portray, but never explore, the situation in which their action occurs. Also in this category is *My Classmate* (1960), a comedy directed by Robert Siodmak, a veteran of the Weimar cinema who had spent many years in the United States. *My Classmate* portrays an old school chum who writes to Reichsmarschall Hermann Göring in 1944 expressing his dismay with the Nazi regime. Göring, as a function of the limits of his own mentality, and as an example of the bureaucratic machinery functioning blind-sidedly, has an official document issued for the fellow certifying him as crazy. For from the State's perspective one can only be crazy if one denies the glory of the Third Reich and the honor of the Führer. Through this irony, of course, the old chum becomes an officially protected critic of the Nazi regime.

Both *08/15* and *My Classmate* were significant for treating the war with a detached neutrality while, at the same time, being able to evoke humor over aspects of the Nazi experience. *My Classmate*, in fact, was scripted by J. M. Simmel who in the 1960s and 1970s became West Germany's best-selling novelist. The overriding notion that these movies, and other films of the 1950s which can be grouped with them, portray a "neutral" position toward the Third Reich demands further exploration, however. That judgment assumes that film content can be identified ideologically in its own right rather than being deter- mined at the moment of any specific individual's reception of it.[37]

We must recognize that the interpretation of a movie may vary greatly. Any given individual may respond to a movie in ways exactly opposite to the inten- tions of its creator.[38] This does not negate, however, describing a movie in terms of its positioning in relationship to other movies in categories or genres akin to it. What is a challenge, however, is to describe and categorize specific films in terms of a historically informed analysis of their contents. This means that while a specific point of view is present in the movie, it will not be necessarily clear to every viewer or agreed upon by all. The contents may well be ambiguous. Even if they are not, the perception of them still will vary.

For the 1950s, distinct patterns exist in West German feature films about the Third Reich and the Second World War. Those patterns may be charac- terized as revealing differing perspectives on the Nazi experience: opposition/ criticism as represented in the resistance movies; a relatively non-judgmental position, as reflected in the neutral movies; a defensive position, often with elements of praise for Nazi heroics in the patriotic films about the Second World War.

In dealing with those patriotic movies, we touch on what is the most volatile and controversial body of works produced in the West German cinema since 1945. Non-Germans, as well as contemporary Germans, likely will have difficul- ty accepting this body of films. Several of these movies ignore Nazism, treating the war as a stage for heroism, either individual or Germanic. Others manifest actions and plots in such a way as can only be interpreted as fascistic.

The Star of Africa, produced in 1956, was made at a cost of two million Marks and directed by Alfred Weidemann. The soundtrack for the movie is based on an intense jazz score, and it is one of the movie's most effective elements. Shot on location in Berlin, Rome, and Madrid, the storyline portrays the exploits of World War Two fighter pilot ace Hans-Joachim Marseilles.

The chronology of the narrative is from 1939 (just before the war begins) to 1941 when Marseilles dies in a plane crash in North Africa. Thus, the plot ends at a point when historically Germany was still winning the war, and when its problematic invasion of the USSR—and Hitler's program to exterminate Jews—had not yet commenced.

The movie's hero is shot down over the English Channel, but manages to swim to shore; he records over a hundred "kills" making him an ace of the Luftwaffe; he falls in love with a schoolteacher in Berlin while on leave. And rather than conveying any tentativeness about him, or ambivalence about his actions, the film lionizes Marseilles uncritically. As the film news service of the Protestant churches in Germany noted in a review of *The Star of Africa*, Marseilles is no tragic hero. He and his companions fly and shoot at will and without hesitation.[39] Other commentary argued that the movie could have been passable fare for the cinema in the Third Reich; it presents war as hard and fair sport.[40] Further, some argued that such a film being produced in West Germany was a great misfortune—in a society where artists claim to be apolitical and where a studied posture of "objectivity" is supposed to reign.[41]

The Star of Africa indeed glorifies the life of the military hero. Marseilles and his girlfriend Brigitte are hosted joyfully by Italian Fascists in Rome. His commander, the Major, speaks of each of the men in his unit as his "sons." While Marseilles is convalescing, after being shot down in the English Channel, he plays pool in a café with an elderly Frenchman. He asks the man what he thinks of the war. The old gentleman has no opinion about the war at all, but he concludes that with it going on he has a much better chance of surviving than any young man.

The ideology of *The Star of Africa* is defined by the attitude of Hans-Joachim's girlfriend Brigitte. They spend several days of his leave together. Just before he returns to the front, in a brief, dramatic monologue she has a great deal to say against dying—but nothing at all to say against the war! The movie is made in a style typical of the 1950s cinema in West Germany, with ample use of documentary footage intercut into the action. Yet unlike attempts to exploit the irony or absurdity of the Nazis through use of original footage of them, here the "documentation" is utilized on behalf of a series and uncritical point of view. Indeed, comradeship and adventure are the abiding values promoted in the movie, just as they are the values that Hans-Joachim promotes when he returns as a hero to talk with the boys at his old school in Berlin.

Sub # 47: Lieutenant Captain Prien, too, takes a Nazi-era war hero as its protagonist. Directed by Harald Reinl, the movie was released in 1958. It portrays the harrowing circumstances of the submarine crews, and is similar to the big-budget West German feature that drew large audiences worldwide, *The*

Boat (1982). One critic called *Sub # 47: Lieutenant Captain Prien* "A mixture of the old-UFA and the new-Hollywood styles."[42] Another Harald Reinl film, *The Green Devils of Monte Cassino*, premiered, appropriately, at the San Sebastian festival in Franco's Fascist Spain in 1958. An article in the *Hannoversche Presse* noted that the movie was "an attempt at rehabilitation of the German soldier; it shows our side as fair and heroic." The article, moreover, applauds the portrayal of the wanton destructiveness of the Anglo-American bombing of Monte Cassino.[43] More critically, the *Stuttgarter Zeitung* accused the movie of being— either consciously or unconsciously—"a rehabilitation of the darkest period of German history."[44] As the promotional material for *The Green Devils* explained Hitler's war machine at work, "it was all dangerous, but beautiful."[45]

Of this group of films the movie adaptation of Heinz G. Konsalik's novel, *The Doctor of Stalingrad* (1958), evoked the greatest international protest. Moscow called the movie unabashed anti-Soviet propaganda.[46] The film was banned in Finnland and, subsequently, in Cuba.[47] East Berlin, of course, found the film objectionable, labeling it a "low point" in West German production, and linking the production company, Bavaria Film, to a major capitalist financial institution, the powerful Deutsche Bank.[48] But criticism was not reserved to Moscow and its friends; the Protestant churches of West Germany also lambasted *The Doctor of Stalingrad*.[49]

There is not a scene, or a single line, in *The Doctor of Stalingrad* that could be interpreted as pacifistic, or as being opposed to the particular circumstances of World War Two and the German invasion of the USSR. The content of the movie coincides with a view—obviously one which had grown in the environment of the Cold War during the 1950s—that the Germans had been victims of Soviet savagery, arbitrariness, and barbarism during World War Two.[50] This view conveniently ignored the German act of military aggression in invading the USSR in June of 1941, while maintaining that incidents of brutality by the Red Army as it forged into German territory in late 1944 and early 1945 somehow overshadowed the German barbarism and extermination programs unleashed upon Soviet citizens, whose losses numbered 20 million during the war.

As disagreeable as *The Doctor of Stalingrad* may have seemed to many observers, however, the most overtly offensive movie of the entire range of patriotic, heroic films in this era was the 1955 production *So Long As You Live*. Directed also by Harald Reinl, and based on a script by him and Joachim Bartsch, the movie is set in the Spanish Civil War (1936–1939).[51]

In the relatively complicated plot several Germans from the Condor Legion who survive a crash of their airplane hide themselves in a cave. A young Spanish woman, Teresa, finds the Germans and befriends them. Her humility and humanity is juxtaposed to a portrayal of the Republicans who hold kangaroo courts and lecherously ogle the women of the town.

Meanwhile Spanish Republican forces have captured the nearby village. The Soviet Commandant Malek is depicted as evil, and the Soviet troops as drunken and brutish. The Mayor of the town, Torquito, is a Communist dupe. His own daughter turns against him and joins Teresa's efforts to protect the

11. Soviet Commandant Malek forces Teresa to reveal where a German
pilot is hiding. An apologia for Hitlerism, *So Long As You Live*, capital-
ized on cold war sentiments. Deutsches Institut für Filmkunde

Germans after the truth about the Republicans' barbarism is revealed. She asks
her father what is done with prisoners: Coldly he answers, "We shoot them, of
course!"

As the film moves toward its climax, carried emotionally for many sequences
on the strength of the music composed by José Muñoz Molleda, the righteous-
ness of the German-aided Loyalists (Franco supporters) becomes ever clearer.
At the end of the movie the badly wounded Michael—Aryan hero of the Third
Reich—even on crutches can get the best of the perfidious commissar Malek.
Footage of German bombers are edited into the film to link their raids positively
with the liberation of the town, and, hence, the throwing off of the yoke of the
oppressor.

Eventually Teresa comes to Michael's aid. From the narrow mountain trail
they see German troops marching toward them through the valley below. There
is triumphant music. Enthusiastic children greet the German liberators, waving
flags. Theresa is reunited with Escosura, an estate owner and an officer in
Franco's forces. They embrace; he opens his clenched fist and shows he a small
cross. The final scenes show the happy Spaniards bidding Michael farewell; he
returns to his German Condor squadron and to its future good works for the
Führer.

So Long As You Live is an unabashedly pro-Fascist film, one that glorifies the role of Hitler's legions in the Spanish struggle, and one that negatively portrays the anti-Franco forces, which were drawn from a broad political range—Constitutionalists, Republicans, Socialists, and Communists. The movie was awarded the official designation of "Worthwhile" by the West German film industry's self-control board in 1955.[52]

In sum, throughout the 1950s films produced in West Germany treating Nazism and the Second World War did so from three different perspectives. The topic was hardly ignored. At the end of the 1950s, moreover, two exceptional movies were produced. They quickly became established as among the most popular productions of the West German industry, both with native audiences and abroad. Nonetheless, they seem to have been overlooked by historians, or at least undervalued. They stand at the pinnacle of the West German cinema in coming to terms with the Nazi experience through fiction.

We Prodigies premiered at the end of October 1958. It was shown in the U.S.A. under the title *Aren't We Wonderful?* and captured a Golden Globe award.[53] It also was the first German-made film ever released in Israel. The movie was banned by the right-wing Salazar dictatorship in Portugal, but it was a triumph with Swiss audiences.[54] Even the East German critics liked *We Prodigies*; they wondered aloud in varous newspaper commentaries how such a movie could be produced in West Germany.[55]

The movie was controversial in the German Federal Republic itself. On the political Left, the review in the Social-Democrat newspaper *Vorwärts* faulted it for putting so much narrative into ninety minutes, and for portraying the rise of Nazism as an overpowering force.[56] On the extreme right, a newspaper for World War Two veterans attacked the movie repeatedly.[57]

We Prodigies attempts to place Nazism and World War Two in a broad historical perspective, to take a critical perspective on the experience, and to develop fully the rich chords of satire and parody. The movie opens with a voice-over talking about the old town of "Newtown-on-the-Nitze." The lives of two boyhood friends, Bruno and Hans, are interwoven to form the movie's narrative. Periodically the action is punctuated by a pair of vaudevillians who play the piano and sing satiric ditties. These interludes fill in the jumps in time throughout the narrative, and steer the interpretation of the action in specific directions. The device also serves to provide for distancing the viewer from the action.

We Prodigies begins on the eve of the First World War. Thereby, two interpretive points are made. First, that the rise of Nazism and the coming of World War Two was related directly to World War One and Germany's fate in it. Second, that the Nazi phenomenon is to be understood in the context of events in Germany which both precede and follow it; Nazism is a part of a continuum in the shared German experience.

The narrative structure of the movie throughout is episodic. The 1920s are portrayed by Hans, angrily throwing down his silverware and rushing off to borrow 20,000,000 Marks, representing the runaway inflation of 1922/23.[58] The

12. *We Prodigies/Wir Wunderkinder* (1958): Distancing on the German past achieved through stylistic devices such as the "film within a film." Deutsches Institut für Filmkunde

highly charged, and often violent, political atmosphere of Weimar is reflected in the scene of a Mardi Gras party where Hitler is being parodied on stage. Storm troopers barge in and a fight breaks out. Hans and the Danish girl Kirstin, whom he has just met, escape while the fight rages, photographed as reflected in a mirror.

Hitler's takeover and the coordination of German life to Nazi ideology is represented through the rapid rise of Hans's old schoolmate, Bruno Tisches, in the Nazi party. Hans finds Bruno and his entourage after 1933 established in a villa that had belonged to a Jewish doctor. A *salon* at Tisches's villa, presided over by his mother-in-law, includes a phrenologist reading the guest's heads, Tisches trying to convince Hans to join the Nazi party, and drunken excess. This sequence fades into the vaudevillians' song about expenditures, taking up on the Nazi slogan "Tomorrow the World."

Just as the war begins Hans marries Kirstin. He is working in a bookstore now, having lost his position as a journalist because he would not give in to pressure to "coordinate" his writing to Nazi ideology. *We Prodigies* handles the war years themselves very briefly, representing them through the single sequence of a bombing raid.

What the movie does do is to carry over into the postwar era, and it does so with a critical posture not found in West German productions prior to it. Hans returns to Neustadt and encounters an old teacher who speculates that the Nazi Bruno Tisches must now really be sitting on the hot seat. The truth, however, is that Tisches has a new name and a spiffy automobile, both courtesy of the Allied occupation forces. Tisches is officially de-Nazified, but in fact unreconstructed; in his view Hitler was a bit crazy, but, after all, he was there to prevent the worst—namely, a Communist political triumph in Germany.

In the first wave of the West German postwar "economic miracle" Tisches rises quickly to wealth and prominence. Hans, too, has regained his job in journalism. Finally he feels himself compelled to attack Tisches in print, detailing his ardent Nazi background. A confrontation occurs when Tisches arrives at the newspaper offices in his limousine to demand a retraction of the article. Hans, however, will not apologize. Tisches demands to know what Hans did against the Nazis, to which Hans replies lamely that all along he had failed to take Hitler seriously.

In anger and frustration, Tisches storms out of the office, races down a corridor, and into an open elevator shaft—to his death. While this seems a weak and contrived ending, the movie does manage to parlay a certain poignancy out of it. The final scene is of Tisches's funeral at which dignitaries of the new West German state are assembled. At the old Nazi's graveside the euology is intoned, "We want to live on in his spirit," and the movie ends.

We Prodigies is nearly unique among West German movies about the Third Reich. The scope of the setting intersects with a point of view that emphasizes the wide range of culpability in German society for the rise and triumph of Hitlerism. The notion of a continuity between the Nazi era and postwar West Germany is, in fact, a staple ideological element in several of the so-called "New German" films of the late 1970s. Yet few of these later films attain to this insight so deftly and compellingly as does *We Prodigies*.

The other film made at the end of the 1950s that warrants special recognition is Bernhard Wicki's *The Bridge* (1959). Wicki, an actor who had established himself in World War Two roles, directed the film, using a script by Richard Mansefeld and Karl-Wilhelm Vivier, with music by Hans-Martin Majewski. *The Bridge* won wide acclaim, both in West Germany and internationally.[59]

A great many German newspapers applauded *The Bridge* as the most "pacifist" German-made movie to be set in World War Two. Its international acclaim was also strong. Comparisons were made between *The Bridge* and Remarque's *All Quiet on the Western Front* or Norman Mailer's *The Naked and The Dead*.[60] Indeed, *The Bridge* was the first postwar German film bought by a major Hollywood distributor, Allied Artists, for exhibition in the U.S.[61] In France the film played well at the box office, too.[62] It also penetrated the Soviet Union which ordered 1,182 prints of *The Bridge*.[63]

The Bridge is so effective because it enters deeply into the situationality of Nazism. Its setting is a town in the Rhineland in the spring of 1945. As the invading American troops move into the area, a group of teenage boys summon their boyish courage, mixed with Nazi zeal and shot through with slogans learned by heart, to defend a small bridge. They have become obsessed with the notion that its defense is important to the war effort and to Germany's salvation.

The choice of setting is especially important temporally. One of the most characteristic elements of the German response to Hitler was the allegiance to him and to the Nazi movement, right to the bitter end of the war. By being pinpointed at this historic moment the movie's narrative is connected with the emotional depth of the German commitment to the Third Reich. That commitment is, overtly, the central theme of *The Bridge*. The boys are so caught up with the message of Hitler's propaganda that all their judgments are subverted to Nazi ideology. The movie provides a rare insight into the way this ideology penetrated life in the Third Reich. In that regard, it gains a measure of specific and unique importance among the movies under discussion here.

In the end the boys' valiant and deadly sacrifice is for naught. After they have fought and died to defend the bridge from a unit of American G.I.s, an SS patrol suddenly arrives. The older members of the Nazi elite dynamite the bridge and speed off on their motorcycles. Its defense was of no importance. The boys were doing nothing of military use or significance to serve their beloved Führer.

13. Teenagers poised to defend a bridge for their Führer. The high point of German film's coming to terms with Nazism in Wicki's *The Bridge* (1959). Deutsches Institut für Filmkunde

The Bridge marks a highpoint for German films set in the Third Reich. It also marks an abrupt end to the wave of West German films about Nazism and the war! They trail off right after *The Bridge* and by 1962, for all practical purposes, had disappeared.

It should be noted that *We Prodigies* and *The Bridge* were produced at the moment when conservative politics were most dominant in West Germany. The only time since the country's founding in 1949 that a single party has won over 50 percent of the vote in a West German parliamentary election was the 1958 victory of Konrad Adenauer's conservative Christian Democrats. Thus we must question the validity of claims that the phenomenon of the Third Reich was addressed only later in West German experience when, by the late 1970s, a more leftist ideology had come to permeate the society and many of the political reforms of the Social Democrats, who took power in Bonn in 1969, had taken hold. The fictional treatment on film of the Third Reich reached its pinnacle just when the conservative consensus in West Germany was at its height.

In the early 1960s the film industry in West Germany declined rapidly. The factors influencing this downturn were many, and sometimes they were similar to those which influenced Hollywood's decay in the decade after 1945: the challenge of television, the impact of a "baby boom," and the burgeoning of a family-oriented, younger middle class oriented to materialist values. As this erosion of the film industry set in, a younger group of German filmmakers and critics, representing various alternative positions, adopted a program of desired reform, expressed in a document called the Oberhausen Manifeste (1962).

Whatever the reasons, West German movies about Nazism and the Third Reich produced during the 1960s were few. The shift toward a "New German" film approach came with Werner Herzog's first feature, *Signs of Life* (1967). Set in Greece in 1942 it portrays the dilemmas of a young German who is recovering from war injuries on an island. Yet, Herzog wished to move beyond the setting of World War Two's framework and beyond direct allusion to the moral dilemmas posed by it. Some observers have maintained that his 1972 feature, *Aguirre, The Wrath of God* is a parable of Hitlerism. The film is set in the sixteenth century, and its protagonist, Aguirre, is a compulsive Spanish conquistador who travels up the Amazon and perishes with his doomed expedition. The claim that this parallels Hitler's destructive leadership of Germany, however, is fraught with problems.[64]

West German production of the 1970s, in number of films set in the Third Reich and World War Two, was no greater in quantity than that of the 1950s. Moreover, the movies in this category from the 1970s and early 1980s fall into the same patterns as those of the 1950s. The claim that they mark distinct new fictional directions based on new awareness of, or insights into, the Nazi experience seems slim at best.

Among the Resistance films of the New German Cinema are two movies about youthful wartime protesters in Munich, *The White Rose* (1982) and *The Last Five Days* (1982). Michael Verhoeven, the director of *The White Rose* claims the story of a small group of young, Catholic critics of Hitler was planned for a filming in the 1950s, but was finally considered inappropriate by the potential producers.[65] West German reviewers found the topic appropriate for filming in the 1980s, but they were generally critical of what Verhoeven put onto the screen. *Suddeutsche Zeitung*, for example, called it a "genre film" in the worst sense, meaning that the reviewer found the characters wooden and the action predictable.[66] The review in *Stuttgarter Zeitung* further objected to "all the thrills" packed into *The White Rose*, "according to movie conventions."[67] Another influential national newspaper, *Die Zeit*, took issue with the claim made at the end of the film that the conviction of the Scholls for treason still stands in West German law, arguing that a U.S. military law of 1945 exonerated all Germans found guilty by the Nazi state of crimes against it.[68]

The White Rose is a conventional narrative of the activities of the "White Rose" group of students at the university in Munich in the early 1940s. Their main protest against the regime was to paint anti-Hitler slogans on walls by night, and to surreptitiously circulate handbills.[69] They were finally arrested for the latter offense, after a zealous university custodian saw them sneaking about while classes were meeting. Sophie Scholl and her brother were condemned to death.

The screenplay, written by Verhoeven and Mario Krebs, is structured as a narrative in which various situations of the young people in the "White Rose" group are portrayed. Very little about their motivation is presented and even less about the actual contours of their political thought. Enough is suggested about the conflict over one of them being enlisted in the German army—whereby the obvious pull in two different directions is created—to portray a plausible and real dilemma. Otherwise, the thematic material of the movie seems oddly flattened, without sharp and distinct forms of conflict and commitment. This may, of course, be considered a naturalistic device meant to draw the film materials closer to an approximation of the actual wartime situation in Germany and of this group's positioning within that situation.

The White Rose has been shown widely in the United States; *The Five Last Days* (also 1982), however, marks a more significant filmic event. Directed by Percy Adlon with his wife, Eleanor Adlon, as co-director, this movie focuses on the last five days in the life of the condemned student Sophie Scholl. Played by the same actress as in *The White Rose*, Lena Stolz, the lead character in *The Last Five Days* is portrayed as far more self-conscious and informed than in *The White Rose*.

In *The Last Five Days* Sophie Scholl confronts a female prison trustee, played by the veteran Irm Hermann. Her encounter with this character, the older, apolitical Else Gebel, is a point of departure for exploring the parameters of political aloofness. The narrative technique is disjointed, experimental, and effective. Adlon punctuates the shift of time from day to day by fading to a blackout to mark the passage of each twenty-four hours, thus making the viewer fully aware of the cut away from one day's dialogues to the next.

The Last Five Days is a far more effective film for raising general issues of political responsibility and commitment than is *The White Rose*. Yet, both are fundamentally pedestrian resistance films, even though the former poses aesthetic and moral challenge to its viewers. Other resistance films, however, have gained far more attention: *The Tin Drum* because it is an adaptation from Günter Grass's monumental novel, and *Lili Marleen* because it was one of the most expensive and popular productions of the extraordinarily prolific director Rainer Werner Fassbinder.

In 1976 Volker von Schlöndorff's version of *The Tin Drum* marked an event in the German cinema that had been long awaited—the filming of Günter Grass's best-selling novel which had been first published in the late 1950s. To some critics, this film marked the beginning of the "adaptation crisis" in the New German Cinema, characterized by the evident inability of the filmmaking community to generate new, original screenplays.[70] For the film industry itself, however, the film version of *The Tin Drum* achieved box-office success at home and garnered favorable response abroad, including an Academy Award "Oscar" for "Best Foreign Film" from the professionals in Hollywood.

The Tin Drum portrays the complicated tale of little Oskar, living in the city of Danzig amidst a mixed German and Polish population at the outbreak of the Second World War. As the film narrative progresses in time, Oskar becomes fixated at an infantile stage of development, and his piercing cries shatter windows and wreak havoc whenever he calls them into play. This thwarted development is, of course, symbolic, just as his piercing cries are a metaphor for his pained resistance toward an adult world seeped in the insanity of Nazism and the duplicity and insincerety that is normative to human conduct.

The Tin Drum, because of its metaphoric characteristics, and because it portrays the war years through the distorted prism of Oskar's perspective, is perhaps too special in its fictional structure and too rarefied in its point of reference to be an effective work that comes to terms with the Third Reich. To make such a claim will be considered anathema by devotees of the book who would hold up *The Tin Drum* as a model of postwar German fiction; nonetheless, as a film, its effectiveness is compromised.

We must recognize, moreover, that the position of *The Tin Drum* in the coming to terms with the recent German past was determined by Günter Grass its author and not by Volker von Schlöndorff its film adapter. That position, indeed, is right at the end of the 1950s—at the moment of the novel's publication in 1959. *The Tin Drum*'s place in time is thus contemporary to the two movies which have been cited earlier as marking the highpoint of film fiction set in the Third Reich and the Second World War—*We Prodigies* and *The Bridge*.

Another adaptation by a skilled filmmaker fails to attain the power of the book. Klaus Emmerich's film, *The First Polka* (1978) offers a teenage perspective on the outbreak of war. *The First Polka* is set in the town of Glewitz at the end of August 1939. It was here that an attack on a German radio transmitter—usually attributed to German units disguised as Polish soldiers—occurred which gave Hitler the pretext for invading Poland. The film ends with a recording of Hitler's proclamation, delivered the morning of the incident, in which he maintains that now "shot for shot and bomb for bomb will be returned," and which he ends with the prophetic and ironic warning that "those who fight with poison will be fought back against with poison gas."[71] Like the film version of *The German Hour* (1971), an adaptation of the Siegfried Lenz novel, *The First Polka* fails to evoke as clear a moral perspective on its material as the original written work did.

One reason that movies like *The First Polka* are less successful than *We Prodigies* is that their narratives do not cover a span of time. They are limited in their political and moral implications, as well as in their potential as historical fiction by being so time-bound, and, in this particular instance, bound at a point at which the issues of history are less compelling than later. It is, to great extent, precisely because of its temporal setting—in the desperate final days of the collapsing Third Reich—that Bernhard Wicki's *The Bridge* is so powerful as a work of fiction in its capacity to explore the obsessive and compulsive characteristics of the Nazi ideology.

It is the end of the Third Reich, when the legacy of its historic course and its crimes against humanity were revealed, that is the most poignant and evocative. Eberhard Fechner's *Winterspelt* (1978) explores the plan of a German officer to surrender his entire unit to advancing American troops as the Third Reich crumbles. Yet, it is obvious that the military mentality cannot accept such an apparently sane and rational move. Instead of exploring the moral burdens of the Nazi war of aggression, however, *Winterspelt* portrays a more limited moment of moral decisiveness that evaporates. More successful is Edgar Reitz's 1976 movie, *The Hour Zero*, set just after the war, in the summer of 1945. For its dramatic point of departure the film utilizes the historic withdrawal of American forces of occupation from around the Leipzig area as part of the postwar settlement permitting Soviet troops to move in.

The Hour Zero focuses on an adolescent boy. He is still caught up in many of the myths and much of the rhetoric of the Nazis, but he has fashioned a fascination for the triumphant Americans. With a teenage girl he plans their flight to the United States, to be financed by selling jewelry and other valuables an SS officer had buried and which the young man mysteriously knows about.

The Hour Zero is, strictly speaking, set in the immediate postwar era. Yet, through its characters and situations it conveys a series of challenging perspectives on the Third Reich itself. The sense of guilt is homely. As the farmhand who was wounded in the war expresses it in anticipation of the Soviets arriving, "There's gonna be some paying for what went on. I'm just gonna sit back and watch those Russians fucking all those women."

The fear of rape is developed in *The Hour Zero* as a constant and imminent threat, only to be resolved anticlimactically when the Soviets actually arrive to begin their occupation. Thematically Reitz's movie contradicts the legend of Soviet brutality and barbarism that was nutured—both officially and unofficially—during the 1950s, and which found its most powerful fictional expression through films such as *The Doctor of Stalingrad*.

The Hour Zero is about illusion, self-deception, self-defensiveness, and the abrogation of responsibility. The folk at the rail crossing where the film is set posture and pose apolitically, refusing to discuss Hitler and Nazism, uninterested in politics as a topic that spoils their relaxation. This is poignantly revealed in the sequence in which the former Polish prisoner Malek, who may well be Jewish (although this is not clarified), questions them about how one becomes a Nazi.

Movies which focus on adolescent experience right at the end of the war and the collapse of the Third Reich, as in Wicki's *The Bridge* or Reitz's *Hour Zero*, are especially effective. Helma Sanders-Brahms adopts a different strategy. Being herself of a younger generation than filmmakers Wicki and Reitz, she fashions a narrative that is part family history and autobiography. *Germany, Pale Mother* portrays her mother and father during the war years and into the immediate postwar epoch of Sanders-Brahms's own childhood.

Germany, Pale Mother begins with a voice-over narration that the viewer identifies with the filmmaker herself. The voice asks what she is guilty of, she who was born admidst the falling bombs of World War Two. And this narration is visualized later in the film in a sequence in which the doctor holds up a newborn, streaked with blood, metaphorically standing for that generation born during the Third Reich and the war itself—blood-stained, blood-splattered, guilt-soaked-in-blood. This imagery, along with that which occurs later in the film when her mother's face is swollen and paralyzed, expresses both the pathology of the Nazi

14. Weary Germany near war's end. Helma Sanders-Brahms's *Germany, Pale Mother* expiates German guilt through a litany of suffering. Deutsches Institut für Filmkunde

experience as well as its legacy that is a natural inheritance—a kind of "birth-curse"—for the subsequent generations of younger Germans.

Another movie that warrants mention is *The Trip to Vienna* (Edgar Reitz, 1974). In it, two young women from the small village of Simmern in the Hunsrück mountains take a wartime journey to Vienna. There they enjoy an interlude of romance and romantic illusion, all of which is subtly juxtaposed to the war itself that is raging elsewhere. In this film, Reitz initiates a dramatic concern that has continued in his later films, and one which perhaps best defines the positioning of the New German Cinema to the Nazi experience most revealingly. It is the exploration of how illusion and human yearning mingled during these years to permit "everyday life" to go on amidst what seems to have been such an era of distorted and traumatic experiences.

These films of the 1970s and early 1980s fall into categories similar to those of the 1950s: resistance films, like *The White Rose*, *The Last Five Days*, and *Lili Marleen*; neutral films, such as *The Trip to Vienna* or *Germany, Pale Mother*; and, finally, titles which might be called Nazi rehabilitation films.

One of the works which may be labeled as "Nazi rehabilitation" is the ambitious cinematic masterwork in four parts directed by Hans Jürgen Syberberg entitled *Hitler—A Film from Germany*. As its framework it takes a panorama of German history from the late nineteenth century through the Nazi era and on beyond it to a point in time that is contemporary, but unspecific. It is a work in which the sweep of time, a hundred years roughly, is embraced without any extension of the camera's point of view into space. Its space is constrained, the darkened area of a relatively small studio stage. The documentary and newsreel footage of the Nazi era, sparingly intercut, never releases the movie from its own spatiotemporal constraints, and pale visually against the still photographs, the mannequins, the puppets which personify the various historical personages of the 1920s and 1930s.

Hitler parallels the rise of the motion picture with the rise of Fascism, but does so neither narratively or ideologically, but simply as a juxtaposing of the one against the other. The filmic self-reflection here proceeds from a puppet of the nineteenth-century Mad King Ludwig of Bavaria holding forth in Edison's first movie studio to the Peter Lorre monologue from Fritz Lang's *M* (1932) when the child murderer confronts his jury of peers, to a depiction of Hitler as the Charlie Chaplin character. The Hitler is in all of us; the murderer, who like the child killer, protests his inability to act differently. The narrator tells of the hell about us; documentary recordings of Nazis dedicating books to the flames are heard; scenes alluding to German filmmakers of the 1920s and the 1970s are cut in. Where will this end? The endless exploitation of Hitler for profit: Hitler books, Hitler films, Hitler newspapers.

The temporality is fractured radically, and this radical fracturing is sustained throughout all four episodes. Only the reappearance of Hitler in disguises, Hitler as a ventriloquist's dummy, Hitler in costume and out, provides unity that is thematic. Through each episode wanders a small girl, dressed in black, playing with dolls, or with Ludwig puppets, cradling the small toy dog with the Hitler

15. Images from German history and twentieth-century culture layered. Syberberg's 4-part *Hitler: A Film from Germany*, which is visually stunning, but morally problematic. Deutsches Institut für Filmkunde

face, standing with it against a projection of the central figure of the great German expressionist movie of 1919, Caligari, on the wall behind her.

At the beginning of the second episode we see the Black Maria (the earliest filmmaking studio) within a glass ball in a snow storm. The little girl with the puppet; an actor playing Karl May, the German inventor of hundreds of popular novels set in the American West, adored by Hitler and proclaimed by a generation (or really two) of Germans. Hitler describes himself in a monologue as the end product of western civilization, followed by a cut to three black GIs dancing with a blond woman at Wagner's grave. In a long tunnel, Hitler's valet begins a rambling monologue on his master's private affairs, enumerating his items of clothing, engaging with sublime patience in the accumulation of the triviality and banality of the Führer and his possessions.

Episode three, "A Winter's Tale" maintains more temporal unity than the others, being set in the last years of the war, but full of references beyond the war. Himmler at an SS banquet expounds on mysticism, the occult, Buddhism, and the like. The valet, eating, between bites gossiping about Hitler; in the background the radio broadcasts voices from the Nazi past. Hitler, the ventriloquist's dummy, explains that having failed at art he turned to politics, and boasts of how much he has changed things: Russians on the Elbe; the Jews with their own State; the United States with a new colony—"Consider where the great new market of Hollywood lies?"

The final episode consists of a long monologue, shared by two different narrators, both male. Projections and sound documents are laid upon it. Toward the end the little girl wanders back to go down a row of gallows. The last war report from the German armed forces is broadcast in the background. A great victory celebration is described. The narrator accuses the Hitler dummy of the trivialization of old German values. The young girl holding the Hitler dog stands, eyes closed. The stars fly and amidst them appears the grail.

The temporal structuring is episodic from the exterior, random and disjointed from the interior. Shortly after I saw the entire film someone asked me about it, and I had to catch myself while responding to keep from referring to it as a nonfiction film. At the one level this seemed utterly preposterous. At another remove, while nonfiction is incorrect as a descriptive phrase, it pointed to the experiencing of the filmic presence as tempo and time structure. The randomness, the disjointedness, the ruptured segments of image corresponding to historical time and all the parallelisms, which fail to reunite, are all very important in the film's ideological position vis-à-vis the reconstruction of the German past. To a great extent this succeeds as an enactment of the interiority of the historical experience revisited cinematographically.

The most expensive, and internationally the most popular, German produced film set in World War Two is the feature *Das Boot*, about which distributors were so self-confident that they released it with the original German title throughout the United States. *The Boat* is a standard "war" movie, which ably exploits the technical and emotional strong points of that genre. It portrays German "U-Boat" men as heroic and dedicated, as slightly irreverent toward the Führer and even as openly rebellious toward the Nazi command, who remain safely on shore. All the usual heroics of the common man are present, and even some of the stereotypes of Nazis, à la Hollywood, are as well.

Yet a major sequence of the book written in the 1950s, on which the film is based, is omitted. In that sequence, which covers a score of pages, a British ship is torpedoed and its crew jumps to the water. The German craft surfaces, and its crew clamber onto the hull of the submarine. They then proceed to gun down the struggling survivors in the water. Indeed, it would seem that in the drive to normalize the experience of Hitler's war from the German side, the film version of *The Boat* has chosen to omit issues of moral culpability, such as the incident just described.

But how are such issues of moral culpability to be presented in fiction and drama; specifically, how in film? Oddly, perhaps the most successful instance of portraying such moral questions occurs in a manner which, when described, must sound distinctively contrived. In the East German film directed in 1966 by Konrad Wolf entitled *I Was Nineteen* the action takes place in the waning days of the war, as Soviet troops advance from the east. With them is the protagonist, a nineteen-year-old boy, born in Germany, whose parents, German Communists, had taken him to Moscow when Hitler had come to power twelve years before. He is torn, as the war ends, and as a future must be built. Even after "unhappy endings" something else comes about. He is caught emotionally between being born German and being raised a Communist. Right in the middle of this movie, the narrative continuity and development is interrupted. An extermination camp has been liberated, and the viewer is exposed to a sequence, shot with the so-called "fast" film stock used in movie newsreels. The camp and its operations are explained: starkly, coldly, factually. Then the narrative line resumes.

While a written description of this sequence is inadequate, a reader may recognize that Wolf has managed to gain the proper distance on his material, and hence what might seem on the surface a contrivance works well. Yet, that question of distance is a vital one to the entire problem here. Wolf, who directed several of the most able movies about aspects of the Nazi experience and the war that Nazism brought with it, had a special personal distancing on the phenomenon, having grown to young adulthood in exile in the USSR. Moreover, as a filmmaker in the German Democratic Republic, his perspective is compounded by the distancing that East Germans have on the Nazi phenomenon, which is treated officially as a scourge brought upon German workers and peasants by the machinations of a dying capitalist system. While this sounds like West German Neo-Marxism, the East German point of view is quite different. This is so because it can be swallowed whole in a society which has broken its ties with the burden of the past by declaring itself to be not a successor state of the German past, but an entirely new one.

Nonetheless, this "distancing" issue is a tricky one. Distance on a phenomenon, in certain instances, brings it into perspective, but not in others where our sensibility demands closeness. Can we assume that the further in time we get from an event the better we shall comprehend it, the greater its significance shall be for us, and the more apt the mechanisms of fiction and drama through which we may portray it? Something resembling this assumption, which we might call historicist, seems widely shared, but highly questionable.

What, indeed, is the entire problematic of any fiction representing the Nazi experience, the Second World War, and the massacre of European Jewry that occurred within the framework of that war? Any contemporary German film that would attempt to deal with the Holocaust becomes subject to demands which can hardly ever be satisfied. How would criticism worldwide have treated, for example, a miniseries produced by German television like NBC's *Holocaust*—so shot through, as it was, with melodrama and the conventions of primetime television? Would not such a German production have run the inevitable risk of condemnation for trivializing and exploiting this most horrifying epoch in human history? Or, what would have been the international reaction had a German filmmaker directed *Seven Beauties* (1974)—which was made by the Italian Lina Wertmuller—so full of moral ambiguity, sexual perversion and provocation, and laced with a kind of survivor's cynicism, all set in a Nazi extermination camp?

The Nazi destruction of European Jewry, in fact, has been one of the most elusive subjects for West German directors. It is a subject that has been avoided, for the most part. At the end of the 1950s in the East German film industry the capacity to deal with this subject, with sensitivity, intelligence, and candor was demonstrated in productions such as *Professor Mamluck* (1957) and *Stars* (1959), both directed by Konrad Wolf. As for productions in the Federal Republic of Germany, few treat the Holocaust directly. Among the films of the best-known New German directors, only Rainer Werner Fassbinder's *Lili Marleen* (1980) can be cited as taking part of its subject the Nazi war against the Jews.

When its narrative structure and its dramatic points are compared to many other fictional portrayals which allude to the Holocaust—as well as to standard

16. Willi, played by Hanna Schygulla, on her way to a private audience with Hitler in R.W. Fassbinder's *Lili Marleen*. Deutsches Institut für Filmkunde

historical interpretations of this event—*Lili Marleen* contains admirable elements. For one thing, in this movie Jews are shown as being actively engaged against the Nazi menace, taking personal risks to try to expose the working of the Nazi extermination machine, and acting in various ways—in one sequence using direct violence against the Nazis—to liberate as many Jews as possible from the Nazi apparatus. This action in the film, and the overall characterization that it supports, goes against the wide-spread, and largely untrue, image of Jewish passivity and resignation in the face of the threat of Hitler's "Final Solution" to the so-called "Jewish problem."

On the other hand, however, the entire pattern of German civilian complacency and military complicity in the SS operations of extermination is never alluded to in the film's plot. The main Jewish characters, with whom the viewer might be expected to empathize are established in the neutral and protected environment of Switzerland. Their foray into Germany itself is in the order of a spy mission. *Lili Marleen* never confronts the actual situation of those threatened Jews living in Nazi-occupied Europe with the death machine poised to devour them.

Among West German films which have tried to deal directly with stories of Jews in Germany, however, yet another criticism must be made. Peter Lilienthal's *David* (1977), for example, which was awarded a prize at the Berlin Film Festival, fails to engage the basic moral and emotional issues of the Nazi's murderous anti-Semitism. It is too much like the made-for-TV film, *The Oppermann Family*, which was broadcast for the first time in January 1983, on the occasion of the fiftieth anniversary of Hitler's coming to power, which like *David* creates a fiction that shows prejudice and some of its consequences, but enters no realm beyond it. And, historically, that is precisely what is at issue—the realm beyond. For the Holocaust was no simple extension of bigotry and prejudice as it is encountered day in, day out, around the globe. Chronologically, both *David* and *The Oppermann Family* are set in the years after Hitler's coming to power, but before the Second World War began. The extermination program itself was ordered only in 1941, and began to be realized—initially outside of Germany's boundaries—only during the invasion of the Soviet Union in summer of that year.

Another movie, *Star Without Sky* (1984), directed by Leoni Ossowski, is set at the other end of the Holocaust chronologically, being placed in Berlin in 1945 just before the war's end. In the film, the city has already been surrounded by Soviet troops, and the young Jewish boy, Abiram, has fled a column of Jews headed for exportation to one of the death camps. He hides in a cellar where a group of Berlin kids have established a storage place for food that they have secreted away from their parents. One of the kids goes off to inform their school principal of the discovery of this undesirable, but the other children set to work trying to find a new hiding place for him. The narrative tension is developed well between elements of fear, peer-pressure and approval, and the simple desire to survive as the war comes to its close.

Indeed, only one West German film, *From a German Life* (1977), penetrates the moral and historical dilemmas contained in the actual Nazi destruction of European Jewry. By focusing on a fictional character, based on the real life Commandant of Auschwitz, Rudolf Hoss, this movie at least succeeds at some level in coming to terms with the death camps and the moral culpability for their existence. Just this, however, is not only rare, but nonexistent, in other West German films, including the products of the New German Cinema which have been critically applauded and acclaimed for the qualities of "breakthrough" in their fiction dealing with the Third Reich. The more common West German mode of representation of the Nazi experience by the New German Cinema at its best has been in a film already mentioned, Helma Sanders-Brahms' *Germany, Pale Mother*, or in the monumental cinematic undertaking by Edgar Reitz, *Homeland* (1985).

The Reitz film runs a full fifteen hours, and is set in the fictional village of Schabbach. Indeed, from its chronology alone it parallels that masterpiece of the West German cinema, which premiered at the end of the 1950s, *We Prodigies*. The temporal setting of *Homeland* extends from the end of the First World War into the 1950s.

Homeland is a brilliant film, especially if we consider the manner in which its narrative deftly, and subtly, plays off many assumptions of both the German cinema and German culture at large. Nonetheless, it does not address the moral dilemmas of Nazism, and, indeed, much of its dramatic effectiveness is in placing the Nazi experience into a continuum of overall German experience. "Schabbach is good," Edgar Reitz has claimed, "because it is so small, and because it is so small it is innocent."[72]

The main issue is how a West German film that is historical and which portrays a dimension of the Nazi experience must do so from a perspective of exploring how this experience is shaped into meaning for Germans attempting to come to terms with their own history. For both generational and cultural reasons during a fleeting period at the end of the 1950s, this engagement with the past seemed to be shifted onto a different plane. The New German Cinema, as well as much of the writing and commentary on it, has succumbed to a Neo-Marxist mythology. There is no evidence that in the 1970s and 1980s German moviemakers have succeeded in achieving any kind of breakthrough in dealing with the experience of Nazism, the Second World War, and the Holocaust. In itself this may be disappointing, but it should not be surprising. We recognize what we perceive to be the special link of contemporary Germans to the Nazi past historically. Yet, at the same time, we acknowledge that Nazism must be viewed as a human—not a German—failure.

In 1980 the film critic Andrew Sarris wrote:

> Why should German film be so fashionable outside of Germany after so long a time of scorn and neglect? It is hardly because German filmmakers have become conspicuously more repentant about Hitler and the Holocaust. Quite the contrary. Remarkably few recent German films have considered, with any degree of realism or historical perspective, the subject of Nazi atrocities.[73]

Correct as Sarris's observation was, he offered a dubious interpretation of this phenomenon. Sarris argued that what this reflected was the moral deficiency of the American audience. The popularity of the New German Cinema in the 1970s, he claimed, was a function of the "decline of moral zeal" in the United States. The lines of his argument, however, are clouded.

In the spring of 1985 the media in the United States debated and criticized President Reagan's visit to a German military cemetery at Bitburg in observance of the fortieth anniversary of the end of the Second World War in Europe. Critics focused on the fact that a number of "SS" members were buried at Bitburg. The argument against the Reagan visit had to do with the perception that the "SS" members must be distinguished from other fallen German soldiers. Interestingly, this perspective contradicted a view held widely in the 1950s that Germans should accept a sense of collective guilt and shame for the crimes of Nazism, which could not simply be blamed on certain members of elite military units.

Our point, however, is not to judge the political or moral wisdom of the Reagan visit to Bitburg, or of West German Chancellor Kohl's invitation. Nazism, and the course of the Second World War, remain so morally complex that even the best-intentioned discourse over the subject is compromised. What is the relationship of today's German population to the Nazi past? How may we judge those other nationalities, from Frenchmen to Ukrainians, from Serbo-Croats to Austrians, who aided and abetted the massacre of Jews and other civilians across Europe from 1941 to 1945? Who are we to judge? What standards do we use?

No matter what our conscious opinions about Germany and its past may be—indeed, we may believe that we hold no such opinions at all—when the lights go out and when the projector goes on an entirely new problem confronts us. When we come into full awareness of being in the presence of a "German" film about that world-historical tragedy that issued forth from "German" soil, a wide range of feelings, biases, assumptions, expectations, and, yes, even demands are evoked in many of us. Do we expect a coming clean? a work of atonement? art made into apology? When the lights go out, both literally and figuratively, are the Nazis not still for us today the "shadow" of our own inner failings, historical references to the darker side of human action and cunning, both loathed and strangely admired simultaneously? These are not easy questions, nor are they pleasant ones.

FOUR

Memory without Pain

Nostalgia is a feeling that we likely all have experienced. In its original Greek meaning, the word nostalgia refers to a "longing for home" which, as the suffix *-algia* suggests, has reached the point of sickness. The pathological nature of this longing, however, is not invariably associated with the term. Often nostalgia is regarded as a mildly pleasant, though somewhat frivolous feeling, which is essentially innocuous. It is a diversion we feel we might manage to summon up consciously, but it is also one which can suddenly, unexpectedly sweep over us. Either voluntarily evoked or involuntarily triggered, nostalgia is, in personal experience, often but a fleeting encounter with a vague longing for a return to some moment or place in our own past.

Essentially we are interested in nostalgia as a social and cultural reaction. It is the collective role of nostalgia as a cultural value in society that is our central point of departure. As an emotion, this collective or social nostalgia may be related to our personal nostalgia, but by dint of its being a mass phenomenon it is also different from anything we might experience individually. The nature of that difference needs exploring, but to do so is not the intention here. We wish to examine through movies the existence of collective nostalgia which occurred in the United States from the late 1960s into the 1980s.

The background to that era of the late 1960s during which nostalgia became apparent as a widely shared social and cultural value is characterized by the escalation of the military involvement of the U.S. in Southeast Asia and the debate, protest, and conflict in American society because of it. That involvement occurred against the background of the unique American experience of the two decades preceding it, from 1945 to 1965.

The uniqueness of that experience was based upon the triumph of the United States in the Second World War and the resulting rapid ascendancy of the fortunes of the United States internationally.[1] Although the industrial potential of the United States had grown rapidly in the first forty years of the twentieth century, it was only after 1945 that this growth translated into the technological, economic, military, and diplomatic preeminence of the United States worldwide. This preeminence lasted until the middle of the 1960s. Then, with unexpected suddenness, this supremacy appeared to begin to unravel.

Internationally that ascendancy was based on the economic and military power of the United States, its domination of alliances throughout the world (NATO, SEATO, etc.), and—to some degree—on the good repute and record that the United States had gathered in the war against fascism in Europe and against Japanese expansionism in the Pacific. Domestically this rising prosperity led to a situation in which by the year 1960, for the first time in U.S. history, over 50 percent of all Americans could be classified by economic status as "middle class."[2] Prior to this breakthrough in 1960, and forming the basis for it, was the post-World War Two baby boom.

The 1950s were in actuality a more complex period than the widely disseminated negative caricature of them would have it. The Eisenhower years were neither so bland, nor so unoriginal, nor so empty culturally as they have often been portrayed. A number of revisionist historians recently have begun reassessing the Eisenhower presidency.[3] Moreover, the lively contribution to culture by the Beat poets and writers, as well as by numerous jazz artists, along with the emergence of rock music, and even the early, golden years of live television production, provide evidence of a creative activity that was hardly ossified.

Nonetheless, the 1950s were a decade of relative quiet, peace, and prosperity. The ethos of family life and of upward mobility was a central facet in the experience of many Americans. It was, in part, against this background that the films of nostalgia emerged in the late 1960s, and flourished during the 1970s, often enough reconstructing dimensions of the experience of the 1950s in order to evoke the nostalgic mode.

Historical experience never coincides precisely with decades, though the use of such conceptualization is common and convenient. In some ways, the quiescence, the cultural values, and the general middle-class optimism we generally attribute to the 1950s had begun as early as 1947 or 1948, or perhaps dated to the war's end itself. This was so, even in spite of postwar economic problems and pressing issues right after 1945, such as the shortage of housing.

Moreover, elements of these moods and values prevailed well into the 1960s, until 1965 at least, and perhaps, even until 1967. Some might argue that a break with the quiescence, prosperity, and increased certitude about America and its role in the world occurred abruptly with the assassination of President Kennedy in November 1963. Others would maintain that Kennedy's election in 1960 meant that the chronological turning point of one decade to the next marked a fundamental transformation in collective experience for American society in general.

It was the escalation of the military involvement of the United States in Vietnam, dating from 1965, that was to connect a few years later with the apparent changes in the mood, culture, values, and perspectives of many Americans. The Vietnam experience is central to the entire problem we are looking at through the films of nostalgia from *Bonnie and Clyde* (1967) to *The Big Chill* (1983). It need not be maintained that the U.S. intervention in Vietnam and its residue dominated that entire period. Nonetheless, it is necessary to offer here at least several observations about the war and the protests against it.

First of all, the military goal of the United States in Vietnam was consistent with the general policy of "containment of communism" articulated first in the "Truman Doctrine" in the immediate postwar epoch and continued by subsequent American administrations. The War in Korea (1951–54) was a model for the escalation of U.S. military involvement in Vietnam ten to fifteen years later.[4] What was different was neither the moral nor the political rightness of the intervention, but simply the outcome of the two episodes. The situations were similar, in that in the long run American policy in Vietnam aimed at maintaining the south of the country as a separate political entity free from communism. This was just what had been achieved through military intervention—and sustained ever since—in Korea.

The different outcomes of the two situations were caused by three factors: (1) The South Vietnamese proved to be less effective allies than the South Koreans had been; (2) the United States was not able to effectively enlist significant direct support from its allies, especially from NATO, for its undertaking in Vietnam; (3) the military undertaking in South Vietnam provoked levels of criticism, dissent, and protest in the United States which had had no parallel during the Korean War.

Nonetheless, it is important to repeat that the Vietnam undertaking was no anomaly in American post-World War Two policy. Nor for that matter were the Vietnamese allies *inherently* less worthy or less defensible than the Koreans. The South Korean leadership in Seoul in the early 1950s had constituted a puppet government of Washington just as later the government in Saigon would. There seems to be, for American policy, few alternatives to relying on the best local political forces one can identify—even if they are far from ideal—in trying to stabilize a system under attack by insurgents. Whether the South Korean leadership was less corrupt than the South Vietnamese is arguable. In the long run, however, the South Koreans were able to enlist greater native support for the anti-Communist effort than could the South Vietnamese leadership. When all other arguments and theories about the failure of U.S. policy and the massive military intervention undertaken by Washington in Vietnam have been considered, a simple truth remains: The Communists took over South Vietnam because the Saigon government proved incapable of mobilizing indigenous resistance to them. The Saigon government, which represented a small elite of the population, proved unworthy of the massive direct diplomatic, economic, and military aid that Washington provided for its defense.[5]

The turbulence that flowed through American society over Vietnam reached its high point between August 1968, the date of the demonstrations in Chicago during the Democratic Party National Convention, and May 1970, when four students at Kent State University were killed by Ohio National Guardsmen. The nature of the "New Left" political protest, which blended with a counterculture shift in values that registered among significant numbers of younger persons in the 1960s requires subtle treatment throughout this chapter rather than a thumbnail sketch of it which might be presented at this point. Just when a widely shared impulse to cultural change was becoming perceptible in the United States, around 1966 or 1967, the first wave of the "baby boom" children who had been born between 1948 and 1955 were coming of age. The perceived cultural changes accelerated into the early 1970s, by which time a great many of them—liberalized attitudes toward sex, drug use, the ascendancy of rock music as the cultural core for American youth, more casual dress, and a changing status of women—became relatively well established and widespread.

Of the movies that characterized the shifting mores, values, and habits among a substantial number of young adults in particular, the most seminal—and in some ways the most improbable—was *Bonnie and Clyde* (1967). Starring Faye Dunaway and Warren Beatty, directed by Arthur Penn, it was scripted by the previously untried team of David Newman and Robert Benton.

When its nationwide release was pending, the production company, Warner Brothers, appears to have concluded that it was a movie that might do reasonably well on the "popcorn circuit" but not elsewhere, in more sophisticated markets. By "popcorn circuit" the distributors meant the smaller midwestern and southern cities where audiences presumably went to the movies simply because there were so few other sources of diversion available, especially to younger people. Initially, this suspicion seemed correct. *Bonnie and Clyde* was reviewed savagely in *The New York Times*, presumably paving the way for the expected attacks by the "better" critics. Opinion, however, became quickly divided in the critical community, though it soon shifted toward finding in this vivid and highly stylized, yet fast-paced, exploration of a man and a woman on a spree of robberies in the early 1930s a highly intelligent, passionate, and finely crafted film. On this count, the youthful moviegoers of 1967 were ahead of those who were writing about *Bonnie and Clyde*.[6]

In its initial review of the movie, *Time Magazine* wrote of the "sheer, tasteless aimlessness" of *Bonnie and Clyde*.[7] In a rare turnaround, however, Stefan Kanter at *Time* reassessed his earlier critical piece, while *Newsweek*'s Joseph Morgenstern called his own review of several weeks earlier "grossly unfair."[8]

Writing in *Films in Review*, Page Cook spared little invective: "The script of *Bonnie and Clyde* by David Newman and Robert Benton is dementia praecox of the most pointless sort. . . . There is *evil* in the *tone* of the writing, acting, and direction of this film, the calculated effect of which is to incite in the young the delusion that armed robbery and murder are mere 'happenings.' "[9] The old, Hollywood warhorse press reviewed *Bonnie and Clyde* as having inconsistent direction and being flawed by erratic performances.[10] Nonetheless, the evidence points toward a misunderstanding on the part of critics not so much about the nature of the movie itself, but rather about the audience response to it. Abe Greenberg, writing in the *Los Angeles Citizen News*, expressed this bewilderment:

> There were the "bad guys" who became "good guys", sort of Robin Hoods in the eyes of one segment of the public. Yet none of this jells with the trail of death and destruction left by the Barrow gang. Therein lies the puzzlement—why did producer Warren Beatty "humanize" these murderous characters and make the lawmen seem heavies?"[11]

In an era in which the "generation gap" seemed to grow geometrically before one's eyes, the debate over *Bonnie and Clyde* seemed to illustrate it in action. Greenberg's puzzlement was shared by hundreds of his colleagues across the United States and ostensibly by hundreds of thousands of his generation. Yet, in the American democracy the taste of the majority of moviegoers prevailed. The box office conquered critical suspicions and moral approbation. By year's end, in its report on cinema for the year 1967, a *Time* report called *Bonnie and Clyde* "the sleeper of the decade," and acknowledged that in the eyes of many it was "the best movie of the year."[12] More important, contemporaries

17. The breakthrough to a new nostalgia idiom in Hollywood feature film: Arthur Penn's *Bonnie and Clyde* (1967). Academy of Motion Picture Arts & Sciences

were able to recognize in *Bonnie and Clyde* elements which differentiated the movie from its predecessor Hollywood productions. Often, there was disagreement over just what it was that *Bonnie and Clyde* foreshadowed, and not all observers—in retrospect—seemed to have been able to identify its components clearly. A review in *Films and Filming* seemed unable to get a handle on the phenomenon: "Bringing nostalgia to heel, sharply and superbly, Arthur Penn's *Bonnie and Clyde* is a film for now, and perhaps posterity."[13]

Yet, in just what way was it a film for now? Had *Bonnie and Clyde* brought nostalgia to heel? Or had nostalgia, through *Bonnie and Clyde* as its vehicle, begun an inexorable seepage into culture and consciousness in the United States? *Bonnie and Clyde* produced an immediate ripple in the fashion world; styles modeled on the 1930s flourished. The "Faye Dunaway" look penetrated magazines and clothing stores. This reflected a response to the surface values of nostalgia in the movie. As one critic wrote in this regard in the *Villiage Voice*, *Bonnie and Clyde* "slithers easily into nostalgia."[14]

Reaching that first level of nostalgia was of no great challenge or consequence. *Bonnie and Clyde*'s exploitation of styles of dress, its re-creation of buildings and interiors of the 1930s, or the myriad chase scenes with vintage automobiles were not definitive of its nostalgia. Rather, its real exploration of nostalgia was located at the juncture between the movie's fictional re-creation of the past and the connectedness of that very re-creation to the present. Observers noted that not since the wildfire response to *Gone With the Wind* in 1939 had any other movie created such "worldwide, intensive excitement."[15]

This worldwide, intensive excitement was a product of the emergence of a self-conscious youth counterculture very much informed by the idea that it was distinct generational phenomenon. A substantial number of young people fashioned themselves as rejecting the crass, superficial, and plastic values of their parents' generation, often citing their felt affinity to their grandparents' generation. *Bonnie and Clyde* premiered at a juncture when the strands of this generational counterculture movement coalesced with the increasing protest against U.S. military involvement in Southeast Asia. Most critics were bewildered by the positive response to the movie. An exception was Pauline Kael, who wrote in *The New Yorker*:

> In 1967 the movie-makers know that the audience wants to believe—maybe even prefers to believe—that Bonnie and Clyde were guilty of crimes, all right, but that they were innocent in general; that is, naive and ignorant *compared with us* [my italics]. The distancing of the sixties version shows the gangsters in an already legendary period, and part of what makes a legend for Americans is viewing anything that happened in the past as much simpler than what we are involved in now.[16]

Bonnie and Clyde stands as a landmark. Its connectedness to the moment of its appearance was riveted in the social and cultural fabric of the United States in the year 1967. This phenomenon cannot be overestimated. As one commentator analyzed Bonnie and Clyde's relationship to its audience:

One can no longer consider the film as a film. It has transcended art to become a psychic convenience. It has gone beyond the pale of criticism to become the rarest of all things, an artifact that is both symptom and cause.[17]

In *Bonnie and Clyde* many viewers found what registered with them as an expression of anti-establishment frustration and a portrayal of deprivation and injustice that had drawn the protagonists, who are sympathetically treated throughout the plot, into a life of crime.

A good deal of the picture's financial success was the fact that the late Sixties audiences related to the rootless alienation of the film's milieu. Bonnie and Clyde are rebels without a cause. . . characters which the so-called "youth movement" of the Sixties turned into campy [*sic*] pop culture heroes. . . .[18]

The great economic depression of the 1930s is only vaguely alluded to in the movie, rather than being significantly manifested in its narrative structure. In only a single scene is the economic and social tension of the era evoked, and, even then, it is done fleetingly. When an old man surprises Bonnie and Clyde as they wake up from having spent the night in an abandoned house, social commentary connecting them to a protest against the establishment and the economic conditions it has produced become clear. Clyde, his pistol drawn, confronts the old man who is poking about the yard of the house. The old man, in bib overalls, backs away. In the distance, behind him, is a car loaded with the family's belongings, in which his wife and children sit in tatters. He explains to Clyde that the house they have been sleeping in used to be his home. Now that the bank has foreclosed on it, he and his family are heading west. Having come back for a last look at the old homestead, he gets an added treat of symbolic revenge—he and Clyde take turns shooting up a billboard the bank has erected in front of the property announcing its ownership.

This direct act of anger and revenge is treated as deeply satisfying, and the viewer is drawn into sharing the feeling of satisfaction by the director. Though the sequence is brief, and not at all pivotal to the narrative, the scene nonetheless sets a tone and gives a basis in value and meaning for all the subsequent exploits in the film. For by placing that brief sequence early in the movie, the association of the entire film with a protest against the establishment is strongly suggested. It is no imaginative exaggeration to point out that in this context the act of shooting up the sign, rendered as a device of social protest, equates neatly with the penchant of protesters in the late 1960s for acts of direct confrontation with police, random acts of destruction and political vandalism, or the greatest favorite of American protestors—the scrawling of incendiary graffiti in public places.

Bonnie and Clyde was an important movie for film history and toward the end of the 1960s marked a potential turning point in Hollywood's direction. Yet, as James Monaco has argued in *American Film Now*, it soon became a model for the "entertainment machines of the seventies," not for powerful, thoughtful movies created in its own vein.[19]

And just how does *Bonnie and Clyde* relate to the overriding concept of nostalgia which is posited here as a central idea around which a substantial part of collective cultural experience focused in the United States from 1967 to 1985? To begin answering that question requires, first of all, additional comment about the notion of nostalgia itself.

A central point in defining nostalgia and, hence, in distinguishing it from other concepts which may be closely related to it is to describe the phenomenon first in terms of popular parlance. This would be to say that nostalgia is "memory without pain."[20] Such a description goes a long way toward indicating something about the qualities of any experience that is felt as nostalgic. It also provides us with a way of getting at an insight into the nature and quality of nostalgia.

Nostalgia is that special type of memory that is not analytical, but rather is recollection sweetened, mystified, or mythified. Nostalgia is not historical; it is often claimed that it should not be confused with that mode of perception called historical. Instead, nostalgia is a manipulation of historical consciousness geared to a particular kind of release of tension. The very nature of history is that the tracings of the past have been taken and molded into intellectual constructs which normally yield causal and explanatory models of how and why events have occurred. We may remember the past, but it is only when the traces in memory that we recall are shaped and molded into structures of explanation—usually narratives—that the historical mode itself is evoked. History may be mythologized, of course, either intentionally or unintentionally. Even more clearly and emphatically the historical may be falsified. History relies upon certain forms of vertification for its claims. Naturally, arguments may be advanced against the overall concept that the data that historians treat as "facts," because they are verifiable, are an acceptable base for reconstructing the past accurately.

Nostalgia, by contrast, is not liable to tests of veracity, nor is nostalgia based on documentation. Nostalgia is a feeling that does not yield casual or explanatory ways of perceiving the past, understanding it, and developing a critical appreciation of it.

We identify nostalgia as a feeling—often a vague one—that refers to past experiences and perceptions. In the present, that feeling provides a basis for cherishing those perceptions emotionally. Nostalgia, however, is not euphoric, and is often tinged with sadness and penetrated by a sense of loss. Indeed, this is perhaps its most salient and commonly felt association. Moreover, this association, and the entire psychological and philosophical complexity that underlies it, is further complicated when we refer to the nostalgic as manifested in fictional works.

The increasing presence in contemporary culture of fiction on film and videotape means that more and more viewers absorb into their awareness a shared body of experience. The issue is not that the fiction created in movies is essentially so different in its nature and character from written fiction. Rather, it is the case that film, and the related medium of television, provide fiction as an immediate, direct, and collective phenomenon to millions of viewers—all of whom experience the fiction of a film within a few short months, or the fiction of a television presentation on a single evening.

Moreover, this widely shared body of collective fiction is increasingly viewed by children and adolescents. More and more the populations of contemporary societies contain persons who have grown up with strongly shared collective images of specific fictional representations. As an example, we might observe that nearly any significant public event or process that has occurred since the 1920s, such as the "Great Depression," has been documented on film. That footage has been widely seen and is still being used and reused in audio/ visual treatments of the topic. The "cowboy movie," similarly, has imbued successive generations with images of the North American West which are deeply ingrained. The collective function of film, and of the subsequent delivery system that broadcasts film primarily, namely, television, is to reinforce images which are shared collectively. Hence, these images become part of the collective memory of certain generational cohorts or portions of the population.

If nostalgia is memory without pain, and if we are to speak of the single film, *Bonnie and Clyde*, as having inaugurated a wave of movies of nostalgia in the United States at the end of the 1960s, we must recognize that the subject matter of *Bonnie and Clyde* and the era in which the action of the movie takes place was not part of the *lived* experience and memory of the vast majority of the younger American viewers with whom the movie became so popular. The persons who flocked to the movie theaters to see *Bonnie and Clyde* were predominantly under thirty years old, and had not lived through the actual Depression of the early 1930s. Yet, it is precisely this that is significant. The Depression has become a part of collective memory, even for those who did not actually live through it. No doubt it was an especially salient emotional and symbolic touchstone for the "baby boomers" who were coming of age in the late 1960s. First of all, they were a generation who had grown up being exposed repeatedly to images of the Depression era in films or on television. Moreover, their parents had, to a great extent, been children of the Depression, who had experienced the dislocations and insecurities of that period through the eyes of children and with the sensitivity of those who are helpless to do anything about the circumstances of life surrounding them. Many a baby boomer drank in lingering anxieties of the Depression era with his or her mother's milk.[21]

Delving into a "reception history" of *Bonnie and Clyde* would be superfluous. Still it can be emphasized that the audience for *Bonnie and Clyde* was prepared by the media and their parents to respond to this movie nostalgically. Upbeat banjo music, the open and free feeling of the pair's escapades, and the sympathetic treatment of the main characters and their exploits, characterizes *Bonnie and Clyde*. These elements create "memory" of a special sort—not only without pain, but with a distinct pleasurableness about it. Even the final, grotesquely violent end, when Bonnie and Clyde are mowed down in a hail of police bullets, is highly stylized. Their deaths are treated in slow motion, muting the visual "pain" by using cinematic devices to mold the scene into a mode of intimacy and pathos.

The self-consciousness of the nostalgic mode in this film is suggested strongly in a scene in which Bonnie reads a poem she was written about them and their exploits. That poem captures the idea of the film; it is about the "legend" of

Bonnie and Clyde rather than being about them. And it might be noted that all legends, insofar as they mark a sentimentalization of the past, are nostalgic in mood.

Bonnie and Clyde deals with the past by stylizing it, extracting the situation from its genuine historical setting, and portraying events, figures, and circumstances which were surely in reality uglier, meaner, and more cruel than the "legend." This generosity of spirit in treating the past, counterpointed to the great attention given cinematically to naturalistic details, is significant. This very mixture of vagueness and precision characterizes the nostalgic. And since movies are so apt a medium in which to realize just this kind of mixture, film is an extraordinary vehicle for the nostalgic mode.

Beyond the storyline of the movie, other elements of nostalgia that sprang from the popularity of *Bonnie and Clyde* became evident. Not only did Faye Dunaway's costumes inspire a wave in clothing design, but also the sound track—featuring "Foggy Mountain Breakdown" by Lester Flatt and Earl Scruggs—produced a craze for the hillbilly strains of bluegrass music which, even if contemporary, evoked a backward part of America caught in a kind of time warp. The success of this music marked the beginning of a period of ascendancy and general popularity for country and western music nationwide.

That a generation which fashioned itself as being one of protest, and embarked on countercultural pursuits, should respond so positively to the image of the 1930s presented in *Bonnie and Clyde* is not surprising. The depression hearkened back to the last great domestic crisis in the United States prior to the protests of the late sixties and the reaction against them. The thirties presented, in terms of the movies from that decade, a combination of gangster films, satiric comedies, and imaginative musicals. These had created images which associated positively with the late sixties counterculture of protesters, draft resisters, political radicals, hippies, and drug users. Marxism in the United States, even among the youthful radicals, remained in the late 1960s more tied to images from the 1930s of Groucho, Chico, Zeppo, and Harpo, than to the convoluted dialectics explored in the nineteenth-century writing of Karl.

Bonnie and Clyde was a film in which many protesters, would-be protesters, and fellow-travelers found fictional inspiration. Interestingly, a film released three years later, in 1970, attracted apparently a large segment of roughly the same audience and also achieved wide box-office success.

Patton, directed by Franklin L. Schaffner, was based on a screenplay co-authored by Francis Ford Coppola and starred George C. Scott in the title role. It is a skillfully made film. In its very ambiguity, and in the resulting numerous dimensions of its appeal it is, in fact, emblematic of that moment—at the end of the 1960s—when it was produced. *Patton* can be interpreted as an anti-war film *or* as a movie that presents an unabashedly nostalgic portrait of the great individualistic military adventurer who is limited by political forces. *Patton*, since it has to do with the Second World War, is overtly more historical than *Bonnie and Clyde*, which is connected, but only tenuously and by indirect allusion, to a shared collective experience—the Depression. *Patton* is based on biographical incidents in this public figure's career, and presents events of standard historical interest in its narration. Moreover, Patton's reaction to the immediate postwar situation in Europe, and his attitude toward the Soviet Union, connects the movie's sequences of resolution to major and ongoing questions for world affairs and U.S. foreign policy since 1945.

Unlike *Bonnie and Clyde*, which depends so much on its complex, interwoven narrative structure, *Patton* relies on strong, direct, visual images, leaving the storyline relatively simple and the narrative progression open. *Patton* opens with the image of a gigantic American flag that fills the entire screen. It is the backdrop against which the general gives his opening speech. It is a monologue, directed within the film's action toward his troops who form the audience for him, but who are never seen on the screen. Yet the power of the scene is that it is so filmed as to be directed right at every viewer in the audience. Abrupt cuts are made: from a side of Patton's face, to his revolver in its holster, to other details. Patton's speech, indeed, sets the tone, not only for his characterization, but for the rest of the film. "Americans want to fight," says Patton, "they will never lose a war. The idea of losing a war is hateful." The visual qualities of the sequence reinforce the characterization of the man: anxious, abrupt, self-certain, obsessed with being in control of a situation. Patton's text intones the virtues of discipline for "making a man," just as, throughout the movie, he embodies and personifies the energetic machismo of the professional soldier and military adventurer.

In its day, *Patton* appealed to a substantial audience who apparently could interpret from the portrayal of military machismo and swaggering old-style heroism the perverse myopia of military types. After all, at several points in the movie Patton speculates—to the strains of distant music evoking the chords of memory—on how he was with the Roman legions who faced the Carthaginians, or how he served as one of Napoleon's lieutenants. Patton later speaks naïvely of Nazism, describing it as simply like any other political movement—like either the Democratic or Republican parties in the United States![22] Moreover, his behavior toward the Soviets—displayed in a scene where he toasts his Soviet counterpart as a "son-of-a-bitch"—reveals a military mentality totally out of touch with political and diplomatic reality. Filtered through a prism of anti-war sentiment in the late 1960s such elements could register interpretively with certain viewers as portrayals which supported criticism of the military establishment. Among many of the younger viewers of *Patton* the movie was filtered through just such a prism. Hence, it was responded to positively on the basis of that filtering. For in Patton's fantasy of military exploits one senses an individual who cares not what he is fighting for or whom he is fighting against. From his political views about Nazis and Soviets we perceive a military man for whom national policy, as formulated by the civilian leadership of the nation, is but an annoyance. Identifying these elements and reaching these interpretive conclusions is problematic. Essentially the point of view established in the film is Patton's own.

The film is set chronologically in the last years of the war, and greatest attention in the narrative structure is given to Patton's leading the sweep of the

3rd army across France and into Germany after he has been "rehabilitated" and returned to its command.

A savvy viewer, so inclined politically, will question Patton's cavalier attitude toward the war policies (as reflected in his relations to the Soviets) or his easygoing attitude toward German fascism and the rehabilitation of prominent Nazis. To do so, however, requires bringing to the movie not only a relatively sharp sense of history, but also a fairly well-defined political focus. Without being so inclined and prepared, the movie itself is more open to interpretation in a different direction: one in which sympathy for Patton and his situation is strongly evoked. His imaginings of military exploits in the past, in which he sees himself as a Roman legionnaire or as a Napoleonic lieutenant, after all, are presented as slightly bizarre, but nonetheless quaint. Moreover, these sequences are not structured into the narrative at moments in which they connect to anything threatening or dire; they remain personal quirks as they are presented. Patton's desire to succeed militarily is not analyzed in any way, nor is the incident in which he slaps a GI in a medical ward whom he thinks is a "goldbricker."

The critical perspective on both these occurrences must be brought to the movie by the viewer entirely. As a hero Patton is flawed, but this only adds to the naturalism of the portrayal rather than detracting from his ethos. The overall presentation is of a character who is not entirely unsympathetic. His failings are entirely personal, rather than opening a pathway for the viewer's analysis of the system in which Patton operates and the values that he represents. President Richard M. Nixon, in the midst of still conducting his aggressive military policy in Vietnam, enjoyed *Patton* enormously, and repeatedly saw it in the White House during the year of its release, 1970.

Patton is a movie of nostalgia that returns to the last victorious stages of the Second World War. Although he is a flawed human, Patton is nonetheless heroic and triumphant. He is the independent, dedicated military adventurer whose grit and daring produce results. *Patton* premiered in 1970, just as U.S. military involvement in Southeast Asia produced a spasm of escalation—incursions into Laos and Cambodia along with the bombing of Hanoi and its harbor—that still created no breakthrough in the military fortunes of the U.S. and its ally. A number of viewers might have been expected to associate the figure of Patton with a kind of military prowess that was missing in the combat being waged. In the movie there is an implication that the headstrong military leader, filled with bravado, makes mistakes, some of which we may dislike. Basically, however, it is implied that it may be his kind of gutsy leadership that is the best source for securing military victory.

In the script of *Patton* nothing occurs to indicate the liabilities of such a figure. Patton is a success on the screen. Interpreted nostalgically, his success suggests reinforcement for a feeling already present in some quarters in the United States when the movie was released. That very feeling has subsequently been forged into a purported explanation for the failure of the United States in its Vietnam intervention. It is a point of view that would have it that the United States failed because the military was thwarted by the government's own policy.[23] If only the military had been unharnessed, so this version goes, it would have run up staggering and convincing victories against the Vietcong and their North Vietnamese allies, rather than falling short of U.S. objectives in the war because the U.S. military was restricted by Washington's politicians to waging limited combat. This view may coincide but little with the nature and reality of the conflict in Southeast Asia, and the myriad strategic problems presented in the attempt to conduct it, but that neither prevents its being widely held nor prevents the movie *Patton*—in its nostalgic mode—from registering fictional/ emotional support for this notion.

The nostalgic mentality that associates most strongly with *Patton* can be brought even more clearly into focus if that film is compared to one released in 1973 that, on the surface, seems but little connected to it. *Save the Tiger*, directed by John Alvidsen (whose later *Rocky*, 1976, evoked many of the classic, Hollywood images of personal struggle and upward mobility), starred Jack Lemmon in a role for which he won an Oscar, with his portrayal of Los Angeles garmentmaker Harry Stoner.

Save the Tiger is set in the present, the early 1970s, and hence it is a different sort of movie than those which resurrect and reconstruct a past epoch directly, and which utilize this "recapturing" to predicate the nostalgic mode. In its uniqueness, *Save the Tiger* evokes its nostalgic elements either through dialogue, or in several of the prolonged and rambling monologues of Harry Stoner.

In spite of being set in contemporary Los Angeles, and having a plot that covers but a day and a half chronologically, *Save the Tiger* ranges over a wide period of time imaginatively. Harry Stoner is a World War Two veteran who has run a successful business with his partner Phil Green for years. Threatened by a cash-flow problem, Harry is now scheming to have one of the company's smaller and less important buildings "torched" for the insurance money. This plan provides the essential dramatic tension, as well as the basic moral dilemma, that runs throughout the movie. Against this central core of suspense Harry and Phil reflect on events and experiences of the past as well as on the eroding values of the present. As his partner, Phil Green, observes to Harry over lunch: "[Today] rats are crawling around babies, they're taking pictures of Mars, and we're in the balcony talking to Charlie Robbins." Charlie Robbins is the gangster who is being hired to burn the building which they own for insurance money. They meet with him several times in the balcony at an X-rated movie theater to discuss details of the arson.

Harry Stoner has named his dress company "Capri," after the island off the Italian coast where he recuperated after the invasion at Anzio in World War Two. He muses that Capri meant to him "brave men who stood together." Increasingly, however, Harry's own questions about the erosion of values and dreams— perhaps, the "American Dream" itself—have become interwoven through the fabric of his life. With simple candor he tells a prostitute he has hired to service one of the out-of-town buyers: "We're both in the same business—we sell imagination." Harry's most revealing verbal wander through memory, lost innocence, fear, and yearning to love and to be loved, however, occurs in a scene toward the end of the film.

Harry has picked up a hitchhiker in her early twenties. She is a caricature of the tail end of the hippie movement. She tells Harry that the three things she wants most are: "Peace, harmony, and to make it with Mick Jagger." At a beachhouse she massages his back, and Harry drifts into a revealing monologue. When Harry mentions his military service in Italy in World War Two to her, the twenty-one year old responds incredulously: "We never fought a war with Italy."

Soon their game of naming heroes past and present turns from the frivolous to the more serious when Harry cites the Nazi war minister Albert Speer. He mentions, too, Hitler's chief adjutant for carrying out the destruction of the Jews, Adolf Eichmann. Then he refers to the "Enola Gay," the name of the plane carrying the atom bomb that the U.S. dropped on Hiroshima. Yet these allusions are intermixed with references to Vietnam, to the "My Lai Hotel, with twelve massage parlors and six swimming pools," and, alas, to "the ditch." This verbal connecting of "My Lai" to the perpetrators of Nazi atrocities in the Second World War is associative. It is not, of course, argued or reasoned out. Its logic is interior, not determinant. Nonetheless, it is a strong suggestive strain, especially because it is presented as part of the increasingly frenzied monologue by Harry who has begun all of this with a prosaic wandering down memory lane—naming music stars of the "big band" epoch and outstanding baseball players of an era long past. The nostalgia strain being played out here connects the Second World War—a time of national consensus in the United States and a point of unabashed national triumph and sense of right—with the U.S. intervention in Vietnam. Harry Stoner, in his confused monologue, reflects the confused situation of the United States as a whole over the Vietnam issue.

The traces of nostalgia in *Save the Tiger* explore effectively the sense of lost innocence that characterized the response of many Americans to the Vietnam war, as well as to the Watergate scandal which followed on its heels. Harry Stoner's personal nostalgia is most suggestive of being that of a man in mid-life crisis. This is the personal, psychological dimension of the movie, and, as such, it is both strong and compelling. He is caught up in the images of the past, represented by baseball players and sundry folk heroes. He is himself like Campbell the whale whom he has read about in the morning's newspaper. He has commented on the demise of this wonderful creature who died after three years of swimming against the current in his tank at the aquarium. And given the title of the film, Harry knows he, too, is an endangered species, like the tiger of which only 556 are left in the world. He, too, has been swimming against the current, fighting a seemingly hopeless battle to maintain the dream that he had fashioned into reality in the preceding years.

Save the Tiger unites the theme of personal nostalgia, generated by Harry's "mid-life" crisis, with the distinctive and provocative strains of collective nostalgia. Thus, *Save the Tiger* connects the sense of deterioration and loss through aging with the perceived erosion of values and purpose that many saw in the U.S. intervention in Vietnam, followed by the Watergate scandal.

Since the personal, or private, dimension of nostalgia is important in this movie, it is worth noting that the perennial allure of the nostalgic mode may, in fact, be most obvious and pressing in a society such as the American. As the perceptive cultural critic Leslie A. Fiedler argued in *The End of Innocence*, which was published in the mid-1950s, culture in the United States offers but scant imaginative symbolism to anyone after young adulthood.[24] American culture, especially as it has developed since the Second World War, can be called increasingly "adolescent." Moreover, the general values of American society tend strongly toward youth, beauty or handsomeness, productivity and accomplishment, and the acquisition of material goods. All of these values are transitory or elusive. Great numbers of individuals are especially prone to insecurity over the possible loss of any one of them. Youth for certain, beauty most likely, and even productivity, will decrease with passing years.

Overall, personal or private nostalgia may be regarded as a compensation that functions to preserve one's identity against the erosive effects of changes, any of which may be either unwelcome or unexpected. But the greatest problem about change, rife in a society that so extensively cultivates rapid transformations of all sorts, is the presence of widespread feelings of ambivalence about the changes once they occur. Seen in this way, nostalgia is a fairly mild—and, some would argue, relatively innocent—defense mechanism which functions emotionally to preserve a sense of continuity. This sense of continuity for the individual denotes the value of nostalgia for sustaining feelings of connectedness to prior experience. At the same time it provides an imaginative device that can assure a notion of uniqueness about the particular experience that is recollected in a nostalgic mood. This emphasis on the uniqueness of our own prior experience, as it is found to predominate in private nostalgia, points to nostalgia being both an excellent defense mechanism and an apt mode of cultural expression. Especially for a culture of "narcissism"—the trenchant term used by the social critic Christopher Lasch to describe patterns of culture and values in America during the 1970s—nostalgia helps preserve the sense of continuity and personal self-importance simultaneously.

The private/personal and the collective/social are by no means separate spheres of human feeling and experience. Nonetheless, our vocabularies have become habituated to falsely divide them in the mind's eye, and to think of them as strictly distinct from one another. Whether considering nostalgia as a personal feeling that sweeps over someone, or perceiving it as a cultural phenomenon that may appear to have developed over time, we recognize the symbiotic interrelatedness of both its private and its public modes. In the late 1960s and throughout the 1970s in the United States the personal impulse to nostalgia intermeshed with an impulse to collective nostalgia brought on by the dislocations caused in society by the Vietnam war, the Civil Rights Movement, Student Protests, Watergate, the First Energy Crisis, the Women's Movement, and the Sexual Revolution.

One favorite setting for the fiction of nostalgia, as well as a kind of touchstone for various fads and obsessions of the nostalgic stripe during the 1970s, became that era of apparent certitude, quiescence, affluence, and relatively unchallenged world supremacy for the United States—the 1950s. The thirties (*Bonnie and Clyde*), the era of the Second World War (*Patton*), other epochs, or even movies in the nostalgic mode set contemporarily (*Save The Tiger*)—none of these settings proved as compelling and popular for evoking nostalgia as the 1950s for the movie industry and its audience.

The range of movies set in the 1950s includes comparatively serious explorations of the phenomenon of rock music, such as *The Buddy Holly Story* (1978), or *American Hot Wax* (1978); stylized rock musicals such as *Grease* (1980); stylized, but essentially naturalistic, milieu films such as *The Lords of Flatbush* (1974); the attempt to capture small-town provincialism as orchestrated by rock music in *American Graffiti* (1973); campus life as in *Animal House* (1978); the painful exploration of relations in a Marine Corps family in *The Great Santini* (1980).

Not only are all these films set in the 1950s, all these films also have in common their focus on adolescence or young adulthood. Hence, they may be assumed to appeal to an audience composed primarily of two age groups: (1) those who had reached adolescence or young adulthood in the period portrayed, roughly from 1953 to 1963; (2) those in adolescence or young adulthood themselves at the time the movies premiered. There then appears to be a demographic reason for the focus on the 1950s, which has to do with selecting an epoch that will presumably broaden the appeal of the movie for a potential audience. Far more intriguing, of course, are the collective psychological grounds for it. Perhaps most interesting is how the two might intertwine.

The collective psychological grounds for this particular focus of nostalgia hinges upon the widely held and widely accepted presupposition that the assassination of President John F. Kennedy in November 1963 marked the end of an era. In turn, that event marked the beginning of a seemingly rapidly downward spiral of the nation and its fortunes—numerous other assassinations and assassination attempts, the unsuccessful Vietnam policy, a rising crime rate, and so forth.

Of all the movies which portray nostalgia, the one that is most clearly anchored in the simple chronology of that transition is *American Graffiti*. It was produced under the inspiration of Francis Ford Coppola in 1973. Coppola rescued the project from apparent rejection by the Hollywood "establishment." This George Lucas movie powerfully reinforces several important aspects of the nostalgic mode in fiction. Although the date of the action is never specified in the film itself, *American Graffiti* was promoted by an advertising campaign in which the main slogan was "Where were you in '62?" That ad campaign theme is revealing, indeed. For it points directly to the personal evocation of connectedness: The question is rhetorical, but inwardly the potential viewer of the movie is pressed to begin his or her relationship to *American Graffiti* on the basis of recollecting where he or she was and what he or she was doing in 1962. Moreover, the date has a powerful collective significance for potential viewers. Chronologically, 1962 is the last year of American quiescence, innocence, and power. Culturally, morally, and in terms of widespread perceptions of American good fortune, 1962 belongs to the fifties psychologically. If we think of the assassination of President Kennedy at Dallas in November 1963 as the single event that most clearly marks a dramatic break in societal stability, in perceptions of American self-confidence, and in the perceptions of the U.S.'s role in the world, we identify immediately the significance of this date.

American Graffiti was a low-budget production in which a substantial portion of the $800,000 production cost was spent on purchasing the rights to the rock music numbers which permeate the text. That music itself was not from the 1960s but, rather, from the preceding decade.

American Graffiti may be considered, in many ways, to be what would be called a *Bildungsfilm*.[26] This German term means literally "a film of education," but only insofar as education refers not to formal schooling, but rather to general patterns of maturation. The movie's narrative portrays an informal rite of passage for the young man, Curt, who is the film's central figure. Unlike much fiction that treats the subject of personal growth and maturation, however, *American Graffiti* is set in but a single night, rather than over a prolonged period of time. Transformation and maturation, then, have been telescoped in *American Graffiti* into an abbreviated fictional timeframe.

American Graffiti begins with shots of teenagers entering and exiting a drive-in restaurant in their cars. The parking lot is the center of visual attention.

18. Mecca for teenage America, *circa* 1963—the parking lot of a drive-in restaurant. *American Graffiti* captured the surface of the favorite era for nostalgia movies. Academy of Motion Picture Arts & Sciences

Of great importance to this opening sequence is the music track that accompanies it—a recording of Bill Haley's "Rock Around the Clock" that evokes a self-reflexive cinematic reference to a film of the mid-1950s. "Rock Around the Clock" provided the central musical theme for Hollywood's breakthrough film in 1955, *Blackboard Jungle*, which had marked the beginning of an initial conscious courting of the adolescent audience by the movie industry. Using the song for its opening, the makers of *American Graffiti*, either intentionally or not, are creating associations between this 1972 film and what might be regarded as a predecessor film from the mid-fifties. More important, beyond these self-reflexive associations of the two films which both begin with "Rock Around the Clock" is the way in which this opening establishes the central importance of rock music for *American Graffiti*. *American Graffiti*, in fact, constructs a subtext to the film which is composed entirely of rock songs from the fifties. This may be called a nostalgic element. It also sets the basis for a further exploitation of nostalgic sentiments based upon it.

One of the verities of popular music in the age of its mechanical reproduction on records and tape is that certain melodies, tunes, and lyrics become increasingly imbued with a sentimentalization. This, in itself, points to their nostalgic value. Clichés, such as "they're playing our song," point to this, as does the market for "golden oldies," as well as the more simple way in which personal memory and imagination can be jarred into specific visions of a person or event in our past when a particular song is heard. We associate music with particular epochs—"jazz" with the twenties, and the big band sound with the thirties—while recognizing that music permeates all our experience. The comparatively unproblematic technologies of the phonograph and the radio have been replaced increasingly by newer devices which permit us to become totally isolated and absorbed in music. Some kind of music may accompany us now almost everywhere—from our automobiles to supermarkets to restaurants, and even may be played for us on the phone as we wait to ask someone about an airplane reservation or a doctor's appointment.

Rock music also is identified with particular moments in time when it has appeared and become popular. Rock music has really come closest to Marshall McLuhan's suggestion of a tribal beat that is responded to spontaneously by millions at once.[27] The success or failure of a rock song occurs with extraordinary rapidness. And rock songs come and go quickly, each etching its place in a very specific time. One need only listen once on the radio to one of the "oldie but goodie," or "Casey Kasem Countdown" shows to recognize how precisely time-bound rock music really is. A specific song is connected inexorably to the month or two in a particular year when it swept the nation and "scored high on the charts."

Along with *Easy Rider* (1969), *American Graffiti* was one of the first movies, which was itself not a musical, to exploit in fiction the centrality of popular music to modern experience. And, of course, the significance of rock music to the experience of adolescents is central, and has only seemed to burgeon, without any significant abatement, since rock's appearance in the early 1950s. By the 1980s, rock had established itself well with pre-adolescents in the U.S.

The fiction of *American Graffiti* is shot through with the sentiments of nostalgia, and this is underscored extensively by the nostalgic allusions which permeate the sound track. Moreover, the movie's text itself contains what might be called several interior suggestions of nostalgia. The character played by Paul LeMat, for example, is a few years older than the other characters who are still in high school or just graduating from it. He is a hot rod jockey admired by many. Yet, in his "advanced years" he is already bemoaning the deterioration of the car cruising culture that he considers to be in decline, speaking about "the way the strip was." Moreover, he adds to this his own perspective in cultural criticism by pointing out that ". . . rock 'n' roll's been going down ever since Buddy Holly died."

American Graffiti, which from its very title, its spirit, and its surface theme is a celebration of American adolescence, nonetheless repeatedly points out that the celebratory moment of youth is extraordinarily fleeting. This, indeed, is a central theme of the film. The entire dramatic problem of the movie centers on whether Curt will choose to accept a scholarship from a local Moose Lodge and go to college in the East, or whether he will reject it and linger awhile longer in the grasp of small-town adolescence.

With absolutely no pretension about being a sociological text, *American Graffiti* nonetheless points to the particular way in which high school exists in American society. As an institution it provides a social, rather than an educational, experience. Pretenses about high school being the latter are empty, even though they are still given lip service extensively. The special nature of adolescence, at least as it is perceived—and likely as it is experienced as well—in American culture is a significant source of awareness. Adolescence, as a concept and a value, apparently continues throughout the lives of many citizens. It is vastly important in our representations of nostalgia, both private or individual and public or collective. High school remains a particular kind of experience, heavy in its emphasis on socialization. It provides an excellent basis for reminiscence about the rite of passage that is encompassed by it.

American Graffiti is held together less by any traditional narrative conventions than by the rock music itself, punctuated by the disc jockey Wolfman Jack's staccato commentary and jive. *American Graffiti* is so completely absorbed in its adolescent ethos, moreover, that its characterizations of adults are rendered skimpy and negative. A high school teacher chaperoning a dance is so portrayed as to suggest a man who has given up. The police are either petulant (giving Paul a ticket) or buffoons (having their squad car sabotaged by Curt at the urging of a teen gang called the Scorpions). A friendly man who will buy booze for underage "Toad" does so, while robbing the liquor store. And when the effects of the alcohol gets the better part of "Toad," he vomits at the curbside while a few adults stand about, fascinated by the display that they treat with curiosity and disdain. The disk jockey Wolfman Jack is the only adult whose role and character is positive. And that is only because he is essentially part of the adolescent world itself.

This fictional depiction in *American Graffiti* resonates well with the perceived reality of a society in which adolescence is accorded special status and characterized distinctively, and in which "high school" is essentially a rite of passage rather than a sustained and challenging academic experience. Much of the appeal of nostalgia is rooted in the uniqueness attached to adolescent experience in Ameican culture.

By extension, John Landis's *Animal House*, which is also set in 1962, is a broad comedy which satirizes small-town college life. With the late John Belushi, who had established himself by the mid-1970s in the often cruel, frequently mean-spirited, and occasionally racist television program *Saturday Night Live*, providing much of its comic core, one might question whether or not the mode of meaning and value in it is one of nostalgia. At first glance nostalgia may seem incompatible with diffuse satire.

In *Animal House* a portion of the humor is either sexist or racist. In many ways the viewer is forced to the conclusion that in this instance nostalgia functions to permit portrayals of women as objects and Blacks as primitives, and that such portrayals are ostensibly legitimized by placing the action in the past—in 1962. *Animal House*, provides an excellent example of how nostalgia may fulfill a specific social, cultural, and ideological function. Put simply, this function is to lend sanction and credibility to reactionary protrayals of women and Blacks. By displacing certain situations from the present in their fictionalization this process is validated. *Animal House* is not structured and executed in a mode that would be called historical. Its fiction provides no pretense for examination of aspects of the past, but simply posits and celebrates these aspects nostalgically. And, since the nostalgic is a mode to be taken less seriously than the historical, its power of suggestion and influence may be potentially even more effective emotionally. Nostalgia here functions in a manner of greater deception than is normally the case.

The sequence in *Animal House* in which a group of men from the fraternity take their dates to a Black nightclub represents this mode at its worst. What transpires is a nasty piece of film work in which Blacks are portrayed as violent, threatening, and their culture—which, in reality is the essential basis of the American youth culture musically—as primitive. Throughout the film women are objectified and treated strictly as targets of adolescent libido.

Animal House nonetheless works plainly and simply as nostalgia for some who experienced collegiate life in the late fifties and early sixties. Take for example, the film critic James Monaco's comments: "It [*Animal House*] is a perspicuous if self-conscious homage to the halls of ivy, circa 1962. The film is lackadaisical, but it is achingly precise. I should know. I vass dere, Sharlie."[28]

It is also a film that satirically alludes to its connectedness to *American Graffiti*. For, perhaps, the most poignant moment in *American Graffiti* comes at the very end. After Curt has made his decision and chosen to leave small-town California, a sequence of still photographs ensues, featuring each of the male characters, accompanied by a brief written description of his individual fate. Toad has been killed in Vietnan, and Paul LeMat on the highway; Curt has gone to Canada [to escape military conscription?], and so on. *Animal House* ends with stop-action shots of the main characters whose fates are likewise detailed. The film ends with a shot of Belushi, who plays the swinish Bulkarski, who is now a U.S. Senator. Thus, does *Animal House* suggest to the viewer who has seen *American Graffiti* a twist on the nostalgic sentiment, and some distancing from it perhaps. Yet *Animal House* is not transcendent of its own nostalgia. Instead, it paves the way for an ideological exploitation of nostalgia. In victimizing the image of women, it points to movies in a similar vein which disguise reactionary social attitudes in the fictional robes of nostalgia such as *Porky's* I, II, and III.

The *Lords of Flatbush*, a low budget production, is, at once, both the most stylized and the most naturalistic film representation of the fifties. As one critic has written, the film clearly established a distinctive 1950s aesthetic.[29] Unlike the other films which have been discussed so far, *The Lords of Flatbush* is set within a lower socioeconomic milieu. Moreover, the community in which the action occurs is distinctively ethnic, although this fact is dramatized only in the last sequence, when the wedding scenes bear evidence of an Italian-American characterization.

The milieu in *The Lords of Flatbush* is urban rather than small-townish. The movie, accordingly, is pitched fictionally to rougher circumstances and to a closer and harsher look at genuine problems of adolescence. Yet, essentially *The Lords* begins with the high school classroom sequence that sets a mood of adolescent fun, and generally portrays the sense of comradeship, both for teenage boys and girls, as pleasant and loyal. There is romance and dating; there are adolescent one-liners and pranks; there are chats at the neighborhood hangout; the adventure of stealing a car and going for a joyride. But there is also Fran's teenage pregnancy and the subsequent marriage, forced—though met with a kind of grudging acceptance rather than with active resistance that ends the film. It is this reality, this dramatic exploring of the consequences of teenage sexuality and the mores of the time and place that focuses this film. *The Lords of Flatbush* affords a special kind of perspective on the complacency of the fifties. The situation is handled with a minimum of sentiment or emotionalism. The film succeeds in evoking naturalistic elements while, at the same time, offering such a stylized characterization of the 1950s.

The Lords of Flatbush captures a dimension of the experience of that decade. While it is stylized and formalized, and while it exploits a number of conventions common to "teen movies," it can be cited favorably for its aspects of psychological and sociological accuracy. The working-class and lower-middle-class milieu of Flatbush is conveyed in a way harking back to the classic movie version of life in its everyday Brooklyn core that was presented in one of the most surprising and pervasive movie hits of the mid-1950s, *Marty*.

The atmosphere of *The Lords* might be described as bittersweet. And if such a term is appropriate here, then it must be added that bittersweet meshes well descriptively with the notion of nostalgia in general. For nostalgia is more complex than being simply "memory without the pain." Nostalgia, if we reflect upon the feeling, may cause us to wonder if its mechanisms point invariably toward a genuine attempt at inquiry into where we have come from. Nostalgia evokes an emphasis on continuity insofar as it poses this question at all. Even those forms of nostalgia which seem most innocuous may be posing this very issue at some level of consciousness.

So far we have been discussing a cluster of films produced during the 1970s which refer to the fifties. But to gain greater insight we must describe their temporal setting even more precisely. The period evoked in these nostalgia movies is generally from about 1955 (the emergence of rock music) to 1963 (the assassination of President Kennedy). Even in this simple description of the time frame we recognize the merging of a cultural innovation (rock music), which has social overtones (youth identity), but which also is connected, albeit obtusely, with a political event (the assassination in Dallas). By its nature, like any form of memory, nostalgia is linked with a variety of elements—personal, generational, societal, and collective. It is an emotional force that can intertwine with any of a variety of elements. Perhaps this richness of variety in nostalgia exists because it is an especially irrational force.

When experienced by most individuals, nostalgia registers as a relatively mild emotional experience that connects epochs in the past with a sense of pleasure, ease, and excitement that is gone forever. To some degree nostalgia must be related to things as they were. The emotion itself, however, always marks an imaginative "improving of the record." Moreover, nostalgia functions most effectively when aspects of the past can be processed through its prism in a mode of continuity. The nostalgic interest during the 1970s for the images of the late 1950s must have evoked a sense of where one had come from for much of the audience. A significant number of the viewers in the 1970s were people who had experienced the late fifties or the early sixties as children, adolescents, or young adults. Even younger people might have been expected to be able to relate the images of the 1950s to themselves. The cultural and social milieu in which they found themselves would be regarded as the result of a change in American life that began in the 1950s.

Nostalgia functions psychologically either to deny or to smooth out change. A movie of the 1970s that emphatically conveys a sense of what rock music meant to transition in American culture at the end of the 1950s is *The Buddy Holly Story* directed by Steve Rash (1978). *The Buddy Holly Story* stands out among movies which explore and develop the connectedness of rock music to cultural change. Moreover, Steve Rash's film manages to do this with a subtlety and insight not usually associated with Hollywood productions. The narrative of the movie is straightforward, and its progression is from 1956 to that day in 1959 when Buddy Holly died in a plane crash along with fellow entertainers Ritchie Valens and J. C. Richardson. It progresses, too, from a garage in Buddy's hometown, Lubbock, Texas, through Nashville to the music world in New York. The genuine deep structure of progression in the film, however, is in its tracing the range of cultural transformations occurring during those three years of the late 1950s when rock music exploded into American culture.

The term "rock 'n' roll" had originated with Cleveland disc jockey Alan Freed at the beginning of the 1950s. Originally it is maintained rock 'n' roll alluded to the act of having sex and was, perhaps, more accurate descriptively than the commonly used "screwing." While this direct reference of the term rock 'n' roll to sex was lost, by the mid-1950s such music was associated, both by parents [negatively] and by teenagers [positively] with a sensuality that challenged traditional American puritanism. Rock was a social and cultural antecedent to the cultural and sexual "revolution" that came a decade later. As the preacher in *The Buddy Holly Story* warns in his sermon against such music, it is "jungle music," hence referring to its cultural primitivism, sensuous quality, and, not least, to its origins in the so-called "race music" of Blacks in the United States. But, then, as Charles Hardin "Buddy" Holly wryly observes, how could it be "jungle music" if it is being written in a garage in Lubbock, Texas?

Racist attitudes toward rock music become evident in Buddy's disastrous recording session in Nashville. He is called a "nigger lover" and, along with his "nigger music," unceremoniously tossed out by the production bosses. In New York, Buddy and his group, the Crickets, fare better. Indeed, their appearance at the all-Black theater, the Apollo, located in Harlem—in spite of the impresario's apprehensions—is a success.

Buddy Holly's music holds the movie together, to some extent emotionally, but primarily as a focus of his own seriousness, energy, and hard work. For while the rock music of the 1950s might be seen as a source of social unrest and cultural change releasing the libidos of teenagers across the length and breadth of the United States, Buddy Holly is portrayed in the film as a man of extraordinary sweetness and a representative of values which are essentially traditional. He is serious about his music, loving and faithful toward his wife Maria, and respectful of authority. He is a child of the fifties at its best. He holds within himself an enormous potential for challenge to past cultural assumptions and, at the same time, a capacity for preserving certain proprieties, traditions, and civilities. In a way quite different from *American Graffiti*, *The Buddy Holly Story* makes music its subject—rather than its crutch. The sociology of the unique situation represented by Buddy, his wife Maria, and the two other young men in his band, presents an accurate metaphor of the process of cultural and social change which began with the emergence of rock music among American youth.

By contrast, the more esoteric and unconventional world of the Beatniks of the 1950s is portrayed in a movie entitled *Heartbeat*. As a biography of the writer Jack Kerouac this film explores the unconventional lifestyle of Kerouac and his entourage against the backdrop of 1950s conservatism and complacency. In its relatively accurate portrayal of the Beats the movie manages, at its end, to associate many of the avant-garde Beatnik interests with the later fully emergent Hippie culture of the late 1960s. This is done by ending the film with a scene of Kerouac's pal Neal Cassady, who is released from prison where he had been incarcerated on drug charges. The final sequences of *Heartbeat* portray him heading off across America surrounded by the requisite long-haired youths in a battered old bus.

To connect the Hippies with the Beatniks who appear to be their soulmates and predecessors seems accurate historically, although the line of connection is not so direct.[30] At least one historian of thought and culture has done just that, writing that ". . . Jack Kerouac and Allen Ginsberg began the degenerate drift toward porn and pot. Two decades later, Beatniks looked like the gentlest of mystics, not always very good poets but authentic human beings, waiting for God . . . [and] rejoicing in the small and real things of life . . ."[31]

That observation, however, raises the question as to just how to balance the claims of historicity against the interpretation that something is nostalgic. All nostalgia pieces, by dint of being set in the past, relate by definition to the historical. Is all history, then, and all interest in things historical, by the same token, to be considered as tinged with nostalgia? This question is not so easily answered, and is confounded by the issue of distancing. Is it correct to label one interest in the past as objective and analytical by contrasting it to another that is subjective and sentimental? This is what we have become accustomed to doing, and it is precisely this distinction that is at the heart of our dividing "nostalgia" from "history." In spite of attempts over the past two centuries, and especially since the Second World War, to make the study of the past more scientific, it remains the case that any reconstruction of the past will be an amalgam of data (facticity) and interpretation (fiction).[32]

Nostalgia is a specific mood from which the past is perceived. Moreover, nostalgia is ostensibly based on the assumption of originating from within the lived experience of the individual responding to it. Strictly speaking, we cannot be nostalgic about the era of the First World War unless we were alive then. This matter, however, is complex, and its complexity points to the function of fiction itself. Many of us feel a connectedness with aspects of the past which we have experienced vicariously through their fictionalization. History, too, by its narrative structure tends to reinforce the basis of our feeling of connectedness to certain images of the past. If "history" is to be, strictly speaking, differentiated from "nostalgia," we must recognize that perceptions of a historical nature still serve as a basis for nostalgic feelings and yearnings, just as history can be approached from a nostalgic mode.

Another film, also set in 1962, raises problems of distinguishing the nostalgic from the historical. John Lewis Carlino's *The Great Santini* was released in 1980. It portrays a stubborn, macho Marine aviator, "Bull" Meechum played by Robert Duvall, with dramatic emphasis on his relationship to his oldest teenage son. The son is quiet in his resentment toward his father, although he once wishes out loud that there would be a war ". . . so King Kong out there would have something to fight." Later he weeps to his mother after "Bull's" accidental death while on a training flight that he often had wished to have his father dead. The story is developed, along with all the complex of emotions in the tension between father and son against a backdrop of a small southern town in the early 1960s, and the situation of the young man's last year in high school.

From its adolescent perspective *The Great Santini* is a *Bildungsfilm*. From another perspective, however, it is a portrayal of a seriously flawed character in mid-life, whose end is tragic. The interpretation is possible that Bull Meechum is meant to represent a dying breed of old-style hero, but such an interpretation is highly biased, and suspect. Indeed, just how *The Great Santini* relates interpretively to the moment of its setting is an open question. To gain closure on that question requires exploring the movie's associative connections to the era in all their richness.

As portraying a specific epoch in the life of the collectivity, that is, as capturing a time in the life of American society, *Santini* is suggestive, even evocative—but unspecific. As a portrayal of a moment in the life cycle—that is, as a film exploring the tenuous coming of age of an adolescent—and the normal struggle between the generations, *Santini* is clearer. Personal nostalgia anchors itself consistently in adolescence and young adulthood. That period in our experience provides each of us the richest wellspring of materials for the nostalgic imagination.

There are allusions throughout the movie to "Bull" Meechum being a warrior without a war, which a viewer might interpret in connection with Vietnam. Such a response, however, originates in the historical sensibility of the viewer strictly and is not based on anything actually given in the film itself. Essentially it is the personal adolescent element that prevails in this movie. One of the most naturalistic and effective scenes in *The Great Santini* is when "Bull" takes his son to the Officer's Club to celebrate the boy's eighteenth birthday and get him drunk. It is a sequence portrayed with great insight and feeling, which connects well with a basic appeal that is rooted in personal nostalgia.

Still here the argument must wander along the edges of definition and perception. *The Great Santini* does not fulfill the definition of nostalgia as "memory without the pain." But then perhaps this particular film serves notice that the real problem is with the definition itself, not with whether or not *Santini* should be called nostalgic.

Santini certainly can be distinguished from simple nostalgia. Its complexity defines it as a work in which the issue of nostalgia itself is reflected upon. Compare, for example, *The Great Santini* with *American Graffiti*. The weakness in the latter is that Curt's decision as to whether he will accept a college scholarship and go East is not of enough psychological import, as scripted into the narrative, to be magnified into emotional significance. The confrontation between "Bull" Meechum and his son in *The Great Santini*, however, generates precisely this kind of significance because as fiction it generalizes the emotional tension of the father-son relationship and fills the screen for the entire length of the film with it. By being set exclusively in an adolescent's world *American Graffiti* lays bare its fictional materials in a simplistic nostalgia mode. The effectiveness that the movie gains by entering a world of adolescence is compromised by the absence of authentic conflict between the generations in the movie. *The Great Santini* evokes a reflexive form of nostalgia, fraught with greater ambiguity.

In a similar style *The Last Picture Show* (Peter Bogdanovich, 1971) reaches a level of interpretive nostalgia. It is not, however, adolescent-parent emotional tension that focuses the power of this film, but rather its relentless exploration of place. Set in a small West Texas town in the 1950s, the movie, based on a Larry McMurtry novel, portrays a lost way of life. In this backwater place during the Korean war the closing of the last movie house marks the end of an era. While not so intended in McMurtry's original literary conceptualization, as a movie *The Last Picture Show* reflects back interestingly on the decline of Hollywood and the cinema itself. It is, essentially, a sociological interpretation, paralleling an aspect of the modernization of the United States with the concomitant erosion of small-town life. *The Last Picture Show* portrays, however, neither simple nor sweet sentimentality for the past.

While the 1950s is the epoch of greatest nostalgic focus, other epochs and decades have clearly drawn attention in such fictional reconstructions of the moods and moments as well. *They Shoot Horses Don't They?* (1969) and *The Way*

19. Robert Redford, Mia Farrow, and a script based closely on F. Scott Fitzgerald's *The Great Gatsby*: At the box office the 1920s did not register well on the nostalgia meter. Academy of Motion Picture Arts & Sciences

We Were (1974), both directed by Sidney Pollack, are set in the 1930s, as was *Paper Moon* (1973, Peter Bogdanovich). Jack Clayton's filming of *The Great Gatsby*, based on a screenplay by Francis Coppola that clung to the original F. Scott Fitzgerald novel closely, was presented as evoking the ethos of the 1920s. Nonetheless, all four films may still be regarded as nostalgia "façades." Interestingly, *Cabaret*, which was based on a series of stories written in Germany shortly before Hitler came to power, succeeded far more than *Gatsby* at the box office. Berlin on the eve of the Nazi takeover had more appeal than Long Island opulence in the 1920s in this nostalgic instance.

The more direct experience the potential audience for movies in the 1970s and early 1980s might be assumed to have had of a period, such as the 1950s, the more varied, naturalistic, and problematic the nostalgia movies set in that epoch. More "distant"nostalgia movies than those set in the 1920s and 1930s become more elusive. The question opens as to just what is it that their nostalgic mode explores. Moviemakers are aware that in such instances nostalgia as an emotion increasingly must play off a media-made "collective memory" that exists in American culture. Such movies evoke nostalgia insofar as certain things are acknowledged as composing a shared perception. The myths, legends, and images of the late nineteenth-century frontier, perpetuated through various modes and forms, for example, especially in that movie genre called the "Western," form such a widely shared perception which is in no way based on direct experience of it and which is then later referred back to in memory. George R. Hill's *Butch Cassidy and the Sundance Kid* (1971) and *The Sting* (1973) are good examples of this displaced form of nostalgia.

Other films have been predicated on nostalgic appeal rooted even more directly in cinematic traditions of the past. Francis Coppola's *One From the Heart* (1982) attempted to recapture that special mood of the era of the movie musical, much as did Martin Scorsese's *New York, New York* (1977), which added in the big-band era appeal. A direct exploitation of the nostalgic mode was MGM's release of *That's Entertainment* (1976). Composed entirely of sequences from musicals, dating from the early 1930s to about 1960, this compilation film explores the past self-reflectively and exhaustively. By contrast, one of the most subtle explorations of this displaced nostalgia" is found in Louis Malle's *Atlantic City* (1975).

Atlantic City is set in the New Jersey coastal resort in the mid-1970s just as the economic exhilaration brought on by the legalization of casino gambling was sweeping the town. The film is about an ambitious young woman from Saskatchewan, seeking to find her break in life by becoming a casino dealer, who becomes paired with an aging numbers runner. It is in the latter character, played by Burt Lancaster, that the mode of nostalgic characterization is manifested. For Lancaster's role soon becomes a self-positing one in which he acts out an established image of the tough guy. This situation permits the film to become, at one level, an examination of the image of the tough guy, or hood, as that image is established in American culture especially for the films, stories, legends, and lore of the 1930s. *Atlantic City* has numerous nostalgic allusions, one of the most charming of them being Lancaster's comment to a young drug dealer as they walk along the beach: "You should have seen the Atlantic Ocean in the old days; that was some ocean!" *Atlantic City* cleverly weaves a contemporary drama of ambition and illusion into a rich set of connecting links to an image of the past.

More directly and more emphatically Woody Allen's *Zelig* (1983) does the same. *Zelig* explores celebrity and our sense of the past. It is a film made so as to replicate the black-and-white hues of film from the late 1920s, as well as the graininess of the image that characterizes nonfiction footage. *Zelig* exists as a form of interpretive nostalgia that inquires cinematographically into our sense of the past and celebrity, raising questions about the nature of the nostalgic response itself. *The Purple Rose of Cairo* (1985) goes further, though in a different direction, in exploring nostalgia self-reflectively. The idea of the movie-within-a-movie twice over emphasizes this. Set in the 1930s, it does not really challenge its own time frame. In a less direct way, Robert Altman's *Come Back to the Five and Dime, James Dean* (1983) is self-consciously "artsy" enough to draw as much attention to recreating an image of the past as it does to its actual exploring of small-town Texas in the 1950s.

Yet in the film of the early 1980s that was the most successful evocation of the nostalgia theme at the box-office, it cannot be said that anything more than an overt statement toward reflecting upon the phenomenon of nostalgia is given. *The Big Chill*, directed by Lawrence Kasdan, was a very successful box-office draw in 1983. It appeared to sweep the viewership of the "yuppie" element in American society, who are also the film's characters—those successful, affluent professionals in their thirties who are reunited at the time of a friend's suicide. *The Big Chill*, in its concept and central idea, is remarkably similar to John Sayles's *The Return of the Secaucus Seven* (1979). The latter, low-budget feature probed the problem of the youth generation of the 1960s and the loss of their vision and inspiration of the "New" Left.

By the same token *The Big Chill* portrays six college friends whose conventional successes (careers in law, medicine, journalism, the sporting goods business, and television acting, as well as marriage to a successful businessman) are juxtaposed against the seventh member of the group who is leading a haphazard existence. Played by William Hurt, he has achieved his most notable success in preserving at least the appearance of being a dropout from the establishment society. He descends upon South Carolina where the funeral is taking place, driving a battered Porsche, and heavily armed with a range of various controlled substances. Eventually, he has a run-in with the local police, but at the end of the weekend he has decided to stay a spell and settle into the position of old friend Alex, the one who had committed suicide.

The Big Chill draws much of its emotional sustenance and social commentary through the subtext of a music sound track consisting of late sixties rock hits. The strains of Aretha Franklin, B.B. King, and the Band underwrite much of the more "serious" intent in the movie. Like *Save The Tiger*, *The Big Chill* makes reference to the past and evokes nostalgia only in the sound track or in the dialogue, not visually. We never see—as we could in a flashback—any of the shared past of the group when they were university students together at the end of the sixties. The only visual evocation of the past, in fact, is a clipping from a university newspaper. But whereas *Save The Tiger* attempts to question self-reflectively the process of nostalgia itself, *The Big Chill* does not. Moreover, the latter film is extraordinarily affirmative about a group of young men and women whose relationship to their past ideas and commitments is extremely distorted.

The Big Chill builds dramatically toward the final major dramatic sequence in which the night is filled with sex. The Atlanta attorney, hoping to become pregnant, is sent off to bed down with the "good stock" husband of her close friend. Dull Richard's frustrated wife (played by JoBeth Williams) romps passionately on the lawn with an old college chum now turned TV star. Even the erstwhile holdout, the dropout played by William Hurt, goes off with the dead friend's girlfriend Chloe, even though, as a result of wounds he suffered in Vietnam, "he can't do anything."

This series of sexual encounters—reaffirming an old emotional attraction; being an act of one woman's generosity toward another; having one friend and soulmate fill the romantic/emotional obligations of another—is a dramatic visual enactment of the ethos of the late sixties counterculture itself. For while that counterculture movement flirted with political protest—as focused narrowly on

20. *The Big Chill*: Late 1960s revolutionaries from the University of Michigan reunite on a South Carolina sofa in the early 1980s. Academy of Motion Picture Arts & Sciences

opposition to U.S. military actions in Vietnam—it was essentially lacking in political ideology. Its true inspiration was an impetus to undo many of the standard American puritan values, through a liberalization of sexual mores, an embrace of more mass and popular culture forms, and a tolerance for drugs.[33] Especially in the area of challenging and altering sexual mores the counterculture impulses of the university generation of the late sixties had their impact on American life and culture, and perhaps a lasting one.[34] Thus, the crescendo of sexuality in the sequence that leads to a kind of dramatic resolution in *The Big Chill* is altogether appropriate. For the generation portrayed did achieve a certain breakthrough in sexual directness, spontaneity, and solidarity, all of which are represented in that sequence. Whether they are, hence, more loving, happier, and more satisfied is an entirely independent issue. In regard to what it portrays the film is historically accurate; whether it intends to be or not cannot be answered. Otherwise, *The Big Chill* is at pains to justify all tendencies toward narcissism, self-centeredness, and smugness. The rejection of any position even resembling political commitment or engagement is sustained.

> What is remarkable about it is that two years, now, after its release, successful young professionals who went to college during the sixties still talk about *The Big Chill*. A reference to its title serves as a reference to a conversation they might have had, or had wanted to have but probably didn't. Among other things it indicates that the evasions of the film are widespread evasions. . . ."[35]

The late sixties produced a spasm in U.S. society. Some observers, both within the youthful counterculture and outside of it mistook a certain malaise about the conduct of the Vietnam war as reflecting a deep political commitment to the ideas of the "New Left." This, however, is far from the truth. The political culture of the United States remained in this period as it has essentially been since the end of World War Two—low on ideological definition, based on consensus within the two established political parties, and characterized by staggering levels of nonparticipation. In 1972, for example, when youthful interest in politics might have been considered high, only 12 percent of persons under age 26 who were eligible to do so voted in the Nixon-McGovern presidential race.[36]

Critics of the antiwar movement may have been correct in citing much of the draft resistance as originating in the self-centered and self-protective responses of young people who did not want to be sent to combat in Vietnam. But the conclusions of those critics, to the point that this discredited the antiwar movement were incorrect. The simple truth was that most young Americans *neither* protested the war *nor* served in the military during it.

> Contrary to the impression given by movies like *Coming Home*. . . . America was not then divided between one army of soldiers blindly and helplessly shipped to Vietnam and another army of committed war resisters back home. The largest army dodged both confrontations.[37]

The nostalgia that became apparent in American-produced movies, and in other cultural forms as well, was geared not only to recapturing a sense of lost innocence, but also to retrieving feelings of self-importance and grandeur which were felt to have been lost. The collective dilemma of post-Vietnam and post-Watergate America, in fact, meshed psychologically with the post-counterculture bursting of the bubble of energy for change that had emerged among younger people in America at the end of the 1960s.

During the height of the counterculture the nostalgic element had been present in the protest movement itself in the late sixties:

> The counterculture response [of the late sixties] to an America without frontiers . . .
> despite their insistence that the frontier's closing had rendered traditional lifestyles
> and institutions obsolete . . . represented a "reactionary nostalgia" whose indi-
> vidualistic hedonism undercut the Left's programmatic calls for cooperative
> sacrifice.[38]

At the time, the central ethos of Dennis Hopper's and Peter Fonda's film *Easy Rider* (1969) was recognized by some as cast in a mode of romantic retreat and nostalgia. Many pedestrian critics found the movie to be revolutionary in both style and content, but no better an authority than French filmmaker Jean-Luc Godard commented:

> The movie is like a blackboard. A revolutionary movie can show how the arms
> struggle may be done. *Easy Rider* is not at all a film of this order. Although it is highly
> tendentious, it wears the mask of disengagement; its atmosphere, in fact, is that of a
> pastoral.[39]

The baby boomers, who produced in the late 1960s what appeared to be a broad cultural revolt against society, seemed increasingly to find a nostalgic absorption in the recent past as the focus of their cultural identity. "The television and movie culture of the 1950s had surrounded them with heroic portrayals of the Old West and World War II, while their parents had raised them in placid suburbs."[40] While this audience seemingly rejected these old myths, they demanded new ones—often based on explorations of the 1950s themselves. The World War Two movie practically disappeared at the beginning of the 1970s. Even though some critics felt that the last of such films were "retreats from idealized concepts and romantic myths," as in *Tora! Tora! Tora!* and *Patton*,[41] the movies themselves were ambivalently shifting certain perspectives on heroism rather than laying such adulation to rest. The Western, a genre which seemed to suddenly vanish in the late 1960s, was revived with the so-called "Vietnam Western."

> The Vietnam or antiwestern, epitomized by Ralph Nelson's *Soldier Blue* (1970) and
> Arthur Penn's *Little Big Man* (1971), portrayed the settling of the frontier as a
> succession of My Lai's. . . . The Vietnam western was a short-lived genre; antimyth

has no substance beyond the myth it is consuming. When it was gone, the classic western, at least the central form in which the Indian plays the role of the Other, was gone with it.[42]

This kind of turning a genre and its myth on its head was time-specific. It came and went quickly. More lasting was a shift in general conceptualizing of movie characters. A new type of star flourished.

> The period's growing self-consciousness about the perceived American myths also promoted a new kind of star, who in Classic Hollywood might have operated only in the margins of straight genre movies. Elliott Gould, Walter Matthau, Dustin Hoffmann, Al Pacino, Robert De Niro, Woody Allen, Gene Wilder, Gene Hackman, Mel Brooks, Jack Nicholson, Jane Fonda, Goldie Hawn, and Jill Clayburgh were all essentially character actors whose self-reflexive, self-doubting pesonae contrasted sharply with the confident, natural imperturbability of Cooper, Grant, Gable, and Wayne.[43]

Nostalgia in movies was at its height in the 1970s. This time-frame of its ascendancy points to its identification with the responses of many in a specific generation of Americans who came of age at the end of the 1960s. When the edifice of myth, legend, and genre that Hollywood had established through decades—from the 1920s to the mid-1960s—crumbled, a new kind of mythos gained enormous appeal.

On the other hand, nostalgia has an inevitable draw upon persons in an advanced civilization. "Instead of directing cultural and individual energies toward relating the self to its larger context, the culture of manager and therapist urges a strenuous effort to make our particular segment of life a small world of its own."[44] Insofar as contemporary culture is one dominated by the managerial mentality and the therapeutic mode, nostalgia as a cultural formation may be considered especially appropriate to it. The essence of the nostalgic remains linked to the individual's *feeling* as if he or she has recaptured a moment or something that is part of his or her past. Even when the nostalgia mode is "social" or "collective," the response to it is predicated on this type of personal identification with the material. This, indeed, is the central way in which the "nostalgic" may be distinguished from the "historical." Whereas the latter invites one to *think* about the past, the former provokes one to *feel* about it. To many observers this distinction is clearly one of a superior mode of awareness, the historical, being compared to an inferior one, nostalgia. Yet, to maintain this is an intellectual conceit.

The burst of nostalgia in Hollywood movies was predicated by the coming of age of the "baby boom" generation in the late 1960s. The ambivalence that was betokened by the late 1960s became apparent through the nostalgic. It may disappear soon, or it might remain central in American culture for some time to come. The counterculture and youth protest movements of the late 1960s produced a rupture in contemporary culture deep enough to prompt parts of that culture to seek to recapture continuity and wholeness through the devices of nostalgia. By the mid-1980s a central cultural problem in the United States remained how the culture as a whole would come to terms with the late sixties. There is evidence of many people attempting or hoping to turn back everything that that epoch meant; there is counterevidence of individuals trying to hold onto that moment in time as evinced in people who have "stuck with the sixties"; there is evidence of people who continue to be caught up in the mentality of the late 1960s; there is evidence of trying, continually, on both sides of the ideological divide, to bring the era of the late sixties to a close.

FIVE

Conclusion

The recapturing of the past, the persistence of memory, the reality of the photographic image: The dialectic between what J. Dudley Andrew has called the "naked power of the mechanically recorded image" and the "learned power of artistic control over such images"[1]—all the films discussed in this book have been involved in these values.

> . . . Inasmuch as the other art forms are not constituted of reality itself, they create metaphors of reality. But photography being itself the reality or the equivalent thereof, can use its own reality as a metaphor for ideas and abstractions. . . .[2]

The personal snapshot is a trigger of nostalgia. One might say that a motive of personal photography, albeit often a subconscious one, is the desire to establish a body of data which can be used at a future date to stimulate recollection, to evoke past feelings, and to engender moods of nostalgia. The notion of preserving a past image in its authenticity was heightened by the advance from still to moving pictures.

Some observers maintain that the basic premise of the photographic is itself nostalgic. One could extend this argument by saying that since the motion picture is based on photographic principles, the nature of the movie is also basically nostalgic.

The relationship of movies to the past, and, by extension, of the cinema to historiography is complex. Movies are not read; they are experienced. When we read we must follow a linear progression on the page. We encounter words, sentences, and paragraphs sequentially in a progression. There is no way around this, even if certain attempts have been made in this century (notably in "stream of consciousness" literature and in experimental writing) to break down or break through this systematization. In reading a narrative we experience, perhaps, a sentence or two of description, a thought presented as an interior monologue, another line of description, then maybe the expression of a conscious thought or comment, more description and so on. Without going into any of the complexities of writing style or the author's point of view, we can recognize that the movie, even though it is most often a narrative of some sort, differs distinctively from the reading experience. The movie image is layered. It exists in depth. In the frame we see action, hear dialogue, and grasp the ambiance, setting, or mood *all at once.* None of this is unfolded, as in writing, but rather is infolded, contained within itself. Often when we see a movie that is an adaptation from a literary work we are disturbed.

We may have read a novel for example, and in doing so, we might have formed an image of the protagonist in our mind's eye. When we view a movie based on that novel, we encounter that protagonist as a given. Our imaginations have nothing left to do by way of "creating" an image of his or her physical being. For many of us this experience is disconcerting. When we encounter a movie adaptation of a work that is particularly dear to us and which portrays a character (or characters) toward whom we feel a deep and intimate emotional closeness that disconcertedness may be especially strong.

In a movie what is portrayed is given directly and experientially (rather than imaginatively). Some maintain that this renders a movie into an inferior form, arguing that our imaginative faculties are not involved in the same way when we see a movie as when we read a book. In part, this is unarguably true—our imaginations are not engaged "in the same way" by the movie experience. They are engaged nonetheless and, I would argue, in ways which are not *inferior* to the reading experience.

The nature of the moving visual image differs greatly from the image created by the word. A word can be modified many times over. We might say the "large, black, rectangular table with gold relief on each corner," for example. And we might continue, elaborating on detail, springing toward the poetic, or coming to talk of function and practicality. But a table on the screen in a movie is that table only—that one table, lit in a special way, concrete as an object, with someone standing next to it. The elaborations upon it are limited by the photographic eye of the camera lens.

For these very reasons movies are especially able to recreate epochs and atmospheres. Motion pictures record the details of verisimilitude while simultaneously making possible the rearrangement of those visions of "reality" through editing. The power of the motion picture is its evocative strength—its capacity to make present an environment, an atmosphere, or an era. Not all films exploit this power by any means. Some ignore it completely; others neglect or fail to nourish it. Still, this ability seems widely acknowledged, if not always recognized by even the most conventional and uninspiring filmmakers.

As the French scholar Pierre Sorlin has noted: "Before the television era—that is, before the middle of the century—there were very few films directly concerned with questions of the day."[3] The past, even if it is the recent past, has been a stable focus of moviemaking. Sorlin's observation is descriptively correct. His choice of wording, referring to the "television era," may mislead, however. The emphasis on contemporary subjects emerged most forcefully with the Italian Neo-Realist directors right at the end of World War Two. They were not responding to the pressures or competition of television:

> Neo Realism was not an aesthetics. . . . Neo Realism was "an ethics of an aesthetics."
> It was the answer of a generation of filmmakers to the question. . . . Shall we ever

have a culture capable of protecting people against suffering instead of just comforting them.[4]

The impetus to more contemporary settings in the cinema is generational. We can connect it primarily to a shared response to the Second World War and its aftermath. That response was likely contingent upon a movement toward contemporary concerns as had occurred in the American cinema during wartime itself. The real shift appears to have come, however, among a generation of Europeans who were forced subsequently to assess the physical and spiritual wreckage brought upon the Continent by the war itself.

The cinema had witnessed realist impulses before: the "New Objectivity" which included a spate of proletarian features made in Germany at the end of the 1920s, or the "Social Realism" of certain French directors during the 1930s, of whom the most prominent was Jean Renoir. Even the Hollywood studios were able to generate some genre films in the direction of a realistic aesthetic during the era of the Depression. Yet it was in Italian Neo-Realism at the end of the Second World War that realism in the cinema became aligned with a moral imperative. The great breakthrough in the cinema in Western Europe that came at the end of the 1950s resulted from renewed attempts to carry out Neo-Realism's essential, original goal.

This moral imperative was felt generationally, in the first instance by many of the *creators* of film fiction. In the long run, however, it was the generational imperative of the *audience* for movies that provided an ambiance in which certain film genres and styles, as well as a certain artistic and ideological independence could flourish. This was the generation that came to age in Europe at the end of the 1950s. They sought satisfaction for their own curiosity; they sought an answer to the shortcomings of their parents' generation; or, at least, they sought to explore those shortcomings more honestly. Their attachment to realism was less literal and aesthetic than it was authentic and existential. The need was to penetrate beneath the surface. This is what all these works share in common. The landmark movies produced at this time, typified by *Hiroshima, mon amour* in France, *We Prodigies* and *The Bridge* in West Germany, Antonioni's triology (*The Adventure, The Night,* and *Eclipse*) and Fellini's *8 ½* in Italy all speak to a particular moment and to a specific audience. Indeed, these films were prominent among those movies which heralded the appearance of a particular kind of audience internationally. This audience was composed of young men and women, normally under thirty years old, often studying at a university or just concluding their studies, predominantly urban, and comfortably middle-class (if not members of the even more affluent upper middle classes). Their political ideology was leftist; their social and cultural views were progressive; in some instances, local conditions dictated that this leftist tendency might be radicalized.

This audience was every bit as identifiable as the different youthful audience that Hollywood began catering to assiduously by the end of the 1960s. When the Vietnam era ended, and the counterculture protest subsided, the courting of youth continued. What came of this was the Hollywood entertainment vehicles—combining special effects, spectacle, and action—which were churned out during the 1970s. Such Hollywood production ". . . may be characterized as formally extraordinarily sophisticated [and] at the same time intellectually preadolescent."[5]

Yet in both instances one must recognize a fundamental verity. The production process was responding to the perceived tastes of clusters within the audience. The European films appear to emphasize greater interiority, more thematic sophistication, more articulate plots, and might be called more "cerebral." They are paced so that reflection on the action in them gives way to contemplation. Yet these are only generalizations, and, as such, are highly limited in their value. Some commentators talk as if such distinctions in movie-type were definitive. Claims are even made that "movies" are an American phenomenon, whereas in Europe "film" is produced.[6] The truth is far more complex. Scant evidence supports the notion that such a distinction existed before the Second World War. Perceptible differences in style and genre may be typified with some accuracy, but such distinctions are hardly definitive. Production on both sides of the Atlantic is diverse.

The collective experience of the United States since 1945 was different enough from that of Western Europe to account for the fact that little change or innovation registered at the end of the 1950s in Hollywood. Such change and innovation was widespread across Europe, including Eastern Europe.

> In literature, *l'ecole du regard*, [the school of looking] with its intention "to let the reader see" via the impassive surfaces of the *nouveau roman* [new novel] was fighting its first battle. Its representatives such as Alain Robbe-Grillet, Michel Butor, and Le Clézio were examining the phenomenal world as it exists apart from the human mind, apart from all human influence and manipulation. In Poland, a new generation of filmmakers established itself, and the Czechs were soon to follow. In Italy, by contrast, it was the "old ones," the representatives of the previous period, who were to achieve the decisive breakthrough.[7]

While Hollywood did not experience significant new directions at the end of the 1950s, such apparent changes did occur late in the 1960s. Nonetheless, the cultural atmosphere which had come to prevail by then in the United States had antecedents which dated back to the late 1950s and the beginning of the 1960s.

> . . .[President John F.] Kennedy (1960–1963) had already catalyzed youthful desire for change that was itself a political power, as yet only dimly recognized, destined to transform the nation later in the decade. Before Kennedy gave it mainstream political meaning, that emerging force had been foreshadowed only in the alienated sullenness of a James Dean, the anarchic sensuality of an Elvis Presley, the restless adventuring of a Jack Kerouac.[8]

We should not be concerned that an apparent redirection in film culture in the United States occurred nearly a decade after it did so in Western Europe. This time gap of seven or eight years was of little real significance. Moreover, a comparative analysis hardly demands exact parallels. The differences are extremely informative.

If we look for explanations of either phenomenon, on the surface the American case may seem easier to explain. The coming of age of the "baby boom" generation, coupled with a series of collective calamities beginning with the widespread criticism of U.S. military involvement in Vietnam, produced in audiences evidence of a demand for nostalgic escapism. Nostalgia movies hardly dominated the entire scope of Hollywood's production. But the appearance of this genre, and its being sustained for nearly two decades points to its appropriateness for the shared mentality of a substantial portion of the audience.

For Western Europe, even given the differences between the three nations we have examined, the end of the fifties marked a distinct epoch of accelerating change in the cinema. The existentialist force that was central to a philosophic repositioning after the Second World War had matured. Prosperity had been reestablished throughout Western Europe. The era of mass terror, which began in the mid-1930s under Stalin, only to be followed closely by Hitler's even more terrifying murder spree, and which had continued to threaten both Western and Eastern Europe, appeared at an end. Khrushchev's denunciation of Stalin in 1956 brought a final, verbal close to it. Beyond these possibilities it appears, however, that the new directions in European cinema at the end of the 1950s were predicated on the appearance of an audience of young men and women who felt a need to break with the past, while at the same time coming to terms with it. On this very terrain the aesthetic and cultural nature of the motion picture enables that medium to meet such desires with particular efficacy.

These youthful European movie goers *circa* 1958–1962 were the sons and daughters of Nazi Germany, Fascist Italy, and Occupied France. By the late 1960s in the United States dilemmas posed by the Vietnam war were being conceived publicly for Americans as morally equivalent to those which were the legacy of World War Two for Europeans. The moral dilemmas of "total" war against civilian populations and of the genocidal practices which had characterized the Second World War offered a basis of comparison for many Americans to look at the U.S.'s military intervention in the Vietnam conflict. Those who promulgated or executed U.S. policy, as well as those who abided these policies by not protesting them, were labeled "fascists" with scant regard for the precise historical or ideological meaning of the word. Moreover, generalized patterns of adjustment in contemporary society could be pointed to as contributing to the impulse toward nostalgia. Throughout human history no area on earth has experienced as rapid development and change as has North America during the last two centuries. Only in the late 1960s did significant numbers of U.S. citizens begin to become critically aware of some of the negative impacts of this rapid development on the natural environment and ecology of the United States.

There are long-term patterns in American culture, as well as immediate precipitating factors, which produced an environment in which receptivity to the nostalgic mode flourished. It must be emphasized that the bent to nostalgia, which some might think to be a characteristic of right wing or reactionary political elements, was not necessarily that at all. A substantial impetus toward the nostalgic manifested itself in the counterculture protesters in the late 1960s who saw themselves as struggling for preservation of environmental natural resources, and so on. No political faction or political agenda has a corner on nostalgia.

Much in the same way no particular political environment guarantees specific innovations in moviemaking. For example, the "New" German Cinema, did not mark a significant redirection in treatment of the Third Reich era in feature-length movies in the late 1970s. An increasingly sensitized leftist movement, responding indirectly to increased antiterrorist measures by the government in Bonn, failed to establish a new consciousness from which filmmakers explore cinematographically the nature of the Nazi legacy in new ways. The high point for West German fictional films set in the Third Reich actually occurred at the end of the 1950s when the conservative political consensus in the Federal Republic was at its pinnacle.

Positing causal links between epochs, public events, and motion picture content and style may be provocative. To do so, however, is speculative. Cultural history does not yield many causal links. To say so may discourage some students of culture and outrage others. But acknowledging this truth opens up the possibility of finding other exciting ways of seeing oblique connections.

Contemporary culture is formed by a constant, complicated dynamic between national traditions and events, generational demands and tastes, and the increasing internationalization of cultural experience through the electronic media. Movie theaters do not do the business they once did, but the transformation of the cinema from mass entertainment to a more specialized form of popular cultural expression does not diminish the social and cultural significance of the medium. The visual/audio work of fiction that we call the movie has become, simultaneously, more varied and more specialized during the last forty years. The potential for expression of complex themes has grown in filmmaking as has the range of convoluted tastes to which movies appeal.

NOTES

The Notes include discursive and explanatory comments which illuminate certain passages in the text, as well as citations. References to reports or commentaries which do not carry a specific author's name or by-line are listed by publication name and date only. For short articles which would be easily located by reference to publication name and date, page numbers have been omitted.

Introduction

1. Henry Ebel has written with special vigor on this topic in various issues of the *Journal of Psychohistory: History of Childhood Quarterly* dating back to 1974. In particular, he has talked about the unique "fantasy partner" that each modern man or woman has in the national state.

2. George Huaco, *The Sociology of Film Art* (New York: Basic Books, 1965), pp. 212, 213.

3. Herbert Gans, *Popular Culture and High Culture: An Analysis and Evaluation of Taste* (New York: Basic Books, 1974), especially pp. 69 ff.

4. The audience for erotic, or x-rated, films, for example, clearly transcends national boundaries. The entire genre of such films would be acknowledged as not being defined by national taste, but by gender (i.e., male) taste. More broadly, we recognize that increasingly the boundaries of national culture are eroding due to the electronic media and modes of culture dissemination. This, moreover, is occurring nearly as quickly in societies which may seek officially to discourage such dissemination (Eastern Europe, Third World nations).

5. Thomas Schatz, *Old Hollywood/New Hollywood: Ritual, Art, and Industry* (Ann Arbor, Mich.: UMI Research Press, 1983), p. 183.

6. Robert Philip Kolker, *A Cinema of Loneliness* (New York: Oxford Univ. Press, 1980), pp. 12, 13.

7. See Paul Monaco, *Cinema and Society: France and Germany During the Twenties* (New York, Oxford, Amsterdam: Elsevier Publ., 1976). The book offers a discussion of the public meaning of popular films in both countries during an age when films were produced for the broadest of mass audiences.

1 Realism, Italian Style

1. Dante Germino & Stefano Passigli, *The Government and Politics of Contemporary Italy* (New York, Evanston, & London: Harper & Row, 1969), pp. 191–193.

2. Mira Liehm, *Passion and Defiance: Film in Italy From 1942 to the Present* (Berkeley, Los Angeles & London: Univ. of California Press, 1984), p. 123.

3. J. Dudley Andrew, *The Major Film Theories: An Introduction* (London, Oxford, & New York: Oxford Univ. Press, 1976), p. 143.

4. Liehm, *Passion and Defiance*, p. 135.

5. Helga Koppel, *Film in Italien, Italien in Film* (Berlin: Henschelverlag, 1970), p. 8.

6. For example, Richard Grunberger, *The Social History Of The Third Reich* (London: Weidenfeld and Nicolson, 1971), offers this interpretation of Nazism.

7. See Elaine Mancini, *Struggles of the Italian Film Industry During Fascism, 1930–1935* (Ann Arbor: UMI Research Press, 1985), pp. 119 ff.

8. George Huaco, *The Sociology of Film Art* (New York: Basic Books, 1965); Huaco concentrates his study on a more limited list of films, pp. 10, 11.

9. Koppel, *Film in Italien*, pp. 13, 14.

10. Huaco, *The Sociology of Film Art*, pp. 15, 16.

11. Cesare Zavattini, *Zavattini: Sequences From a Cinematic Life*, tr. by William Weaver (Englewood Cliffs, N.J.: Prentice-Hall, 1970), p. 9.

12. Italo Calvino, *The Path to The Nest of Spiders*, tr. by William Weaver (New York: Ecco Press, 1976), pp. v, vi.

13. François Debreczeni, "Origines et evolution du Neo-Réalisme," in *Etudes Cinématographiques*, (2ème trimestre, 1964), pp. 20–54.

14. The late nineteenth century saw a great wave of melodrama on the Italian stage which fed into the activities of a populist kind of theater that blended with vaudeville. Such Italian melodrama was performed commonly in the first three decades of this century in Italo-American communities.

15. Guido Aristarco, "Les quatre phases du cinéma italien de l'après-guerre," in *Cinéma '61*, no. 56, (March, 1961).

16. Huaco, *The Sociology of Film Art*, section on Soviet Expressive Realism, pp. 95–154.

17. Felix A. Morilon, O.P., "The Philosophical Basis of Neo-Realism," in *Springtime in Italy: A Reader on Neo-Realism*, ed. by David Overby (London: Talisman Books, 1978), pp. 115–124.

18. Huaco, *The Sociology of Film Art*, pp. 175–176; 182–183; 203–206.

19. David Overby, ed., *Springtime in Italy; A Reader on Neo-Realism* (London: Talisman Books, 1978), introduction.

20. Koppel, *Film in Italien*, p. 84.

21. Overby, ed., *Springtime in Italy*, introduction.

22. B. Singerman, "Gorizon neo-realizma," *Iskusstvo Kino*, no. 4 (Moscow, 1958).

23. As quoted in Overby, *Springtime in Italy*, introduction.

24. Ian Cameron and Robin Wood, *Antonioni* (New York: Frederick Praeger, 1968), p. 43.

25. Liehm, *Passion and Defiance*, p. 115; for decades Fellini fought with Alberto Lattuada over who should claim directorial credit for the film. Since he gets only half-credit, he called his autobiographical exploration of the filmmaker's artistic dilemma *8 1/2*.

26. The "fumetti" are books of actual photographs that resemble the drawn comic books with which Americans are acquainted. These creations of Italian popular culture might be considered akin to the movies because they are based on actual photographs.

27. Liehm, *Passion and Defiance*, p. 117.

28. André Bazin, "On the Other Side of Neo-Realism," in *Federico Fellini*, ed. by Gilbert Salachas, tr. by Rosalie Siegal (New York: Crown Publ., 1969), pp. 178–179.

29. Ibid., p. 179. The kind of phenomenological understanding Bazin is pointing to may best be illustrated in the developed aesthetic theory advanced by Robert Plant Armstrong in *The Affecting Presence* (Champaign/Urbana: Univ. of Illinois Press, 1971) and *Wellspring* (Berkeley: Univ. of California Press, 1976).

30. Peter Bondanella, *Federico Fellini: Essays in Criticism* (London, Oxford, New York: Oxford Univ. Press, 1978), p. 9.

31. Stuart Rosenthal, *The Cinema of Federico Fellini* (Cranbury, N.Y.: A.S. Barnes, 1976), pp. 15–16.

32. Ibid., p. 16.

33. Renzo Renzi, "The Courage to be Self-Destructive," in *Federico Fellini*, ed. by Gilbert Salachas, tr. by Rosalie Siegal (New York: Crown Publ., 1969), p. 195.

34. Ibid., p. 189.

35. Liehm, *Passion and Defiance*, p. 177.

36. Ibid.

37. Cameron and Wood, *Antonioni*, p. 111.

38. See Sergei M. Eisenstein, *Notes of a Film Director*, tr. by X. Danko (Moscow: Foreign Languages Publ. House, 1949), as well his two famous books on film theory: *Film Form: Essays in Film Theory*, tr. by Jay Leyda (New York: Harcourt, Brace, & Co., 1949) and *The Film Sense*, tr. by Jay Leyda (New York: Harcourt, Brace, 1942).

39. See André Bazin, *What is Cinema?* tr. by Hugh Gray (Berkeley: Univ. of California Press, 1967) and *What is Cinema? Volume II*, tr. by Hugh Gray, Berkeley: Univ. of California Press, 1971. Also, Siegfried Kracauer, *Theory of Film: The Redemption of Physical Reality* (London, Oxford, New York: Oxford Univ. Press, 1960).

40. Siegfried Kracauer, *Theory of Film: The Redemption of Physical Reality*, p. 212.

41. Ibid.

42. Nietzsche first expounded the view that western man had gotten rid of the need for God through the triumphs of modern science, but still clung desperately to pre-scientific beliefs and values in *The Genealogy of Morals* (1874). Nietzsche saw this contradiction pushing humanity toward the brink of nihilism, and Antonioni's films often seem to be exploring this very theme.

43. Phenomenology promotes the idea of an observer "bracketing out" all preconceived perspectives on any phenomenon, and, hence, being able to encounter it in such a manner as to penetrate through to its essence. One might say that objectivity, in the phenomenological mode, is a matter of authenticity of relationship between subject and object, rather than a product of analysis.

44. Liehm, *Passion and Defiance*, p. 301.

45. Ibid., p. 302.

46. Ibid., pp. 299, 300.

47. Nietzsche's famed observation was expressed in his parable of the madman who entered the town square proclaiming that God was dead—and that western man had killed him. This was a stunning interpretation in cultural history on Nietzsche's part.

48. An existential point-of-view in the cinema would mandate the most authentic possible shot, and perhaps ideas of direct cinema come closest to this goal. Formalistic intervention in the filmmaking process would be limited. Hence, an emphasis on the long shot, a reduction in the amount of editing, and a naturalism that captured silence as much as filling the sound track with sound would conform as cinematic style with the existentialist viewpoint. Of all directors, Antonioni's approach to filmmaking best conforms to these tendencies.

49. Germino and Passigli, *The Government and Politics of Contemporary Italy*, pp. 84 ff.

50. Franz Brentano, "The Distinction Between Mental and Physical Phenomena," in Roderick M. Chisholm, ed., *Realism and the Background of Phenomenology* (New York: The Free Press, 1960), p. 42.

2   The First Crest of the New Wave

1. After 1945, Christian-Democratic parties were founded both in Italy and in West Germany where traditional conservatives often seemed discredited morally by their (possible) association with the right-wing excesses of fascism and Nazism. In France, the M.R.P. was similar. All of these parties might be seen as coalitions of conservative bodies, hence rallying these forces under a single banner rather than dispersing their strength as had been the case before World War Two.

2. Michel Crozier, "France's Cultural Anxieties Under Gaullism: The Cultural Revolution Revisited," in *The Impact of the Fifth Republic on France*, ed. by William G. Andrews and Stanley Hoffman (Albany: SUNY Press, 1981), p. 81.

3. Structuralism provides a basic philosophical premise from which to approach the analysis and understanding of a great variety of phenomena. It might be said that the

structuralist imperative was first advanced in the field of linguistics, and, moreover, that structuralism has always had definite links to anthropology. Structuralism originated in the French academic and philosophical establishment.

4. The "New Wave" heralded the beginning of the markedly increased respectability of the cinema as art, even in the United States. The variety of films from Europe which found increasingly positive responses from intellectual and cultural elites was stimulated most notably by the New Wave at the beginning of the 1960s. The cultural respectability of motion pictures had to come into the U.S. from abroad for American denizens of culture and the intelligentsia to be able to take the medium seriously.

5. The *auteur* theory has been most extensively promoted in the United States by the New York critic Andrew Sarris. In spite of being French in origin, the concept itself seems particularly apt to American culture, which is so caught up in the cult of personality and celebrity.

6. J. Dudley Andrew, *The Major Film Theories: An Introduction* (London, Oxford, New York: Oxford Univ. Press, 1976), p. 4. Andrew points out that the so-called *auteur* theory is, more accurately, a "critical method."

7. James Monaco, *The New Wave* (London, Oxford, New York, 1976), p. 5.

8. See Herbert Marshall McLuhan, *The Gutenberg Galaxy: The Making of Typographic Man* (Toronto: Univ. of Toronto Press, 1962).

9. George Bluestone, *Novels into Film* (Baltimore: Johns Hopkins Univ. Press, 1957), is still likely the best source in English on distinguishing the virtues and limitations of movies as compared to literature.

10. In 1908 a company was founded in Paris to produce prestige films. Even in the pre-World War One silent era, the notion was that the cinema could draw from the legitimate stage directly.

11. See Paul Monaco, *Cinema and Society: France and Germany During the Twenties* (Amsterdam, Oxford, New York: Elsevier Publ., 1976), chapter four. The advent of sound production in 1929 meant a boom to filmmaking in France. Between 1930 and 1935, the French industry underwent rapid growth; production, in fact, outstripped Germany's for the first time since 1916.

12. José Ortega y Gasset, "Notes on the Novel," in *The Dehumanization of Art: And Other Writings on Art and Culture*, (Garden City, N.Y.: Doubleday-Anchor Books, 1966), pp. 53 ff.

13. In the last thirty years of the nineteenth century, photography supplanted painting in the quest for realistic depictions of portraits, landscapes. and urban scenes. Painters who were forward looking responded by developing a variety of techniques and approaches to their works which paved the way to a variety of innovations which are the basis of "modern art"—canvases which express the painter's interior thoughts and mood, techniques which fracture the material world as we normally perceive it, etc.

14. Alain Robbe-Grillet has increasingly embraced the film as a mode of expression. His most renowned contribution to the cinema, however, still remains his screenplay for *Last Year at Marienbad* (1961).

15. See Herbert J. Gans, *Popular Culture and High Culture: An Analysis and Evaluation of Taste* (New York: Basic Books, 1974), pp. 69 ff. So far as I know Gans coined the valuable term "taste culture"; this 1974 essay remains a fundamental text for examining the concept.

16. Michel Simon, "Les Enfants Terribles," in *American Film*, December 1984.

17. The standard aesthetic in the western world, since the time of the Renaissance, might be called an "aesthetic of virtuosity." Emphasis is on the skill and imagination of an individual to manipulate the materials of an art form, as well as his/her genius for innovation and elaboration. This would be the opposite of aesthetic of power or invocation, in which the individual's talent was paramount, by emphasizing the forcefulness of the work instead.

18. Both France and the United States suffered similar fates in Vietnam. It should be kept in mind, however, that France had far more at stake directly, for she lost a colony she had established over a century earlier. That defeat, for all practical purposes, marked an end to an era in which France's claim to being a world power had been based on traditional territorial claims of world empire. The U.S. defeat in Vietnam may have been more surprising than France's loss in the 1950s, but it was not nearly as devastating to national pride or to the national interest.

19. Edgar Ansel Mowrer, "France's Economic Malaise," in *France in Crisis*, ed. by Elizabeth Davey (New York: The H.W. Winston Co., 1957), p. 36. Later accounts have maintained that the U.S. underwrote the entire military cost of France's undertaking against Ho-Chi-Minh and the Communists from 1950 on. Just this view, for example, is advanced in the documentary film *Hearts and Minds* (1976). Whatever the case, the military involvement appears to have placed a significant burden on France's meagre postwar treasury.

20. In June 1940, when German troops occupied the country, a number of the French fled to Great Britain. There, under the leadership of DeGaulle, the Free French established a wartime government-in-exile.

21. Mowrer, "France's Economic Malaise," p. 35.

22. Ibid., p. 37.

23. Ibid., p. 44.

24. See David S. Landes, *The Unbound Prometheus* (Cambridge: Harvard Univ. Press, 1969) for a thorough consideration of this theory.

25. AJYM was a production company established by Chabrol. It was prominent for the next several years in promoting new filmmakers in France.

26. See Paul Monaco, *Modern European Culture and Consciousness, 1870–1980* (Albany: SUNY Press, 1983), pp. 44 ff.

27. The concept of the dialectical—that is, the tension between forces whose struggle constitutes the dynamic of history—as propounded by nineteenth-century German philosophers Georg Friedrich Hegel and Karl Marx relates to more commonplace notions of transformation. Indeed, the issue of change is a central one to modern social thought. Various philosophic positions, too, are intertwined with the notion of change and its dynamic.

28. Eugene P. Walz, *François Truffaut: A Guide to References and Resources* (Boston: G.K. Hall & Co., 1982), p. 10.

29. Georges Franju, "Entretien avec F. Truffaut," in *Esprit* (28th yr., no. 285, June, 1960).

30. Subjectivity in the cinema is obtained when the camera-eye identifies fully with the perspective of one of the characters, rather than remaining focused from an objective, third-person point of view. The establishing of subjectivity in film is most often attributed to the German director Friedrich Wilhelm Murnau who first advanced this technique in a sequence of *The Last Laugh* (1924).

31. The other two Antoine Doinel films were made by Truffaut at intervals of roughly a decade each. *Stolen Kisses* (1968) portrays Antoine's maturation and his development of a personal and a sexual identity. In *Love on the Run* (1979) adult illusion is crushed, but, more importantly, Antoine reflects upon his life and development.

32. Postwar critics in France labeled a number of productions from Hollywood, such as *The Maltese Falcon* (1941) and *Double Indemnity* (1944), as "black films." Aside from the deceptive plots and the moral message which underlie such films, they are characterized by darkly lit interiors, a great number of night scenes, and particular camera styles. Eventually, the U.S. imported the term "film noir" itself from France to refer to these productions, or to sequences in certain other films.

33. Lazslo Kovacs was the name of the cinematographer of *Casablanca* (1941), directed by Michael Curtiz.

34. John Kreidl, *Jean-Luc Godard* (Boston: G.K. Hall, 1980).

35. To "live life dangerously" is a maxim expressed in print by the late nineteenth-century German philosopher Friedrich Nietzsche. As he is considered a prime forerunner of existentialism, so the phrase might be thought of as expressing a fundamental existential credo.

36. One good example would be the detective novel. As a literary genre, it seems to embody the values of a certain point of view. The genre expresses faith in human ability to fathom all orders of phenomena, to act logically and analytically on data, and, in so doing, to affirm the human capacity to right all wrongs.

37. Jacques Sichier, *Nouvelle Vague* (Paris: Editions du Cerf, 1961), p. 22.

38. R. Basan and R. Lefevre, "Jean-Luc Godard," in *La Revue du cinéma*, no. 390, January, 1984.

39. Georges Sadoul, "Quelques sources du nouveau cinéma français," in *Esprit*, 28th year, no. 285, June, 1960.

40. Charles Ford, *Histoire du cinéma français contemporain* (Paris: Editions France-Empire, 1977), p. 189.

41. Jean-Pierre Jeaucolas, *Le Cinéma du français* (Paris: Editions Stock, 1979), p. 124.

42. Michel Mesnil, "A la recherche d'une signification," in *Esprit*, 28th year, no. 285, June, 1960.

43. François Courtade, *Les Malédictions du-cinéma français* (Paris: Editions Alain Moreau, 1978), p. 218.

44. W. Schwanzer, ed., *Materialien zu Filmen von A. Resnais* (Frankfurt am Main: Filmforum, Duisburg/Kommunales Kino, 1976).

45. Bluestone, *Novels into Film*, p. 182.

46. Jeaucolas, *Le Cinéma du français*, p. 139.

47. *Die Welt* (Hamburg), 2 June 1959.

48. Alexandre Astruc, in *L'Ecran français*, no. 144 (30 March 1948).

49. Mesnil, "A la recherche d'une signification."

50. France was, in fact, the only European country that had not subsidized pre-World War Two film production. See Paul Monaco, *Cinema and Society* (1976), chapter two. State subsidy had hardly assured creative innovation in other instances.

51. H.C. Hagenthaler, "Le System de production" in *Esprit*, 28th year, no. 285 (June 1960).

52. Jeaucolas, *Le Cinéma du français*, p. 114.

53. M. Martin, in *Cinéma*, no. 46 (May, 1960).

54. See Jacques Ellul, *The Technological Society*, tr. by John Wilkinson (New York: Alfred Knopf, 1964). Elsewhere, Ellul often referred to Gaullism as a movement, and to DeGaulle as a personality, embodying the most clear exploitation of "image" to the ends of political manipulation.

55. Ian C. Jarvie, "Seeing Through Movie," in *Journal of the Philosophy of the Social Sciences*, vol. 8, no. 4 (December, 1978). Jarvie's article concludes with a perceptive argument on behalf of recognizing the "social significance" of *all* firms presented publicly.

3   The Bitburg Syndrome

1. See Paul Monaco, "Across the Great Divide: New German Cinema in the 1970s," in *Mundus Artium*, Spring 1979.

2. Eric Rentschler, *West German Film In the Course of Time* (Bedford Hills, N.Y.: Redgrave Publ. Co., 1984), p. 19.

3. Tony Pipolo, "German Filmmakers Seldom Focus on Legacy of Nazism," in "The Sunday New York Times Magazine," in *The New York Times*, August 1, 1982, pp. 1, 15. Specifically, Pipolo cites the highly respected Miriam Hansen of Rutgers University, who argues that an abrupt shift toward film treatment of the Nazi era occurred in the late 1970s.

4. *Kölner Stadt-Anzeiger* (Cologne), 31 December 1954. Since the end of the First World War Germany has had an industry-sponsored system of designating certain films in categories such as "especially worthwhile," "educational," etc. In addition to lending prestige and positive attention to a movie, such designations are accompanied by official, governmental tax-breaks. This system has often recognized films of genuine artistic merit. The same system has, at times in the past, been highly controversial and subject to political manipulation.

5. *Der Spiegel* (Hamburg), 23 June 1954; *Neue-Zeitung* (West Berlin), 8 January 1955; *Flensburger Tagesblatt* (Flensburg), 22 January 1955.

6. *Berliner-Zeitung* (East Berlin), 20 January 1955.

7. *Nordsee-Zeitung* (Bremerhaven), 22 June 1955. A serious dispute over rights to the film story brewed between two production companies, CCC-Herzog and Ariston.

8. See Siegfried Kracauer, *From Caligari to Hitler* (Princeton: Princeton Univ. Press, 1947), for a discussion of Pabst, and, especially, of his film *Kammeradschaft*.

9. *Schwäbische Landeszeitung*, 19 November 1954.

10. DIFK (German Institute for Film Information), Frankfurt am Main, File # 12 U 70.

11. *Nürnberger Zeitung*, 27 April 1957.

12. See *Courrier de l'ouest*, 25 February 1956, and reviews by Jacques Daniel-Valcroze and Claude Brule from *France Observateur* and *Paris Presse* respectively as quoted in *Der Mittag* (Dusseldorf), 6 March 1956; also in *Hamburger Anzeiger*, 17 February 1956.

13. *Freie Presse* (Bielefeld), 26 February 1958.

14. In spite of the enormous postwar influence of Hollywood on the West German film market, this appears to be the only actual U.S.-F.R.G. co-production of the 1950s to be identified as such. Hollywood money, of course, controlled a number of German film companies as subsidiaries.

15. *Hamburger Freie Presse*, 8 November 1955. The state government in Hessen (Frankfurt area), a region traditionally Social Democrat, defended the film; the state regime in Bavaria, an arch-conservative state, through its Minister of Culture, condemned the movie.

16. *Westdeutsche Allgemeine*, 10 April 1963.

17. *8-Uhr Blatt*, 4 April 1953.

18. *Welt der Arbeit* (DGB), 28 November 1952; this publication was an organ of the trade union movement, closely linked to the Social Democrat party.

19. *Abendzeitung* (Frankfurt am Main), 8 November 1952.

20. The critical acclaim the film received in France was summarized in *Der Mittag* (Dusseldorf), 18 January 1955.

21. *Le Parisien libéré*, 7 January 1955.

22. Ibid.; in his review André Bazin makes much out of her falling in no man's land, which he believes is a most significant choice in the script.

23. *Aufwärts* (SPD Party Newspaper), 9 December 1954.

24. *Der Mittag* (Dusseldorf), 18 January 1955.

25. *Le Soir Sports* (Paris), 17 March 1957.

26. *Frankfurter Rundshau*, 28 March 1955.

27. *Frankfurter Allgemeine*, 28 March 1955.

28. *Neue Presse* (Oberfranken), 20 January 1955.

29. One of the young men is actually a younger brother, not a son.

30. See Rentschler, *West German Film*, pp. 103 ff. Rentschler offers an insightful discussion of the bases for—and nuances of—the "Heimatsfilm" in German tradition.

31. A.J.P. Taylor, *From Sarajevo to Potsdam* (New York: Harcourt, Brace, and World, 1966), p. 134.

32. *The Good Soldier Schweik* (1919) was a Czech novel that established the lovable, bumbling character of "Schweik," a recruit to the Austro-Hungarian Army. By following

instructions in the most literal-minded way he deceives the bureaucrats and military officers into regarding him as an idiot. He is a forerunner of characters such as Yossarian in Joseph Heller's *Catch-22*.

33. *Dundee Evening Telegraph*, 27 October 1954.

34. *Mindener Tageblatt*, 14 January 1956.

35. *Les lettres française*, 27 January 1956.

36. *Suddeutsche Zeitung* (Munich), 3 October 1954.

37. Reception theory has been growing increasingly in literary studies during the past decade. It has, so far, made fewer inroads into film studies where its application faces problems of understanding viewer response in a manner as standardized as reader response.

38. See Ian C. Jarvie, *Movies as Social Criticism* (Metuchen, N.J.: Scarecrow Press, 1978). Throughout this essay the author points out that actual audience responses to a given movie may be antithetical to the maker's intention.

39. *Evangelischer Filmbeobachter*, 12 September 1957.

40. *Der Untan*, 4 September 1957.

41. *Wege Zueinander*, 29 September 1957.

42. *Stuttgarter Zeitung*, 26 April 1958.

43. *Hannoversche Presse*, 17 April 1958.

44. *Stuttgarter Zeitung*, 26 April 1958.

45. DIFK (Frankfurt), film packet for *Monte Cassino* (no identifying number).

46. *Kölner Rundschau* (Cologne), 17 October 1958.

47. *Deutsche Film-Korrespondenz*, 10 January 1961.

48. *Berliner Zeitung* (East Berlin), 12 August 1958.

49. *Union-Pressedienst*, Heft 10, 1958.

50. Certainly, the Soviet Union could be held culpable for barbarous acts throughout much of East Europe in the years following the Second World War. The Stalinist Soviet leadership pursued a policy of purges, deportations, and exterminations, the model for which had been given during the period of forced industrialization in the USSR itself during the 1930s. Nonetheless, it seems difficult to establish definite patterns of murderousness by Soviet troops of occupation in the eastern regions of Germany. Whatever "facts" there may be, it appears that Germans in the West exploited tales of Soviet savagery to the maximum during the Cold War era. It is also difficult to judge what punitive measures would have been justified, given the heinous acts of German troops during the war and the criminal record of Nazism.

51. The Spanish Civil War, 1936–1939, provided the Hitler regime an opportunity to aid the forces of Francisco Franco and the Falangists (whose ideology resembled Nazism to some extent). This opportunity, in particular, gave the German air force practice in bombing civilian targets, a method soon to be applied in the early stages of the Second World War.

52. DIFK (Frankfurt), file packet for *So Lange Du Lebst!* (no identifying number).

53. The original German title *Wir Wunderkinder* means literally "We Prodigies." I have chosen to translate the title thus in the text. The film premiered in the U.S. under the title *Aren't We Wonderful?* While appreciating the ironic intent of this choice, I find it misleading, and I have, therefore, chosen to omit reference to this title under which the film is normally listed in the U.S.

54. *Die Tat*, 21 June 1959.

55. *Freiheit* (Halle, GDR), 6 May 1959. This article offers a complete summary of critical opinion voiced in various sources published across the German Democratic Republic (East Germany).

56. *Vorwärts*, 6 March 1959.

57. *Deutsche Soldaten-Zeitung*, 6 March 1959.

58. The inflationary madness reached enormous, almost mythic, proportions in Ger-

many. Stories are told of workers needing wheelbarrows to collect their wages, paid thrice daily as money lost value from morning to noon to evening. Magazines or newspapers cost millions of marks, as did trolley car tickets. See, for example, A.J. Nicholls, *Weimar and the Rise of Hitler* (New York: St. Martin's Press, 1979), pp. 74 ff.

59. *Allgemeine Wochenzeitung der Juden* 25 December 1959; *Der Spiegel*, 4 November 1959; *Deutsche Woche*, 4 November 1959; *Berliner Morgenpost*, 15 November 1959, present an excellent range of positive comments.

60. *Nazione* (Rome), 12 March 1960; *The New York Times*, 3 May 1961; *New York Mirror*, 8 May 1961.

61. *Westfälische Nachrichten* (Munster), 7 December 1960.

62. *Cinéma*, Paris, May, 1960.

63. *Neue Presse* (Frankfurt), 19 February 1963; *Mannheimer Morgen*, 17 August 1963; *Neue Tagespost* (Osnabruck), 13 July 1963.

64. Such interpretations are discussed in Kent Casper and Susan Linville, "Nazi Reframes: Negative Stereotyping in American Reviews of New German,"*Literature/Film Quarterly*, no. 4, vol. 13, 1985, pp. 250–258. With regard to *Aguirre* as an allegory of Nazi Germany, see their discussion of David Denby's 1977 *Horizon* article and Stanley Kaufmann's review, p. 252.

65. *TIP* (West Berlin), 19 November 1982. The article in *TIP*, a popular guide to the arts and entertainments in Berlin, endorses the view that the subject matter of *The White Rose* would have been impossible to produce as a film during the 1950s.

66. *Suddeutsche Zeitung* (Munich), 19 September 1982;

67. *Stuttgarter Zeitung*, 25 September 1982.

68. *Die Zeit* (Hamburg), 25 October 1982.

69. *TIP* (West Berlin), 19 November 1982. The handbills themselves, posted by the Scholls, read "Down With Hitler!"

70. Rentschler, *West German Film*, pp. 129 ff.

71. Hitler evidently had a personal obsession with fear of poisoning, and with gassing, dating back to his own wounding by mustard gas in the First World War. The ending of the film is the actual sound recording of Hitler declaring war. For a psychohistory of Hitler's obsession and the politics he derived from it see Rudolph Binion, *Hitler Among the Germans* (New York, Oxford, Amsterdam: Elsevier, 1976).

72. *The New York Times*, 24 April 1985.

73. Andrew Sarris, "The Great New Movie Wave From Germany," *Vogue*, October, 1980, p. 34.

4 Memory without Pain

1. The emergence of the U.S. as a world superpower after 1945 was abrupt. After the First World War, the U.S. had eschewed its potential new role in the world by entering into isolationism. After World War Two, the U.S. embraced its global role with sudden rigor and tenacity.

2. Landon Y. Jones, *Great Expectations: America and The Baby Boom Generation* (New York: Ballantine Books, 1980), p. 79.

3. See, for example, Stephen F. Ambrose, *Eisenhower* (New York: Simon & Schuster, 1983, 1984).

4. At the time, of course, many protesters wished to see the intervention in Southeast Asia as an anomaly, or as an aberration, in American policy. It was wishful thinking on anyone's part to consider the policies of four successive administrations (Eisenhower's, Kennedy's, Johnson's, and Nixon's) toward Vietnam to be other than consistent.

5. Here it is important to note that the term "unworthy" is being used in a neutral, not a judgmental, manner. The unworthiness of the South Vietnamese leadership was simply

functional—necessary support for it and its policies could not be engendered in the populace. However, most persons would use the word unworthy as implying moral culpability, and I suspect that most readers would be inclined to interpret it in this way as well.

6. Lawrence L. Murray, "Hollywood, Nihilism, and the Youth Culture of the Sixties: Bonnie and Clyde," in John O'Connor and Martin Jackson, eds. *American History Film*, (New York: Fred Ungar Publ., 1979), pp. 237–256.

7. *Time*, August 25, 1967.

8. *Variety*, December 13, 1967.

9. *Films in Review*, December 1967.

10. *Variety*, August 9, 1967.

11. *L.A. Citizen News*, August 23, 1967.

12. *Time*, December 8, 1967.

13. *Films and Filming*, October 1967.

14. Charles Marowitz, "Bonnie & Clyde Symptom and Cause," *Village Voice*, December 21, 1967.

15. *L.A. Citizen News*, March 15, 1968.

16. Pauline Kael, "Bonnie & Clyde," *New Yorker*, February 1, 1967.

17. Charles Marowitz, "Bonnie & Clyde Symptom and Cause," *Village Voice*, December 21, 1967.

18. Ibid.

19. James Monaco, *American Film Now* (New York, London & Scarborough, Ont.: New American Library, 1979), p. 51.

20. Fred Davis, *Yearning for Yesterday: A Sociology of Nostalgia* (New York: Free Press, 1979), p. 22.

21. Glen H. Elder, Jr., "Social Structure and Personality: A Life Course Perspective," in H. Graff and P. Monaco, eds., *Quantification and Psychology: Toward a "New" History* (Washington, D.C.: University Press of America, 1980), pp. 147 ff.; see Glen H. Elder, Jr., *Children of the Great Depression: Social Change in Life Experience* (Chicago: Univ. of Chicago Press, 1974).

22. Patton's notion, of course, might be widely shared in the popular imagination, although it is assumed most people distinguish Nazism as a particularly pernicious force—not just as another party. On record, however, the entire postwar history of the U.S. Occupation, and its often ambivalent and ambiguous policies of de-Nazification shed light on the fact that Patton's view—which coarsely expressed—may have been widely held.

23. George C. Herring, *America's Longest War: The U.S. and Viet-Nam, 1950–1975* (2nd Ed.; New York: Alfred A. Knopf, 1986), pp. 277–278.

24. See Leslie A. Fiedler, *An End to Innocence: Essays on Culture and Politics* (Boston: Beacon Press, 1955); cited also in Fred Davis, *Yearning for Yesterday: A Sociology of Nostalgia* (New York: Free Press, 1979), p. 60.

25. See Christopher Lasch, *The Culture of Narcissism: American Life in An Age of Diminishing Expectations* (New York: Warner Books, 1979).

26. The *Bildungsroman*, the traditional novel of education, explores maturation, the awakening of feeling, and tension between an adolescent and the society. In these terms, this standard "modern" genre, which was at greatest prominence from the last quarter of the nineteenth century to World War Two, is a special kind of literary work tracing rites of passage. *American Graffiti* fits many of the categories well, and Lucas's first film is, indeed, like many a first novel in this regard.

27. See Marshall McLuhan, *Understanding Media* (New York: McGraw-Hill, 1964), pp. 241 ff.

28. J. Monaco, *American Film Now*, p. 224.

29. Ibid., p. 103

30. See Gerald Nicosia, *Memory Babe: A Critical Biography of Jack Kerouac* (New York: Grove Press, 1983), pp. 656 ff. and passim.

31. Roland N. Stromberg, *After Everything: Western Intellectual History Since 1945* (New York: St. Martin's Press, 1975), p. 41.

32. "Introduction," in Graff and P. Monaco, eds., *Quantification Psychology: Toward a New History*, pp. 11 ff.

33. See Herbert Marcuse, *Eros and Civilization* (Boston: Beacon Press, 1966), in which the author anticipates the "cooptation" by the establishment of such forms of cultural revolution.

34. The Reagan presidency, for example, has not pressed its social agenda legislatively. While the wish to legislate more traditional values would seem to be strong in portions of the electorate, it would also appear that even the statistics support the notion that a majority of Americans have accepted vastly altered sexual mores. Moreover, the evident epidemic of cocaine use in middle-age professional groups seems to support the notion that the "establishment" has been willing, indeed, to expand its drug culture from one based almost exclusively on alcohol.

35. Michael Ventura, *Shadow Dancing in the U.S.A.* (Los Angeles: Jeremy P. Tarcher, Inc., 1985), pp. 56, 57.

36. Jones, *Great Expectations*, p. 338.

37. Ibid., p. 109.

38. Robert B. Ray, *A Certain Tendency of the Hollywood Cinema, 1930–1980* (Princeton, N.J.: Princeton Univ. Press, 1985), p. 255. Ray quotes Leslie Fiedler with regard to his assessment of "reactionary nostalgia."

39. Quoted in Diana Trilling, "Easy Rider and Its Critics," *The Atlantic*, September 1970.

40. John Hellman, *American Myth and the Legacy of Viet-Nam* (New York: Columbia Univ. Press, 1986), p. 71.

41. Jerzy Toeplitz, *Hollywood and After: The Changing Face of American Cinema*, tr. by Boleslan Sulik (London: George Allen and Unwin, Ltd. 1974), p. 41.

42. Hellman, *American Myth and the Legacy of Viet-Nam*, pp. 94, 95.

43. Ray, *A Certain Tendency of the Hollywood Cinema*, p. 260.

44. Robert N. Bellah et al., *Habits of the Heart: Individualism and Commitment in American Life* (Berkeley, Los Angeles, and London: Univ. of California Press, 1985), p. 50.

5 Conclusion

1. J. Dudley Andrew, *The Major Film Theories: An Introduction* (London, Oxford, & New York: Oxford Univ. Press, 1976), p. 143.

2. Maya Deren as quoted in Donald M. Lowe, *The History of Bourgeois Perception* (Chicago: The Univ. of Chicago Press, 1982), p. 125.

3. Pierre Sorlin, *The Film in History: Restaging the Past* (Oxford: Basil Blackwell, 1980), p. 16.

4. Lino Micciche as quoted in Mira Liehm, *Passion and Defiance: Film in Italy From 1942 to the Present* (Berkeley & Los Angeles: Univ. of California Press, 1984), p. 129.

5. James Monaco, *American Film Now* (New York, London, & Scarborough, Ont.: New American Library, 1979), p. 51.

6. Tomm O'Brien, Humanities Series Public Lecture, Montana State University, Bozeman, Montana, November 22, 1985.

7. Liehm, *Passion and Defiance*, p. 172.

8. John Hellman, *American Myth and the Legacy of Vietnam*, p. 73.

SOURCES

FILMS

Each film is listed alphabetically by the English title used in the text. In instances in which another title may be used for prints in distribution in the U.S., it is in parentheses. The original foreign language title, director's name (with co-directors or assistants in parentheses), and date of first public release follow.

1   Realism, Italian Style

The Adventure/L'Avventura, Michelangelo Antonioni, 1959
Amarcord, Federico Fellini, 1973
Bicycle Thief/Ladri di biciclette, Vittorio De Sica, 1948
The Big Loafers/I vitelloni, Federico Fellini, 1953
Bitter Rice/Riso amaro, Giuseppe De Santis, 1949
Blow Up, Michelangelo Antonioni, 1966
Casanova/Il Casanove di Federico Fellini, Federico Fellini, 1970
Chronicle of a Romance (Chronicle of a Love)/Cronaca di un amore, Michelangelo
    Antonioni, 1950
Chung Kao (China)/Chung Kao, Michelangelo Antonioni, 1972
The City of Women/La Città delle donna, Federico Fellini, 1980
The Clowns/I Clowns, Federico Fellini, 1970
The Cry/Il Grido, Michelangelo Antonioni, 1957
La Dolce Vita, Federico Fellini, 1960
The Earth Trembles/La Terra trema, Luchino Visconti, 1948
Eclipse/L'eclisse, Michelangelo Antonioni, 1960
8 1/2/Otto e mezzo, Federico Fellini, 1963
Germany, Year Zero/Germania, anno zero, Roberto Rossellini, 1947
The Girlfriends/Le Amiche, Michelangelo Antonioni, 1955
Identification of a Woman/Identificasione di una donna, Michelangelo Antonioni, 1982
Juliette of the Spirits/Giuletta degli spiriti, Federico Fellini, 1960
Love in the City/Amore in città, Michelangelo Antonioni (Fellini, Lattuada, Lizzani, Risi,
    & Maselli), 1953
The Night/La Notte, Michelangelo Antonioni, 1960
Nights of Cabiria/Le Notti di Cabiria, Federico Fellini, 1957
The Orchestra Rehearsal/Prova di orchestra, Federico Fellini, 1979
Paisan/Paisà, Roberto Rossellini, 1946
The Passenger, Michelangelo Antonioni, 1974
Red Desert/Il Deserto rosso, Michelangelo Antonioni, 1964
The Road/La Strada, Federico Fellini, 1954
Roma (Fellini's Rome)/Fellini Roma, Federico Fellini, 1972
Rome, Open City (Open City)/Roma, città aperta, Roberto Rossellini, 1945
Rome, 11 O'Clock/Roma, ore undici, Giuseppe De Santis, 1952
Satyricon (Fellini's Satyricon)/Fellini-Satyricon, Federico Fellini, 1969
The Ship Sails On/El e nava va, Federico Fellini, 1983
Shoeshine/Sciuscià, Vittorio De Sica, 1947
Umberto D, Vittorio De Sica, 1951
Variety Lights/Luci del varieta, Federico Fellini (Lattuada), 1952
The White Sheik/Lo sceicco bianco, Federico Fellini, 1952
The Woman without Camellia/La signora senza camelie, Michelangelo Antonioni, 1953
Zabriskie Point, Michelangelo Antonioni, 1969

2 The First Crest of the New Wave

Breathless/Un bout de souffle, Jean-Luc Godard, 1959
The 400 Blows/Les quatre cent coups, François Truffaut, 1959
Handsome Serge/Le beau Serge, Claude Chabrol, 1958
Hiroshima, mon amour, Alain Resnais, 1959
The Little Soldier/Le petit soldat, Jean-Luc Godard, 1960

3 The Bitburg Syndrome

Aguirre, The Wrath of God/Aguirre: Der Zorn Gottes, Werner Herzog, 1972
Betrayal of Germany/Verrat an Deutschland, Veit Harlan, 1955
Between Two Wars/Zwischen Zwei Kriegen, Hans Farocki, 1979
The Boat/Das Boot, Wolfgang Petersen, 1982
The Bridge/Die Brücke, Bernard Wicki, 1959
Canaris, Alfred Weidemann, 1954
The Children from No. 67/Die Kinder aus 67, Heil Hitler, ich hatt gern 'n paar Pferdeappel, Usch Berthelerz-Weller and Werner Mayer, 1982
Children, Mothers, and a General/Kinder, Mutter, und Ein General, Lazlo Benedek, 1955
Comradeship/Kameradschaft, G.W. Pabst, 1931
David, Peter Lilienthal, 1979
Decision before Dawn/Entscheidung in Morgengrauen, Anatole Litvak, 1950
The Delinquent's Bridge #999/Strafbatallion 999, Harald Philipp, 1960
The Devil's General/Der Teufels General, Helmut Käutner, 1955
The Doctor of Stalingrad/Der Arzt von Stalingrad, Geza von Raavanyi, 1959
The Fair/Kirmes, Wolfgang Staudte, 1960
The First Polka/Die Erste Polka, Klaus Emmerich, 1979
The Fox of Paris/Der Fuchs von Paris, Paul May, 1955
From a German Life/Aus einem deutschen Leben, Theodore Kottula, 1977
The German Hour/Die Deutsch Stunde, Parts I and II, Diethardt Klant, 1971
Germany in Autumn/Deutschland im Herbst, Rainer W. Fassbinder (Kluge, Reitz, Von Schlöndorff), 1977
Germany, Pale Mother/Deutschland, bleiche Mutter, Helma Sanders-Brahms, 1979
The Green Devils of Monte Cassino/Die Grunen Teufel von Monte Cassino, Harald Reinl (Joachim Fuchsberger), 1956
Homeland/Heimat, Edgar Reitz, 1985
The Hour Zero/Die Stunde Null, Edgar Reitz, 1976
I Was Nineteen/Ich War Neunzehn, Konrad Wolf, 1966
In Those Days/In Jenen Tagen, Helmut Käutner, 1947
The Jew Suss/Jud Süss, Veit Harlan, 1939
The Joyless Street/Die Freudlose Gasse, G.W. Pabst, 1926
The Last Bridge/Die Letzte Brücke, Helmut Käutner, 1957
The Last Five Days/Letzte Fünf Tage, Percy Adlon, 1982
Lili Marleen, Rainer Werner Fassbinder, 1980
The Love of Jeanne Ney/Die Liebe von Jeanne Ney, 1929
M (M: The City Seeks a Murderer)/M: Die Stadt Sucht einen Mörder, Fritz Lang, 1932
Marriage in the Shadows/Ehe in Schatten, Kurt Maetzig, 1948
The Murderers Are among Us/Die Morder Sind Unter Uns, Wolfgang Staudte, 1946
My Classmate/Mein Schulfreund, Robert Siodmak, 1960
The Opperman Family/Die Geschwister Oppermann, Egon Monk, 1983
Pandora's Box/Die Buchse der Pandora, G.W. Pabst, 1927
Professor Mamluck, Konrad Wolf, 1961
Seven Beauties/Pasqualino Settebelleze, Lina Wertmuller, 1974

Signs of Life/Lebenszeichen, Werner Herzog, 1967
So Long As You Live/Solange du Lebst! Harald Reinl, 1955
The Star of Africa/Der Stern von Afrika, Alfred Weidemann, 1955
Star WithoutSky/Stern Ohne Himmel, Leoni Ossowski, 1985
Stars/Sterne, Konrad Wolf, 1958
Sub #47: Lieutenant Captain Prien/U-47: Kapitanleutnant Prien, Harald Reinl, 1957
The Tin Drum/Die Blechtrommel, Volker von Schlöndorff, 1976
Three Penny Opera/Die Dreigroschenoper, G.W. Pabst, 1932
The Trip to Vienna/Die Reise nach Wien, Edgar Reitz, 1974
The Twentieth of July/Es Geschah am 20ten Juli, G.W. Pabst, 1955
We Prodigies (Aren't We Wonderful?)/Wir Wunderkinder, Kurt Hoffmann, 1958
The White Rose/Die Weisse Rose, Michael Verhoeven, 1982
Winterspelt, Eberhard Fechner, 1977

4   Memory without Pain

American Graffiti, George Lucas, 1973
American Hot Wax, Floyd Mutrux, 1978
Animal House (National Lampoon's Animal House), John Landis, 1978
Atlantic City, Louis Malle, 1975
The Big Chill, Lawrence Kasden, 1983
Blackboard Jungle, Richard Brooks, 1955
Bonnie and Clyde, Arthur Penn, 1967
The Buddy Holly Story, Steve Rash, 1978
Butch Cassidy and the Sundance Kid, George Roy Hill, 1969
Cabaret, Bob Fosse, 1974
Come Back to the Five & Dime, James Dean, Robert Altman, 1982
Coming Home, Hal Ashby, 1978
Easy Rider, Dennis Hopper, 1969
Gone With the Wind, Victor Fleming, 1939
Grease, Randal Kleiser, 1978
The Great Gatsby, Jack Clayton, 1974
The Great Santini, John Lewis Carlino, 1980
Heartbeat, John Byrum, 1980
The Last Picture Show, Peter Bogdanovich, 1971
Little Big Man, Arthur Penn, 1970
The Lords of Flatbush, Steven Verona (Martin Davidson), 1974
Marty, Delbert Mann, 1955
New York, New York, Martin Scorsese, 1977
Paper Moon, Peter Bogdanovich, 1973
Patton, Franklin Schaffner, 1970
Porky's, Bob Clark, 1982
The Purple Rose of Cairo, Woody Allen, 1985
One from the Heart, Francis Coppola, 1983
The Return of the Secaucus Seven, John Sayles, 1981
Rocky, John Alvidsen, 1976
Save the Tiger, John Alvidsen, 1974
Soldier Blue, Ralph Nelson, 1970
The Sting, George Ray Hill, 1973
That's Entertainment, Jack Haley, Jr., 1974
They Shoot Horses, Don't They, Sydney Pollack, 1969
Tora! Tora! Tora! Richard Fleischer (Kellogg, Masuda, Fukasaku), 1970

The Way We Were, Sydney Pollack, 1973
Zelig, Woody Allen, 1983

BOOKS

Complete bibliographic information, including place and publisher, may be found in the "Notes" section.

Ambrose, Stephen F., *Eisenhower*, 1983
Andrew, Dudley J., *The Major Film Theories: An Introduction*, 1976
Armstrong, Robert Plant, *The Affecting Presence*, 1971
Armstrong, Robert Plant, *Wellspring*, 1976
Bazin, André, *What Is Cinema?* tr. by Hugh Gray, 1967
Bazin, André, *What Is Cinema? Volume II*, tr. by Hugh Gray, 1971
Bellah, Robert N., *et al. Habits of the Heart: Individualism and Commitment in American Life*, 1985
Binion, Rudolph, *Hitler among the Germans*, 1976
Bluestone, George, *Novels into Film*, 1957
Bondanella, Peter, *Federico Fellini: Essays in Criticism*, 1978
Calvino, Italo, *The Path to The Nest of Spiders*, 1976
Cameron, Ian, and Robin Wood, *Antonioni*, 1968
Courtade, François, *Les Malédictions du-cinéma français*, 1978
Davis, Fred, *Yearning for Yesterday: A Sociology of Nostalgia*, 1979
Deren, Maya, as quoted in Donald M. Lowe, *The History of Bourgeois Perception*, 1982
Eisenstein, Sergei M., *Film Form: Essays in Film Theory*, tr. by Jay Leyda, 1949
Eisenstein, Sergei M., *The Film Sense*, tr. by Jay Leyda, 1942
Eisenstein, Sergei M., *Notes of a Film Director*, tr. by X. Danko, 1949
Elder, Glen H., Jr., *Children of the Great Depression: Social Change in Life Experience*, 1974
Ellul, Jacques, *The Technological Society*, tr. by John Wilkinson, 1964
Fiedler, Leslie A., *An End to Innocence: Essays on Culture and Politics*, 1955
Ford, Charles, *Histoire du cinéma français contemporain*, 1977
Gans, Herbert, *Popular Culture and High Culture: An Analysis and Evaluation of Taste*, 1974
Germino, Dante, & Stefano Passigli, *The Government and Politics of Contemporary Italy*, 1969
Grunberger, Richard, *The Social History of The Third Reich*, 1971
Hellman, John, *American Myth and the Legacy of Viet-Nam*, 1986
Herring, George C., *America's Longest War: The U.S. and Viet-Nam, 1950–1975*, 1986
Huaco, George, *The Sociology of Film Art*, 1965
Jarvie, Ian C., *Movies as Social Criticism*, 1978
Jeaucolas, Jean-Pierre, *Le Cinéma du français*, 1979
Kolker, Robert Philip, *A Cinema of Loneliness*, 1980
Koppel, Helga, *Film in Italien, Italien in Film*, 1970
Kracauer, Siegfried, *From Caligari to Hitler*, 1947
Kracauer, Siegfried, *Theory of Film: The Redemption of Physical Reality*, 1960
Kreidl, John, *Jean-Luc Godard*, 1980
Landes, David S., *The Unbound Prometheus* 1969
Lasch, Christopher, *The Culture of Narcissism: American Life in an Age of Diminishing Expectations*, 1979
Liehm, Mira, *Passion and Defiance: Film in Italy From 1942 to The Present*, 1984
Mancini, Elaine, *Struggles of the Italian Film Industry during Fascism, 1930–1935*, 1985

Marcuse, Herbert *Eros and Civilization*, 1966
McLuhan, Herbert Marshall, *The Gutenberg Galaxy; The Making of Typographic Man*, 1962
McLuhan, Herbert Marshall, *Understanding Media*, 1964
Monaco, James, *American Film Now*, 1979
Monaco, James, *The New Wave*, 1976
Monaco, Paul, *Cinema and Society: France and Germany During the Twenties*, 1976
Monaco, Paul, *Modern European Culture and Consciousness, 1870–1980*, 1983
Nicholls, A.J., *Weimar and the Rise of Hitler*, 1979
Nicosia, Gerald, *Memory Babe: A Critical Biography of Jack Kerouac*, 1983
Nietzsche, *The Genealogy of Morals*, 1984
Overby, David, ed., *Springtime in Italy: A Reader on Neo-Realism*, 1978
Ray, Robert B., *A Certain Tendency of the Hollywood Cinema, 1930–1980*, 1985
Rentschler, Eric, *West German Film in the Course of Time*, 1984
Rosenthal, Stuart, *The Cinema of Federico Fellini*, 1976
Schatz, Thomas, *Old Hollywood/New Hollywood: Ritual, Art, and Industry*, 1983
Schwanzer, W., ed., *Materialien zu Filmen von A. Resnais*, 1976
Sichier, Jacques, *Nouvelle Vague*, 1961
Sorlin, Pierre, *The Film in History: Restaging the Past*, 1980
Stromberg, Roland N., *After Everything: Western Intellectual History Since 1945*, 1975
Taylor, A.J.P., *From Sarajevo to Potsdam*, 1966
Toeplitz, Jerzy, *Hollywood and After: The Changing Face of American Cinema*, tr. by Boleslan Sulik, 1974
Ventura, Michael, *Shadow Dancing in the U.S.A*, 1985
Walz, Eugene P., *François Truffaut: A Guide to References and Resources*, 1982
Zavattini, Cesare, *Zavattini: Sequences From a Cinematic Life*, 1970

ARTICLES

Aristarco, Guido, "Les quatre phases du cinéma italien de l'après-guerre," in *Cinéma '61*, no. 56, March, 1961
Astruc, Alexandre, in *L'Ecran français*, no. 144, 30 March 1948
Basan, R., and R. Lefevre, "Jean-Luc Godard," in *La Revue du cinéma*, no. 390, January, 1984
Bazin, André, "On the Other Side of Neo-Realism," in *Federico Fellini*, ed. by Gilbert Salachas, tr. by Rosalie Siegal, 1969
Brentano, Franz, "The Distinction Between Mental and Physical Phenomena," in Roderick M. Chrisholm, ed., *Realism and the Background of Phenomenology*, 1960
Casper, Kent, and Susan Linville, "Nazi Reframes: Negative Stereotyping in American Reviews of New German," *Literature/Film Quarterly*, no. 4, vol. 13, 1985
Crozier, Michel, "France's Cultural Anxieties Under Gaullism: The Cultural Revolution Revisited," William G. Andrews and Stanley Hoffman, eds., in *The Impact of the Fifth Republic on France*, 1981
Debreczeni, François, "Origines et evolution du Neo-Realisme," in *Etudes Cinématographiques*, 2eme trimestre, 1964
DIFK (German Institute for Film Information), Frankfurt am Main, File # 12 U 70.
DIFK (Frankfurt), file packet for *Monte Cassino* (no identifying number)
DIFK (Frankfurt), file packet for *So Lange Du Lebst!* (no identifying number)
Ebel, Henry, various issues of the *Journal of Psychohistory: History of Childhood Quarterly* dating back to 1974.
Elder, Glen H. Jr.,"Social Structure and Personality: A Life Course Perspective," in H. Graff and P. Monaco, eds., *Quantification and Psychology: Toward a 'New' History*, 1980

Franju, Georges, "Entretien avec F. Truffaut," in *Esprit*, 28th year, no. 285, June, 1960.

Gasset, José Ortega y, "Notes on the Novel," in *The Dehumanization of Art: And Other Writings on Art and Culture*, 1966

Graff, Harvey J., and Paul Monaco, "Introduction," in *Quantification Psychology: Toward a New History*, 1980

Hagenthaler, H.C., "Le System de production," in *Esprit*, 28th year, no. 285, June, 1960

Jarvie, Ian C., "Seeing Through Movie," in *Journal of the Philosophy of the Social Sciences*, vol. 8, no. 4, December, 1978

Kael, Pauline, "Bonnie & Clyde," *New Yorker*, February 1, 1967

Marowitz, Charles, "Bonnie & Clyde Symptom and Cause," *Village Voice*, December 21, 1967

Mesnil, Michel, "A la recherche d'une signification," in *Esprit*, 28th year, no. 285, June, 1960

Monaco, Paul, "Across the Great Divide: New German Cinema in the 1970s," in *Mundus Artium*, Spring, 1979

Morilon, O.P., Felix A., "The Philosophical Basis of Neo-Realism," in *Springtime in Italy: A Reader on Neo-Realism*, ed. by David Overby, 1978

Mowrer, Edgar Ansel, "France's Economic Malaise," in *France in Crisis*, ed. by Elizabeth Davey, 1957

Murray, Lawrence L., "Hollywood, Nihilism, and the Youth Culture of the Sixties: Bonnie and Clyde," in John O'Connor and Martin Jackson, eds., *American History/ American Film*, 1979

Overby, David, "Introduction," in *Springtime in Italy; A Reader on Neo-Realism*, 1978

Pipolo, Tony, "German Filmmakers Seldom Focus on Legacy of Nazism," in "The Sunday New York Times Magazine," in *The New York Times*, August 1, 1982

Renzi, Renzo, "The Courage to be Self-Destructive," in *Federico Fellini*, ed. by Gilbert Salachas, tr. by Rosalie Siegal, 1969

Sadoul, Georges, "Quelques sources du nouveau cinéma français," in *Esprit*, 28th year, no. 285, June, 1960

Sarris, Andrew, "The Great New Movie Wave From Germany," *Vogue*, October, 1980

Simon, Michel, "Les Enfants Terribles," in *American Film*, December 1984

Singerman, B., "Gorizon neo-realizma," *Iskusstvo Kino*, no. 4, Moscow, 1958

Trilling, Diana, "Easy Rider and Its Critics," *The Atlantic*, September, 1970

NEWSPAPERS/MAGAZINES

Abendzeitung (Frankfurt am Main), 8 November 1952

Allgemeine Wochenzeitung Der Juden, 25 December 1959

Aufwärts (SPD Party Newspaper), 9 December 1954

Berliner Morgenpost, 15 November 1959

Berliner Zeitung (East Berlin), 20 January 1955

Berliner Zeitung (East Berlin), 12 August 1958

Cinéma, Paris, May, 1960

Courrier de l'ouest, 25 February 1956

Der Mittag (Dusseldorf), 18 January 1955

Der Spiegel (Hamburg), 23 June 1954

Der Spiegel, 4 November 1959

Der Untan, 4 September 1957

Deutsche Film-Korrespondenz, 10 January 1961

Deutsche Woche, 4 November 1959

Deutsche Soldaten-Zeitung, 6 March 1959

Die Tat, 21 June 1959

Die Welt (Hamburg), 2 June 1959

Die Zeit (Hamburg), 25 October 1982
Dundee Evening Telegraph, 27 October 1954
8-Uhr Blatt, 4 April 1953
Evangelischer Filmbeobachter, 12 September 1957
Films and Filming, October 1967
Films in Review, December, 1967
Flensburger Tagesblatt (Flensburg) 22 January 1955
Frankfurter Allgemeine, 28 March 1955
Frankfurter Rundschau, 28 March 1955
Freie Presse (Bielefeld), 26 February 1958
Freiheit (Halle, GDR), 6 May 1959
Hamburger Anzeiger, 17 February 1956
Hamburger Freie Presse, 8 February 1955
Hannoversche Presse, 17 April 1958
Kölner Rundschau (Cologne), 17 October 1958
Kölner Stadt-Anzeiger (Cologne), 31 December 1954
L.A. Citizen News, August 23, 1967
L.A. Citizen News, March 15, 1968
Les lettres française, 27 January 1956
Le Parisien libéré, 7 January 1955
Le Soir Sports (Paris), 17 March 1957
Mannheimer Morgen, 17 August 1963
Mindener Tageblatt, 14 January 1956
Nazione (Rome), 12 March 1960
Neue Presse (Frankfurt), 19 February 1963
Neue Presse (Oberfranken), 20 January 1955
Neue Tagespost (Osnabruck), 13 July 1963
Neue-Zeitung (West Berlin), 8 January 1955
New York Mirror, 8 May 1961
The New York Times, 3 May 1961
The New York Times, 24 April 1985
Nordsee-Zeitung (Bremerhaven), 22 June 1955
Nürnberger Zeitung, 27 April 1957
Schwäbische Landeszeitung, 19 November 1954
Stuttgarter Zeitung, 26 April 1958
Stuttgarter Zeitung, 25 September 1982
Suddeutsche Zeitung (Munich), 3 October 1954
Suddeutsche Zeitung (Munich), 19 September 1982
Time, August 25, 1967
Time, December 8, 1967
TIP (West Berlin), 19 November 1982
Union-Pressedienst, Heft 10, 1958
Variety, August 9, 1967
Variety, December 13, 1967
Vorwärts, 6 March 1959
Wege Zueinander, 29 September 1957
Welt der Arbeit (DGB), 28 November 1952
Westdeutsche Allgemeine, 10 April 1953
Westfalische Nachrichten (Munster), 7 December 1960

INDEX